Stratford-upon-Avon

second series

General Editor: Jeremy Hawthorn

Professor of Modern British Literature
University of Trondheim, Norway

Propaganda, Persuasion and Polemic

Editor: Jeremy Hawthorn

Edward Arnold

© Edward Arnold 1987

First published in Great Britain 1987 by
Edward Arnold (Publishers) Ltd, 41 Bedford Square, London WC1B 3DQ

Edward Arnold (Australia) Pty Ltd, 80 Waverley Road, Caulfield East,
  Victoria 3145, Australia

Edward Arnold, 3 East Read Street, Baltimore, Maryland 21202, USA

British Library Cataloguing in Publication Data

Propaganda, persuasion and polemic.——
  (Stratford-upon-Avon studies; Second series)
  1. Propaganda
  I. Hawthorn, Jeremy   II. Series
  303.3'75   HM263

  ISBN 0-7131-6497-2

Index compiled by Peva Keane

Text set in 10/11 pt Garamond Compugraphic
by Colset Private Limited, Singapore
Made and printed in Great Britain by
Richard Clay Ltd., Bungay, Suffolk

Contents

Acknowledgements

The editor and publishers would like to thank the following for permission to quote copyright material: Delacorte Publishing and Hodder & Stoughton Ltd for extracts from James Clavell's *The Children's Story* © 1963, 1981 by James Clavell. Reprinted by permission of Hodder and Stoughton Limited; Pacific Publishers for an extract from *Home Management and House Care* by Emily Carpenter, 1977 and Longman-Cheshire, Melbourne, for extracts from *Settlement Patterns and Processes* by Harris and Stehbens, 1981.

Preface

Perhaps one of the best known of all literary depictions of the act – and art – of persuasion is that of Antony's speech in Act 3 Scene 2 of Shakespeare's *Julius Caesar*, in which he mourns the death of Caesar and effectively transforms what we would now refer to as 'public opinion'. In many ways this literary example can serve to illustrate the interlocked complex of problems and issues which this volume seeks to explore. For the sake of clear exposition it is convenient to divide these into two categories – matters of *technique*, and matters of wider social, political and moral *context*.

Starting with technique we can note the following.

1 *The act of persuasion involves deceit*. Antony lies to his listeners about his true intentions, claiming that he has 'come to bury Caesar, not to praise him', and that 'I speak not to disprove that Brutus spoke'. We will see in many of the essays in this volume how one essential component in many acts of persuasion is the denial of any intention to persuade – or to persuade to a given end. John M. MacKenzie gives us a classic example of this in his essay, in which we can learn how the BBC freely used the word 'propaganda' in internal memoranda, but banned its use in broadcasting (p. 45). We will see that in almost every essay in this collection the topic of deceit and deliberate misrepresentation is naturally raised – either in theoretical or in concrete terms – by the discussion of persuasion. And deceit is a topic which it seems impossible to avoid when the discussion extends to such topics as propaganda or to advertising. Although I introduce this as a matter of technique, it is clearly one which is at the heart of the moral disquiet associated with persuasion.

2 *The persuader disclaims the possession of any rhetorical ability*. 'I am no orator, as Brutus is': because persuasion has increasingly become associated with manipulation by means of specific rhetorical tricks, a necessary part of the act of verbal persuasion has become that of assuring one's listeners that they are persuaded not as a result of their having succumbed to rhetorical skill, but as a result of their legitimate and justified response to 'the facts of the case'. We see a similar claim being made by Plato's Socrates, to whose speech of defence Chris Emlyn-Jones draws our attention

in his essay, and it is as if the birth of modern rhetoric is accompanied by a simultaneous need to deny the possession of persuasive power – perhaps the original deceit in the act of persuasion in the modern world.

3 *The persuader starts by asserting common ground with his listeners.* 'Friends, Romans, countrymen . . .'; 'Good friends, sweet friends'; 'you know me all, a plain blunt man'. Throughout Brutus's speech we find an assumed humility, an apparent willingness to admit that, like his listeners, he is an ordinary man. In his essay Justin Lewis draws our attention to the significance of 'pronoun shifting', and we can note the crucial lines in Antony's speech where he declares that, 'Then I, and you, and all of us fell down/Whilst bloody treason flourish'd over us'. The solidarity asserted at the start of the speech has been extended into a declaration of common *interest*. Gunther Kress points out how many advertisements seek to reposition the reader, and a similar process is depicted in Shakespeare's scene.

4 *The persuader works as much in terms of hints and implications as of direct statements.* Indeed, the speech is a masterly example of how a speaker can keep repeating a statement which, by juxtaposition with other statements, he can succeed in getting his listeners to reject. Early on in his speech, when we assume (and we take it he assumes) his listeners to be at their least sympathetic, no direct defence of Caesar, no frontal attack on his murderers, is provided. Instead we have hesitations, qualifications, a refusal to present a problem-free picture of what has happened, all of which forces his listeners to seek for the missing consistency – and to find it in the place Antony intends that it shall be found. It is perhaps only in extreme circumstances, and in those in which a positively inclined audience can be assumed, that direct statement replaces indirect claim and hinted meaning. Gordon Williams provides us with a classic illustration of one such extreme circumstance, but it is striking that in most of the essays in the volume we find a concern with the hint rather than the declaration. One crucial element in this is that it gives the audience the illusion of being active, rather than of passively absorbing what is provided by a skilled persuader. James Clavell's *The Children's Story*, as we see in Jan-Ola Östman's essay, provides another superlative literary illustration of the way in which such indirect means of persuasion can succeed in their aim.

Particular mention should be made of what is perhaps the most striking feature of Antony's speech, its use of repetition ('And Brutus is an honourable man') to raise questions indirectly rather than directly. The journal *Private Eye* has, more recently, perfected the technique of circulating information and opinion while claiming to deny it; Antony's repetitions even though they attribute honour to Brutus keep dragging his listeners back to the issue of honour, and force them to consider it in the light of 'facts' with which they are presented. Such pretended adoption of an opponent's point of view is close to the parodic techniques explored by Andrew Crisell in his essay: we see an attempt to get an audience to reconsider something from an opposed camp by exhibiting it in a changed form or an altered context.

5 *The persuader appeals to his listeners' emotions.* Even though Antony maintains a relatively emotion-free tone early on in his speech, he seizes the first opportunity to appeal to his listeners through their emotions rather than their reason. Persuaders of all times have recognized that action is triggered off more quickly and completely by emotional pressure than by rational agreement – especially when the emotional pressure masquerades as rational agreement. As all of the essays in this collection reveal, the association between successful persuasion and the ability to arouse an emotional response in one's audience is an intimate one. And because the emotions have been seen as more volatile and extreme in their operation than reason, so have rhetoric and propaganda been seen as dangerous in view of the suddenness and force of their potential effects. As Antony puts it, 'Mischief, thou art afoot, / Take thou what course thou wilt.'

6 *The persuader makes use of non-verbal as well as verbal techniques.* Antony's red eyes are commented upon by his hearers, and his appearance is as crucial to his success as is that of the New Teacher in Clavell's *The Children's Story.*

7 *The persuader seeks always to encourage interpretation.* Known facts are presented in a particular light, and relationships between them are suggested. Unknown facts are revealed or manufactured. The persuader never reveals facts in isolation, but in a declared or implied interpretative context. In particular, the persuader relies upon families or complexes of belief: ideologies, cultural assumptions, systems of thought. The audience is encouraged to 'join up the facts' in a particular way, and in particular to *categorize* people, or events or beliefs. A range of sub-techniques is at hand to direct this categorizing activity. *Stereotypes* are of particular value to the persuader, and – as John Smith's essay demonstrates – the act of persuasion often involves convincing a person or people that their beliefs are not *consistent.* The implication of Antony's speech is, for much of its early stages, that if this and this were, as you know, true of Caesar, then how can what is alleged of him by Brutus also be true? The audience is, implicitly, being told that its beliefs are not coherent, and is being invited to achieve such coherence through replacement of some beliefs by others. Arguers instinctively home in on what are seen to be inconsistencies in an opponent's case.

8 *An opposition grouping is defined and then denigrated.* The persuader seeks to reposition his target – or, rather, to get his target to reposition him or herself. Again, stereotyping is most useful here. Persuasion involves alliances – in terms both of alliances between ideas ('systems of thought') and also between people.

If we turn now to matters of the wide social, political and moral context of persuasion, we again see much that is typical in Shakespeare's depiction – and much that at first thought we might find surprisingly modern. Let us, again, sum up the different relevant points.

1 *Persuasion stems from and generates power.* It is power that Antony is concerned with, and although he uses techniques which come from inter-personal communication his speech seeks to intervene in matters of state,

Propaganda, Persuasion and Polemic

in wider political struggle. That much is obvious, but it is this mixture of interpersonal techniques and political ambitions and effects that is at the root of much frightened disapproval of the persuader. Antony pretends to be what, in the context in question, he is not: an ordinary individual. In fact he is a man in search of state power. In their article Kevin Robins, Frank Webster and Michael Pickering insist on the fact that the modern democratic state is, 'necessarily and inescapably, the propagandist state' (p. 7). The exercise of power requires the control of information as much as does the attainment of power; revolutionaries head for the radio station as determinedly as the government tries to hang on to it. And if control of information gives power, so power gives one greater control over information. Persuasion is not a clean topic, in the sense that it can be, or is, carried out clinically and in isolation from social and political interests. Even in those theatres in which most lip-service is paid to the virtues of disinterested debate (universities, for example), argument has social and political sources as well as effects.

As Chris Emlyn-Jones's article illustrates, from the birth of the modern world those with persuasive power have been feared, and this fear is related to a dread of the great (and often seemingly incomprehensible) amount of power enjoyed by the person with rhetorical skill or persuasive skill. John M. MacKenzie's article shows how some recent governments have come only slowly to realize that power comes out of pens and radio transmitters almost as much as out of the barrels of guns. Gordon Williams's article makes it clear that First World War propaganda paid real military dividends for those who were good at it. And Gunther Kress's contribution suggests that the persuasive power of advertising does not just get individuals to purchase certain products, but also positions readers of advertisements with regard to the distribution of power and authority in their society.

Persuasion, moreover, is not just a matter of what people are told but as much of what they are not told. John M. MacKenzie's article is as interesting in terms of what it shows was omitted from BBC overseas broadcasts as in terms of what we learn was included. In the words of Kevin Robins, Frank Webster and Michael Pickering, what we have is 'an ever more intensive and extensive regulation of the information environment' (p. 13), a regulation which is not necessarily perceived by those at whom it is directed. Joseph Heller knew what he was doing when he made ex-Pfc Wintergreen the man who controls the war in *Catch 22*; he is the man who is in control of communications, who decides which messages will circulate.

2 *The further persuasion is from an interpersonal context, the more crucial power becomes.* On the interpersonal level power is mainly relevant to persuasion in terms of the threat of sanctions; in the context of the modern state the contribution that power can make to persuasion is related not just to the threat of sanctions but to control of information. If you are the chairperson you can draw up the agenda – and the agenda-setting function of the media is crucial. Antony cannot threaten sanctions, but his

authority with the crowd is crucial to his success in changing their opinions. We can reverse the words at the head of this paragraph and say that the further persuasion is from an interpersonal context, the more powerful information becomes. As Rosalind Brunt and Martin Jordin suggest in their contribution, many people in contemporary developed Western societies react to these facts by attempting to live in a world of personal experience rather than one which is defined and created by external information agencies.

3 *Skill in textual interpretation becomes progressively more valuable in a world of 'information management'*. Shakespeare's plebs have no intimate knowledge of Caesar as private individual. Their judgement of the truth and falsity of the speeches they hear has to involve processes very different from those used to assess the arguments of their intimate friends. In Joseph Conrad's *Under Western Eyes* the exiled student Razumov, talking to the English teacher of languages about a newspaper report of an assassination of which Razumov has personal knowledge, asks, 'How can you tell truth from lies?' The question has the ring of universality, but it is asked in a very modern context and with a set of very modern presuppositions behind it. The answer he gets refers to certain 'trifles one can go by'. These include 'The character of the publication, the general verisimilitude of the news, the consideration of the motive, and so on'. Learning to weigh such evidence is an acquired skill, a skill which it is the moral responsibility of humane education to disseminate as widely as is possible. The plebs who hear Antony are clearly lacking in such skills, and Shakespeare's portrayal of them gives us a fairly typical example of the conservative belief that the volatility of the mass or the mob requires that information be managed. A number of contributors point out that to talk of persuasion or propaganda is willy nilly to talk of censorship and the suppression of information. Chris Emlyn-Jones reminds us of the flourishing of the arts of verbal persuasion in Athenian democracy; Kevin Robins and his fellow writers see a similar relationship between an increasing concern for the issue of propaganda and a fear of what could happen in a modern democracy were the 'free market of ideas' to be unregulated by paternalistic controls. If information is productive of power, then too information needs to be powerfully regulated.

By now it may be possible to understand some of the reasons why it is that although verbal persuasion is something in which we all indulge, it is something of which most of us claim to disapprove. Central to this negative attitude is the idea that persuasion involves deceit: our epitome of the persuader is the con-man or salesman. To denigrate someone all we have to do is to assimilate them to a class of people whose job it is to persuade – think how effective the association of Nixon with used-car salesman was. Politicians, PR men, salesmen, missionaries – for all of us perhaps these are only a thin line away from the brainwasher or the indoctrinator. (Perhaps least of all for the missionary, who has done his or her persuading in a safely distant land.) All of these we believe to lack sincerity, and in this demand for sincerity rather than for truth we reveal our fear of being duped to be greater than our fear of being misinformed.

The analysis of persuasion needs to concern itself with the different components of the persuasive process and their interconnections if it is to make sense. We can summarize these components as (i) the persuader (ii) the persuasive text or discourse (iii) the persuadee (iv) the determining and interlocking context – social, political, historical. Objection to the *deceit* involved in persuasion normally indicates an individual's perception of an irregularity in the declared or displayed relationships between these different components. We have a conception of an ideal situation in which all relationship of this sort are open and transparent, when the persuadee can 'read off' truths about the persuader and the determining context from the text or discourse, for example. But as our Shakespearian example has shown, successful persuasion too often involves the opposite: a concealment of links and implications in the interest, or in pursuit, of power.

Perhaps one of the classic texts of 'impression management' is to be found in the collection (made posthumously) of Lord Chesterfield's letters to his natural son. Letter after letter gives his son instructions on how to appear to best advantage, and letter after letter assumes that it is appearances rather than essences that are important: 'I am much more anxious about your doing well, than about your being well'; 'Give me but virtuous actions, and I will not quibble and chicane about the motives'.[1] It is not an accident that in Chesterfield's time and in our own more readers have tended to sympathize with Samuel Johnson's opinion that Chesterfield's letters 'teach the morals of a whore, and the manners of a dancing-master',[2] than with Chesterfield's desire to make his son presentable – and thus powerful – in society. (The fact that he singularly failed has gratified the wish of many that such an undiluted desire to manipulate should not prove to be successful.) Our objection is to, in Boswell's words, 'that dissimulation which Lord Chesterfield inculcated as one of the most essential lessons for the conduct of life'.[3] In interesting contrast is our relative tolerance, even enjoyment, of the arts of the satirist and parodist, a tolerance that perhaps confirms Andrew Crisell's argument that there is less conscious moral purpose and more self-indulgence (and, thus, less dissimulation) in the art of the satirist than in the impression-management of a Chesterfield.

To be duped is to be treated like a child, and it may be that part of our resentment of the professional persuader comes from the way he or she forces us into the role of an instructed child. Both Gunther Kress and Jan-Ola Östman give us examples which depict the instruction of a child, and in different ways both contributors suggest that in the situation of a child being educated or instructed we can see a crucial model for a wide variety of

[1]Charles Stokes Carey, ed., *Letters Written by Lord Chesterfield to his Son* (London, Wm. Reeves, 1912), pp. 192, 205.
[2]James Boswell, *The Life of Samuel Johnson* (2 vols., Dent, London, reprinted 1925) I, p. 159.
[3]Boswell, p. 158.

persuasive processes in society. Significantly, in neither example is the adult fully open with the child, although the scales of deception or subterfuge vary very considerably. But in all attempts by an adult to educate a small child through conversation there is an element of role-playing or deception on the part of the adult, who holds back part of his or her knowledge and pretends to a limited sharing of the child's perspective while trying to bring the child nearer to an adult understanding of things. What we accept as legitimate with young children we resent as adults; the politician or salesman who pretends to share our view of the world while trying subtly to shift our opinion in a particular direction makes us feel as if we are being forced into the role of instructed child again.

In our demand for 'sincerity' then, we rebel against the gap between sign and referent, or between the word and the world. We long for that prelapsarian existence in which there was no potential separation of language and reality, the separation which, Chris Emlyn-Jones points out, began to be recognized at the time that 'rational speculation about the origins and nature of the universe' emerged (p. 61).

Such an account suggests that a fear of the persuader is a reaction to the curse of Adam, an unwillingness to accept the inevitable corollaries of rationality. To be able to understand the world through representations is, inescapably, to be able to misrepresent and to mislead. But such an interpretation perhaps takes too little account of the issue of power. We resent the attentions of the professional persuader because they are (in this case accurate) tokens of inequalities of power in society. It is not that we rebel against the potential for misrepresentation that is contained in language, but that we rebel against the use of language to establish or maintain a power structure which in turn gives power over language. In the words of Basil Bernstein, 'Historically, and now, only a tiny percentage of the population has been socialized into knowledge at the level of the metalanguages of control and innovation, whereas the mass of the population has been socialized into knowledge at the level of context-tied operations.'[4] To resent the 'metalanguage of control', then, is not necessarily to resent language as such but perhaps more to react against social inequality as revealed through the differential control of words. In this respect the issue of power enters into our attitudes towards persuasion on the ground floor; it is striking that every single essay in this collection concerns itself with the interpenetration of social power relationships and the act or attempt to persuade at some point or other. Clearly, when Bob Dylan sings that 'propaganda all is phoney' we recognize this as a comment on the exercise of power in society rather than on the nature of language.

Conversely, we are quick – and normally correct – to recognize that a desire for power lies behind the attempt to persuade. Keats suggested that we 'hate poetry that has a palpable design upon us', resisting what he saw as the Wordsworthian wish to bully the reader 'into a certain Philosophy

[4]Basil Bernstein, *Class, Codes and Control* (4 vols., London, Routledge, 1971) I, p. 175.

engendered in the whims of an Egotist'.[5] In Keats's resistance to Wordsworth's poetry we see a classic resistance to words which have 'a palpable design upon us', a resistance which declares a refusal to accept an attempt to assert and gain power through the use of language. In the contribution from Rosalind Brunt and Martin Jordin we can find evidence for a comparable reaction on the part of ordinary people to the palpable designs perceived or half-perceived in media messages. Such attempts to live in a world of personally attested facts may seem like a rejection of the word, but on closer inspection turn out – surely – to involve a rejection of a particular relationship of power in society. Whether such forms of rejection are effective is debatable, but at least to be understood they have to be recognized and respected for what they are.

What is perhaps reassuring when one studies persuasion is precisely that healthy suspicion that ordinary people have for professional persuaders and propagandists. This is not to say that no one is ever taken in; if the argument of Kevin Robins, Frank Webster and Michael Pickering is correct then clearly many are – at least in part. But as Gunther Kress suggests it is possible to educate readers to resist particular forms of persuasion, forms which are concerned to reproduce social inequalities. Suspicion can be transformed into active resistance. The inculcation of habits and skills of critical intelligence – a process which in contrast to many of the persuasive processes considered in this book presupposes an essential equality between instructor and instructed – has never been more in need than in today's world. At a time when significant social forces are announcing that those disciplines concerned with the development of such a critical intelligence are socially redundant, there is an overwhelming case for an oppositional view which states precisely the opposite. It is to be hoped that this book can contribute to the development of the critical intelligence needed to understand, and change, the hidden determinants of many attempts to persuade in today's world.

Jeremy Hawthorn

[5]Letter to John Hamilton Reynolds, Tuesday 3 Feb., 1818. Maurice Buxton Forman, ed., *The Letters of John Keats* (London, Oxford University Press, 1947), p. 96.

Note

Our purpose in this article is to explore some neglected aspects of propaganda research as developed in the United States during the early decades of this century. This theoretical work, we argue, must be situated in the context of fundamental social and political shifts then taking place in the West, and of the 'communications revolution' (film, radio and the mass-circulation press) that accompanied them. From what has now become the dark side of this material, we salvage a repressed theoretical tradition and elaborate a political, or political-economic, approach to the study of propaganda. This approach, we suggest, has particular relevance, in the 80s, for understanding the upheavals and transformations associated with the so-called 'information revolution' (born out of the convergence of video, computing and telecommunications technologies). Insofar as these recent developments do no more than extend, intensify and complete processes set under way in the early part of the century – and this is our argument – the concerns and preoccupations of many early social science researchers remain highly pertinent.

1

Propaganda, Information and Social Control

Kevin Robins, Frank Webster, Michael Pickering

All social problems turn out finally to be problems of social control.
Robert E. Park (1924)

Propaganda is a concession to the rationality of the modern world.
Harold D. Lasswell (1927)

Propaganda, communication and public opinion

It is ultimately in the context of industrialization, urbanization and the formation of the nation-state in the late nineteenth and early twentieth century that we must situate the widespread concern with, and about, propaganda in social science research. These transformations, brought about by the accelerating growth of capitalism, were, of course, central issues in the classical tradition of sociology. They are reflected in Tönnies's concepts of *Gemeinschaft* and *Gesellschaft*, and in Durkheim's distinction between mechanical and organic solidarity. But concern about their impact reaches its most distilled form in American mass society theory:

> The movements of population and the contact between people from the ends of the earth, the opening of world markets, and the spread of modern technology, the growth of cities, the operation of mass media of communication, the increasing literacy of the masses of people all over the world, have combined to disintegrate local cohesion and to bring hitherto disparate and parochial cultures into contact with each other. Out of this ferment has come the disenchantment of absolute faiths which expresses itself in the secular outlook of modern man.[1]

As traditional bonds and values have weakened, it is argued, so has the individual become increasingly segregated, isolated and alienated. As society becomes ever more subject to the principles of rationalization,[2] so

[1] Louis Wirth, 'Consensus and Mass Communication', *American Sociological Review* (vol. 13, no. 1, February 1948), p. 7.
[2] See Ferdinand Tönnies, *On Sociology: Pure, Applied and Empirical* (University of Chicago Press, 1971) ch. 19.

1

do the mechanisms of social cohesion break down. As De Fleur and Ball-Rokeach emphasize, 'the most important element of this idea was that ineffective social organization failed to provide adequate linkages between individuals to maintain an integrated and stable system of social control.'[3]

It was in this context of mass society theory that communications sociology came into being. The new communications technologies of the early twentieth century were clearly destined to play a crucial role in what came to be called the Great Society. For Louis Wirth, it was upon the mass media that 'to an ever increasing degree the human race depends to hold it together. Mass communication is rapidly becoming, if it is not already, the main framework of the web of social life.' His argument is that 'in order to communicate effectively with one another, we must have common knowledge, but in a mass society it is through communication that we must obtain this common body of knowledge'.[4] But if the mass media had become central channels of communication and information dissemination, then the implications remained open and uncertain. On the one hand, they might be appropriated by dictatorial regimes 'to orchestrate the sensibilities of rootless, volatile populations detached from traditional sources of orientation'; alternatively, they had 'enormous potential for spreading knowledge and establishing rational standards of judgement in an enlarged democratic public'.[5] For better or for worse, mass communications would henceforth play a formative role in the political process. In a world in which 'impersonality has supplanted personal loyalty to leaders' and 'literacy and the physical channels of communication have quickened the connection between those who rule and the ruled', Lasswell argues, 'most of that which formerly could be done by violence and intimidation must now be done by argument and persuasion'.[6]

What Lasswell is advocating here is not free and open networks of communication. The logic of his position moves less towards argument as an end in itself than towards the persuasive use of communications channels to engineer public opinion and consent. In democratic as in totalitarian systems, Lasswell reminds us, the communications process is underpinned by relations of power. It is at this point, of course, that we address the question of propaganda: ours 'is an atomized world, in which individual whims have wider play than ever before, and it requires more strenuous exertions to coordinate and unify them than formerly. The new antidote to wilfulness is propaganda. If the mass will be free of chains of iron, it must

[3]Melvin L. De Fleur and Sandra Ball-Rokeach, *Theories of Mass Communication* (New York, David McKay Company, 3rd edn, 1975), pp. 138–9.
[4]L. Wirth, 'Consensus', p. 10, 4–5.
[5]Albert Kreiling, 'Television in American Ideological Hopes and Fears', *Qualitiative Sociology* (vol. 5, no. 3, Fall 1982), p. 200.
[6]Harold D. Lasswell, 'The Theory of Political Propaganda', *American Political Science Review* (vol. 21, 1927), p. 631.

accept its chains of silver. If it will not love, honour and obey, it must not expect to escape seduction.'[7]

What we want to argue is that within the abundant literature on propaganda and communications there are two distinct theoretical paradigms. In saying this, we are not referring to antagonistic or opposi- tional stances, but, rather, to divergent emphases which invariably coexist within the same texts. The most familiar approach – but, in our view, the least interesting or productive – is that which, from the perspective of communications theory, applies a psychological model to the study of propaganda. Essentially what it does is to transpose a behaviourist stimulus–response framework onto the sender–receiver model of the com- munication (and propaganda) process. Thus, Harold Lasswell, writing in the late 20s, suggests that 'the strategy of propaganda . . . can readily be described in the language of stimulus–response': 'the propagandist may be said to be concerned with the multiplication of those stimuli which are best calculated to evoke the desired responses, and with the nullification of those stimuli which are likely to instigate the undesired responses'.[8] James Carey refers to this as a transmission or transportation view of commu- nication, one that understands communication as fundamentally and essentially a matter of 'persuasion, attitude change, behaviour modifica- tion, socialization through the transmission of information, influence or conditioning'.[9] Propaganda is 'the attempt to affect the personalities and to control the behaviour of individuals'.[10] Intrinsic to this model is the idea of an active communicator-propagandist (stimulus) and a passive, inert receiver (response). Propaganda entails a process of deliberate manipula- tion or seduction, and this manipulation is performed on isolated, susceptible individuals (the detached and alienated monads described in mass society theory). Furthermore, the assumption is that this process of persuasion appeals to the emotions and works by 'emotional possession': the individuals in the mass audience are 'likely to be influenced by excited appeals as those appear in the press or over the radio – appeals that play upon primitive impulses, antipathies and traditional hatreds'.[11]

The development of effects studies in mass communications research has largely been a matter of the displacement of this 'hypodermic' model in favour of a more situational approach. Mass media have, quite rightly, come to be seen as working amidst other influences on attitudes and behav- iour, in a broader social arena. Variables have been introduced between

[7]Harold D. Lasswell, *Propaganda Techniques in the World War* (London, Kegan, Paul, Trench, Trubner & Co., 1927), p. 222.

[8]H.D. Lasswell, 'The Theory of Political Propaganda', p. 630.

[9]James Carey, 'Mass Communication Research and Cultural Studies: an American View', in James Curran, Michael Gurevitch and Janet Woollacott, eds., *Mass Communication and Society* (London, Edward Arnold, 1977), p. 412.

[10]Leonard W. Doob, *Public Opinion and Propaganda* (London, Cresset Press, 1949), p. 240.

[11]Herbert Blumer, 'The Mass, The Public and Public Opinion', in Bernard Berelson and Morris Janowitz, eds., *Reader in Public Opinion and Communication* (New York, Free Press, 2nd edn, 1966 [1946], p. 45.

sender/stimulus and receiver/response: psychologists have, for example, elaborated personality and learning theory and developed concepts of selective perception and cognitive dissonance; and sociologists have emphasized the mediating influence of both interpersonal relations and structural variables like class or sex. The theoretical orthodoxy has progressively shifted away from the idea of powerful media towards an acknowledgement of the active receiver, the obstinate and recalcitrant audience. What has become clear is that, whilst the media may have agenda-setting and reinforcement functions, they are 'not omnipotent in terms of controlling the minds and behaviour of members of the mass audience'.[12] Whilst we don't, by any means, want to dissent from the idea of an active audience, we do think it significant that, as the 'hypodermic' model has been discredited, so has the concern with propaganda evaporated. It has been banished to a lonely and peripheral region of mass communications theory: the study of psychological warfare and operations. The reason for this, we would suggest, lies in the (fundamentally behaviourist) communications model that informs this approach. The problem, for us, is its limiting emphasis on effects at the level of the individual, in terms of individual attitude, opinion or behaviour changes. Propaganda has, regrettably, been conceptualized exclusively in narrow psychological terms, and, moreover, identified with the strong ('hypodermic') version of this model. Consequently, as more sophisticated and attenuated variants have emerged, so has the very notion of propaganda been depreciated and discredited.

As communications and propaganda became the preserve of psychology and sociology, rather than of political philosophy and political economy, so were crucial issues obscured and important debates deferred. We are entirely behind Terence Qualter when he suggests that, 'preoccupied with the mechanics of empirical research and the trivia of detailed case studies, scholars turned away from such still unanswered questions as the role that public opinion can or ought to play in a democracy, and the impact of propaganda and the manipulation of public opinion on the theory and practice of democratic government.'[13] It is here that we come to our second theoretical paradigm for the study of propaganda, one that conceptualizes propaganda within a broader political theory and political economy of communications. Whilst this approach has invariably been overshadowed, and even eclipsed, by the narrower communications paradigm, it is, in our view, more productive and raises fundamental and urgent questions about

---

[12]Donald F. Roberts, 'The Nature of Communications Effects', in Wilbur Schramm and Donald F. Roberts, eds., *The Process and Effects of Mass Communication* (Urbana, University of Illinois Press, revised edition, 1971), p. 376. For relevant overviews of audience and effects studies, see, *inter alia*, Joseph T. Klapper, *The Effects of Mass Communication* (New York, Free Press, 1960); Denis McQuail, 'The Influence and Effects of Mass Media', in James Curran, Michael Gurevitch and Janet Woollacott, eds., *Mass Communication and Society* (London, Edward Arnold, 1977); Terence H. Qualter, *Opinion Control in the Democracies* (London, Macmillan, 1985), chs. 4–5.

[13]T.H. Qualter, *Opinion Control*, p. 29.

the relation between communication, information and the political process in our society.

What this approach does is to locate the study of propaganda and communication within the wider context of political phenomena and theory: legitimation, democracy, bureaucracy, social administration, public opinion, social control, the nation-state. Its fundamental concern is with the principles of administration and governance necessary to ensure integration and cohesion in the Great Society. The indispensable pre-requisite for administrative control across the expansive territory of the modern nation-state is, of course, an effective communication and information infrastructure. William Albig notes that 'communication is the fundamental human institution in that it sets the limits of community size and by its nature affects all types of human association. And the integration of any social unit', he continues, 'is dependent upon the capacity to transfer ideas, to transmit administrative orders and to prevent disintegration at outlying points'.[14] Only through the extensive flow of communication and information can administrative unity and integrity be assured. In this sense we can argue that the nation-state is essentially and intrinsically an information society.

If communication and information underpin administrative cohesion and power, then it is all the more crucial for political management and integration. With the dissolution of traditional and localized communities, and with the emergence of a communications infrastructure, Alvin Gouldner suggests, 'social interaction was less requisite for cultural communality. People might now share information and orientations, facts and values, without mutual access and interaction.'[15] Through this process there evolved the idea of a 'public' as an audience for communication, and of public opinion as a political force: 'The organized sway of public opinion in the Great Society was possible only when opinion could be formed and expressed by large groups within relatively short time periods.'[16] Now, much of the early literature on propaganda, we must emphasize, intersects with the study of public opinion.[17] The common concern is with the flow of communication and information between citizens, and between citizens and government in the Great Society. There is a recognition in public opinion research that 'the quality of public opinion depends to a large extent on the effectiveness of public discussion, [and that], in turn, this effectiveness depends on the availability and flexibility of the agencies of public communication.'[18] Free circulation of,

[14]William Albig, *Public Opinion* (New York, McGraw-Hill, 1939), p. 21, 47.

[15]Alvin Gouldner, *The Dialectic of Ideology and Technology* (London, Macmillan, 1976), p. 95.

[16]W. Albig, *Public Opinion*, p. 47.

[17]See, *inter alia*, L.W. Doob, *Public Opinion and Propaganda*; Bruce Lannes Smith, Harold D. Lasswell and Ralph D. Casey, *Propaganda, Communication, and Public Opinion* (Princeton University Press, 1946); Daniel Katz *et al*, eds., *Public Opinion and Propaganda* (New York, Henry Holt, 1954).

[18]H. Blumer, 'The Mass, the Public', p. 50. See also Bernard Berelson, 'Democratic Theory and Public Opinion', *Public Opinion Quarterly* (vol. 16, Fall 1952), pp. 313–30; Paul F.

and access to, information is considered to be crucial for the effective articulation of public opinion, and, thereby, for the democratic process.

What this ideal presupposes, of course, is a rational *public*. It invokes a rational process of judgement and decision-making on the basis of freely available information and effective communication. This faith in rationality is particularly apparent in the work of the Chicago School. Thus, for Robert Park, 'public opinion is determined by conflict and discussion. . . . The public is never ecstatic. It is always more or less rational. It is this fact of conflict, in the form of discussion, that introduces into the control exercised by public opinion the elements of rationality and of fact.'[19] This faith in the possibility of a rational 'universe of discourse' reflects and perpetuates eighteenth-century Enlightenment philosophy. It presumes that process of 'public reasoning' (*das öffentliche Räsonnement*) – the 'public use of reason' – which, Habermas argues, characterized the eighteenth-century public sphere (*Öffentlichkeit*).[20]

Not all observers, however, were as sanguine as Robert Park and the Chicago School. For many, the Enlightenment ideal of rational political discourse had proved to be an empty utopia: channels of communication and information were imperfect and inefficient; and the citizens of the Great Society often proved to be quite irrational and 'often poor judges of their own interests, flitting from one alternative to the next without solid reason or clinging timorously to the fragments of some mossy rock of ages'.[21] What became particularly apparent was the ambiguous role of the new communications media in the process of information dissemination and rational decision-making. Whilst the new technologies were indispensable for 'public conversation' in the twentieth-century nation-state, they also made possible the manipulation of public debate and the public sphere. Rational discourse could be skewed by the mechanisms of propaganda. Whilst signalling the importance of 'public discussion' and the 'availability and flexibility of the agencies of public communication', Herbert Blumer argues that 'there is interference with effective public discussion' and that 'today most students of public opinion find that their chief concern is the study of propaganda.'[22] Insofar as public opinion research was concerned with the possibilities for rational and democratic public discourse, it had necessarily to confront those forces that might subvert, obstruct or influence the process of opinion formation.

Whilst propaganda was commonly associated with the exploitation of mass media by dictatorial and totalitarian governments, what was more

Lazarsfeld, 'Public Opinion and the Classical Tradition', *Public Opinion Quarterly* (vol. 21, Spring 1957), pp. 39–53.

[19]Robert E. Park, *On Social Control and Collective Behaviour: Selected Papers*, (ed. Ralph H. Turner) (University of Chicago Press, 1967 [1924]), pp. 219–220.

[20]Jürgen Habermas, *Strukturwandel der Öffentlichkeit* (Darmstadt, Luchterhand, 1962), p. 41, 129.

[21]Harold D. Lasswell, 'The Vocation of Propagandists', in *On Political Sociology*, (University of Chicago Press, 1977 [1934]), p. 236.

[22]H. Blumer, 'The Mass, the Public', p. 50.

important, in the longer term, was a growing recognition by political theoreticians that propaganda was, in fact, an integral feature of democratic societies. An increasingly pragmatic and 'realistic' appraisal of the political process suggested that 'in a world of competing political doctrines, the partisans of democratic government cannot depend solely upon appeal to reason or abstract liberalism.'[23] What became apparent was that 'propaganda, as the advocacy of ideas and doctrines, has a legitimate and desirable part to play in our democratic system.'[24] Writing on the eve of the Second World War, one commentator suggests that 'the peculiar weakness of democracy' is 'that of allocating disproportionate freedom to the individual at the expense of authority and of the security which authority guarantees. . . . Democracy is always in danger of dissolving into anarchy, political and moral.' In the face of this always potential instability, democratic societies must elaborate propaganda that is 'positive and affirmative of new freedoms': although 'democracy stands by the principle of free discussion, [it need not] be squeamish about the efficient use of propaganda, as emotionalized ideology, in making its views persuasive.'[25] The modern democratic state is, necessarily and inescapably, the propagandist state. The very complexity of the developed nation-state appears to be such that a 'free market' of ideas and debate must be superseded by the (scientific) management and orchestration of public opinion. Lasswell makes the point succinctly: 'The modern conception of social management is profoundly affected by the propagandist outlook. Concerted action for public ends depends upon a certain concentration of motives.' 'Propaganda', he continues, 'is surely here to stay; the modern world is peculiarly dependent upon it for the coordination of atomized components in times of crisis and for the conduct of large scale ''normal'' operations.'[26]

What emerges in this political science research is an approach to propaganda that is quite distinct from the behaviourist emphasis, with its stimulus–response paradigm, its focus on attitude and behaviour modification, its concern with the atomized individual, its theory of 'emotional possession', and so on. This alternative perspective, which places the study of propaganda in the context of political science, has in our view considerable relevance and interest. Whilst we would dissent from many of the substantive judgements made by Lasswell *et al.*, we believe that their fundamental theoretical paradigm raises crucial issues about the interrelation of propaganda, public opinion and mass communications, and about transformations in the nature of political control in the early part of the twentieth century. In drawing our attention to the relation between

[23]W. Albig, *Public Opinion*, p. 301.
[24]Harwood L. Childs, *Public Opinion: Nature, Formation, and Role* (Princeton, Van Nostrand, 1965), p. 282.
[25]George E. Gordon Catlin, 'Propaganda as a Function of Democratic Government', in Harwood L. Childs, ed., *Propaganda and Dictatorship* (Princeton University Press, 1936), pp. 142–3.
[26]H.D. Lasswell, 'The Vocation of Propagandists', pp. 234–5.

information/communications and power, we shall argue, this approach identifies perhaps *the* central axis of the political order, and one that is crucially important in the 1980s.

In developing the understanding of propaganda, this perspective makes two fundamental points. The first is that *propaganda is a matter of the politics of information*. It is a question of accessibility and restrictiveness in the flow of information within the modern nation-state. At one level this is about information management and 'special pleading' (propaganda, public relations, advertising). According to Albig, special pleading is 'an inevitable concomitant of the growth and organization of society during the past century'.[27] But just as important as the manipulation of information is its restriction and censorship. For public opinion to function, 'there must be access to information on the issues with which public opinion is concerned';[28] censorship undermines the principles of free and rational public discourse. Censorship and secrecy are, moreover, complementary to explicit propaganda and information control. In Walter Lippmann's words 'without some form of censorship, propaganda in the strict sense of the word is impossible. In order to conduct a propaganda there must be some barrier between the public and the event': 'Every official is in some degree a censor. And since no one can suppress information, either by concealing it or forgetting to mention it, without some notion of what he wishes the public to know, every leader is in some degree a propagandist.'[29]

The second important point is that *propaganda and information management are normative aspects of modern democratic societies*. Far from being exceptional, anomalous or aberrant elements in the democratic process, propaganda is a *constitutive* aspect of 'actually existing' democracy, democracy in the mass society. Whereas propaganda was, in the words of William Albig, 'incidental to the development of tribes or simple folk peoples', it is 'essential to the development of unanimity in modern states'.[30] Contrary to the behaviourist emphasis on the individual, the point to be made here is that the 'relevant audience' of propaganda is the public;[31] only with the emergence of the public and of democratic public opinion can and does propaganda become an important social force. Whilst the pure theory of democratic government through public debate sounds lofty, its reality is more problematic and unmanageable. We have already referred to Lasswell's argument that, given the complex and atomized nature of modern societies, the 'concerted action' of

[27]W. Albig, *Public Opinion*, p. 283.
[28]Hans Speier, 'Historical Development of Public Opinion', *American Journal of Sociology* (vol. 55, January 1950), p. 377.
[29]Walter Lippmann, *Public Opinion* (London, George Allen & Unwin, 1922), pp. 43, 247. On the close relation between censorship and propaganda, see Kevin Robins and Frank Webster, 'The Media, the Military and Censorship', *Screen* (vol. 27, no. 2, March-April 1986), pp. 57–63.
[30]W. Albig, *Public Opinion*, p. 296.
[31]David L. Altheide and John M. Johnson, *Bureaucratic Propaganda* (Boston, Allyn & Bacon, 1980), p. 10.

propaganda is necessary to ensure 'a certain concentration of motives'. Ellul makes the further point that 'public opinion is so variable and fluctuating that government could never base a course of action on it; no sooner would government begin to pursue certain aims favoured in an opinion poll, than opinion would turn against it.'[32] The implication is that a central, directive agency must both articulate and orchestrate public opinion to ensure 'rational' government. Modern societies, Wirth suggests, 'have learned that in the face of their size and complexity and their internal heterogeneity, the engineering of consent is one of the great arts to be cultivated.'[33] The management of consent is, however, a delicate matter insofar as any government remains ultimately accountable to public opinion. It 'cannot follow public opinion', argues Ellul, 'but it cannot escape it either.' Since 'the government cannot follow opinion, opinion must follow the government': 'the point is to make the masses demand of the government what the government has already decided to do.'[34] This management of public discourse and opinion – ultimately through control over the various channels of information – has become an intrinsic aspect of 'normal' political rule in democratic society.

In this context, Harold Lasswell suggests that 'propaganda attains eminence as the one means of mass mobilization which is cheaper than violence, bribery or other possible control techniques.'[35] Idealistic (Enlightenment) debate on the public sphere and rational democratic government here metamorphoses into concern with the mechanics of social management and social control. From the earliest days of propaganda and opinion research, with an acute sense of the disruptions entailed in the transformation from *Gemeinschaft* to *Gesellschaft*, great attention was paid to the possibilities of social cohesion in the mass society. For Robert Park, the new social order 'is more or less of an artificial creation, an artifact. It is neither absolute nor sacred, but pragmatic and experimental'.[36] And this for him raised the issue of social control. The same issue is raised by Louis Wirth in terms of the manufacture of consensus. He argues that the 'lack of a social mind to go with the social body is the deficiency that we must supply if organized social life, on the scale on which we must now live it, is to endure', and he goes on to suggest that 'the only reasonable equivalent of "mind" in the individual organism that we can think of as an essential in the social organism can be supplied through consensus.'[37] The central issue is that of creating social and moral integration in a society in which the public and public opinion count as a social

[32]Jacques Ellul, *Propaganda: The Formation of Men's Attitudes* (New York, Alfred A. Knopf, 1965), p. 124.
[33]L. Wirth, 'Consensus', p. 9.
[34] J. Ellul, *Propaganda*, pp. 126, 132.
[35]H.D. Lasswell, 'The Vocation of Propagandists', p. 231.
[36]R.E. Park, *On Social Control*, p. 5, cf. pp. 209–10. See also Elisabeth Noelle-Newmann, *The Spiral of Silence: Public Opinion – Our Social Skin* (University of Chicago Press, 1984), pp. 95–6.
[37]L. Wirth, 'Consensus', p. 4.

force, and in which coercion has been delegitimized as a form of social control. As Morris Janowitz argues, concern with social control within this intellectual tradition does not focus on the social psychology of conformity; it stands for 'a comprehensive focus on the nation-state and a concern which has come to be called "macrosociology" '.[38] Social control is a political concept: it addresses the extended social reproduction of mass society particularly, and, the role of information, communications and public opinion in this process.

With this emphasis the Enlightenment ideal of Reason becomes translated into rationalization and the technocratic regulation of society. Faith in a rational public gives way to the invocation of expertise and to the scientific management of public opinion. In the blessed name of Science and Rationality and Efficiency, political rule becomes a matter of social engineering, and the machinery of propaganda and information management becomes more pervasive. 'There has always been some propaganda', Albig points out, 'but in the modern age, it is organized, intentional and relatively more effective.'[39]

This subsumption of propaganda into the very form and structure of social control in the modern nation-state is particularly clear in the writings of Walter Lippmann during the early 20s. Lippmann points to two dilemmas of mass society. The first is that of the competence of public opinion: 'The ideal of the omnicompetent, sovereign citizen is, in my opinion, such a false ideal. It is unattainable. The pursuit of it is misleading. The failure to produce it has produced the current disenchantment.'[40] The second problem is that of the increasing complexity of social organization; it has attained 'a complexity now so great as to be humanly unmanageable.'[41] The implication of this is that central governments have been compelled to assume responsibility for the control and coordination of increasingly diffuse societies. In this process, they have realized 'the need for interposing some form of expertness between the private citizen and the vast environment in which he is entangled'.[42] They have created 'a technocracy which has sought to coordinate and manage the Great Society, and at the heart of this project is systematic intelligence and information control'. The gathering of social knowledge, Lippmann argues, is, on the whole, still haphazard; not, as it will have to become, 'the normal accompaniment of action'.[43] If mass society is to be governed effectively and rationally, then control over the circuits of information is essential. 'It is no longer possible', Lippmann continues, 'to believe in the original dogma of democracy; that the knowledge needed for the management of human affairs comes up spontaneously from the human heart.' The

[38]Morris Janowitz, 'Sociological Theory and Social Control', *American Journal of Sociology* (vol. 81, no. 1, July 1975), p. 83.
[39]W. Albig, *Public Opinion*, p. 309.
[40]Walter Lippmann, *The Phantom Public* (New York, Harcourt, Brace & Co., 1925), p. 39.
[41]W. Lippmann, *Public Opinion*, p. 394.
[42]*ibid.*, p. 378.
[43]*ibid.*, p. 408, cf. p. 292.

whole process has now become a matter of scientific management, of social engineering. In a phrase that seems to invoke F.W. Taylor, Lippmann suggests that the manufacture of consent has 'improved enormously in technic, because it is now based on analysis rather than on rule of thumb'.[44] Society as a whole, it seems, is to be run on the same lines of rationality and efficiency as the Taylorist factory. The same technocratic note is present in Edward Bernays's writings on the 'engineering of consent': 'Engineering implies planning. And it is careful planning more than anything else that distinguishes modern public relations from old-time hit or miss publicity and propaganda.'[45] With the scientific management of public opinion through the centralization of communications, information and intelligence activities, Lippmann suggests, 'persuasion has become a self-conscious art and a regular organ of popular government.' His judgement on this – and it is one with which we entirely agree – is that 'a revolution is taking place, infinitely more significant than any shifting of economic power.'[46] What makes it a revolution of such importance? It is to the clarification of this question that we now turn.

Social control and information management

On the basis of this reading of early propaganda and public opinion research we want now to draw out two themes that seem to us to have general and continued importance. The first relates to the growing significance of information flows and information management, and the second to the nature of social control, within contemporary capitalist societies. What our arguments point to, we would claim, is the increasingly systematic and systemic presence, in these societies, of propaganda and information control.

(i) *When was the Information Revolution?*

It is now, in the 1980s, frequently argued that information is becoming a determining social resource and phenomenon. Daniel Bell has gone so far as to argue that we are witnessing the transformation from industrial to post-industrial society, in which the 'axial principle' is the 'centrality of theoretical knowledge . . . as the director of social change', and in which

[44]*ibid.*, p. 248.
[45]Edward L. Bernays, 'The Theory and Practice of Public Relations: A Résumé', in Edward L. Bernays, ed., *The Engineering of Consent*, (Norman, University of Oklahoma Press, 1955), p. 22, cf. p. 4. On the wider cultural influence and implications of Taylorism, see Kevin Robins and Frank Webster, 'Cybernetic Capitalism: Information, Technology, Everyday Life', in Vincent Mosco and Janet Wasko, eds., *The Political Economy of Information* (Madison, University of Wisconsin Press, 1987); Kevin Robins and Frank Webster, 'The Revolution of the Fixed Wheel: Television and Social Taylorism', in Philip Drummond and Richard Paterson, eds., *Television in Transition* (London, British Film Institute, 1985); Frank Webster and Kevin Robins, *Information Technology: A Luddite Analysis* (Norwood, NJ, Ablex, 1986), Pt. 3.
[46]W. Lippmann, *Public Opinion*, p. 248.

'knowledge, not labour, is the source of value'.[47] Recent developments in information technology (telecommunications, data processing) argue a future 'information society' of freedom, plenty and harmony. Within this futurological perspective, the information explosion is seen as intrinsically beneficial. The greater the flow of information and communication, the better: 'with increased communication can come increased knowledge, increased creativity and increased understanding among people.'[48] The particular importance of information technology, however, is for 'managing the mass society, since it is the mechanism that orders and processes the transactions whose huge number has been mounting almost exponentially because of the increase in social interactions'. Information technology, as an 'instrumental mode of rational action', permits the scientific and efficient coordination of a complex social organization.[49]

What undoubtedly characterizes such invocations of the coming 'information society' is a strongly technocratic orientation. The new information technologies are seen as (socially neutral) instruments, capable of enhancing social rationality, planning and efficiency. What this perspective represses and censors, however, are relations of power in contemporary society. Richard Swift puts forward an alternative interpretation of the 'managed society': 'Management has become normal. It taps into all of us. We don't expect anything else. We are told what to do at work, what to buy at home and increasingly how to think. The modern world is too complicated. We can't imagine any other way for things to run.'[50] What Swift sees is not rationality but rationalization. From this perspective the new technologies of information articulate and express relations of domination; they extend and intensify the rationalization of control.

If one examines the growing role of information in society, the evidence, we would argue, does indeed point to control rather than efficient social management – or, more accurately, it suggests that control is an integral part of social scientific management. There is not space here for detailed evidence.[51] It must suffice just to outline the panoply of industries and apparatuses that make up the machinery of information control. There are, we believe, four closely related forces underpinning this system of information management and control. Firstly, there are the institutions of active persuasion, such as propaganda agencies, public relations and advertising. Then, there are the various mechanisms of secrecy, security and censorship,

[47]Daniel Bell, 'The Social Framework of the Information Society', in Tom Forester, ed., *The Microelectronics Revolution* (Oxford, Basil Blackwell, 1980) p. 501, 506. For an extended critique of Bell, see Kevin Robins and Frank Webster, 'Information as Capital: A Critique of Daniel Bell', in Fred Fejes and Jennifer Daryl Slack, eds., *Ideologies of the Information Age* (Norwood, NJ, Ablex, 1987).

[48]Jacques Maisonrouge, 'Putting Information to Work for People', *Intermedia* (vol. 12, no. 2, March 1984), p. 33.

[49]D. Bell, 'Social Framework', pp. 509, 503.

[50]Richard Swift, 'Everything under Control', *New Internationalist* (no. 146, April 1985), p. 7.

[51]See, Frank Webster and Kevin Robins, 'The Mis-Information Society', *Universities Quarterly* (vol. 37, no. 4, Autumn 1983).

which try to restrict popular access to 'classified' categories of information.[52] Thirdly, there are the increasing developments towards the commodification and commercialization of information, which subordinate the flow of information to business values and priorities (*via* market forces, patents, copyright, etc.).[53] And, finally, there is the proliferation of information gathering by corporate and political interests (opinion polls, market research, social surveys, but also more sinister forms of surveillance); it is this collection of 'increasingly detailed information about individuals and family units that not only threatens their privacy, but dramatically increases the power of those with access to the data to create and deliver specialized propaganda'.[54] What we have, then, is an ever more intensive and extensive regulation of the information environment. Our argument is that propaganda, from being a process of *ad hoc* information manipulation, has become transmogrified into the increasingly systemic and integrated machinery of global information control. In his pioneering study of the information industries, Herbert Schiller describes this 'control of the information and ideational apparatus' as a cohesive system of 'mind management'.[55]

The mobilization of information and knowledge resources is, as we have suggested, generally seen as an expression of the late twentieth-century 'information technology revolution', which is supposed to take us from industrial to postindustrial society. Our argument here, however, is that, whilst the new microelectronics-based technologies may enhance and streamline the management of information, this does not mark some qualitatively new phase of social evolution. It seems to us that they do no more, and no less, than extend processes of rationalization and control under way since early in the century. The scientific management of information resources – contemporaneous with the scientific management of the factory – was the crucial mechanism for assuring the organizational coherence of the nation-state (mass society). And the governance of this Great Society demanded the development of a systematic and coordinated management of public opinion. It was in this (pre-silicon) period that the apparatus of 'mind management' took shape. It was at this time that the information industries – mass communication, advertising, public relations, opinion polling, market research – took shape, and propaganda became the 'scientific' and systematic engineering of consent. What we

[52]See, *inter alia*, Donna Demac, *Keeping America Uninformed* (New York, Pilgrim Press, 1984; Des Wilson, ed., *The Secrets File: The Case for Freedom of Information in Britain Today* London , Heinemann, 1984).

[53]See Information Technology Advisory Panel, *Making a Business of Information* (London, HMSO, September 1983).

[54]Oscar H. Gandy and Charles E. Simmons, 'Technology, Privacy and the Democratic Process', *Critical Studies in Mass Communication*, vol. 3, no. 3, June 1986.

[55]Herbert I. Schiller, *The Mind Managers* (Boston, Beacon Press, 1973), p. 4. Whilst Schiller has often been accused of pessimistic and determinist tendencies, his proper emphasis on propaganda and information control by no means implies its comprehensive success and effectiveness. The space and potential for opposition is a difficult issue and requires discussion at much greater length than available to us here.

want to argue is that this, rather than developments in the 1980s, marks the inauguration of the information revolution. It was, we would emphasize, not a technological, but a political revolution. Propaganda and information management must, in Lasswell's words, constitute the pre-eminent 'means of mass mobilization' in the modern nation state. When Walter Lippmann writes of a revolution more significant than any shifting of economic power, it is precisely this information revolution that he designates. Contrary to the arguments of Bell and other futurologists, we would argue that industrial societies have long been information societies: the technocratic strategy of information, communication and opinion management has been integral to political rule through most of the twentieth century.

(ii) Keeping Control: The Dialectic of Enlightenment

Within the early twentieth-century research on propaganda we have sought to disentangle two distinct intellectual strands. And we have argued that the approach which locates propaganda in the context of political theory is of far greater importance, theoretically and politically, than that which works within the framework of behaviourist psychology. The former, macrosociological, approach is concerned with propaganda, information and public opinion in terms of the democratic process and of social control in the modern nation-state. Within this literature we can identify apparently divergent positions on the nature and significance of propaganda in democratic society. There is that which sees democracy as a process of rational and informed debate within the public sphere, and propaganda as the wilful obstruction or manipulation of rational political discourse. And, over against this, is the more pragmatic approach which, despairing of the growing complexity of society and doubting the 'ideal of the omnicompetent, sovereign citizen', concludes that 'the problems that vex democracy seem to be unmanageable by democratic methods.'[56] From this perspective, propaganda – no longer a pejorative term – has a vital role to play in the management of democratic opinion and the engineering of democratic consent. Faith in the rational, informed citizen becomes belief in the rational, scientific technician and expert; the need is felt for 'trained professionals who can deal with increasingly difficult problems of adjustment, interpretation and persuasion'.[57] If these approaches seem divergent, and perhaps even contradictory, there is a sense in which this is more apparent than real. Both, in fact, share a common philosophical tradition and foundation; both have their roots in the Enlightenment principle of Reason and Rationality. In the first case, appeal is made to the reason and judgement of the individual citizen. In the second, it is to the scientific rationalism of the expert, and to the rationality of the social system. Within this latter perspective, the more 'objective' rationality of scientific management and administration seems to promise a more

[56]W. Lippmann, *The Phantom Public*, pp. 189–90.
[57]E.L. Bernays, 'The Theory and Practice of Public Relations', p. 5.

'efficient' democratic order than the often inarticulate, irrational and uninformed citizen. In this historical and philosophical shift from Reason to Rationalization we have the Dialectic of Enlightenment.

Within the early propaganda and public opinion research, this techno-cratic perspective assumes that the scientific management of society, information and opinion is axiomatic if democracy is to be preserved in the mass society. As Albig noted, the partisans of democratic government cannot depend simply upon appeal to reason or abstract liberalism. Lass-well might suggest that the 'practice [of propaganda] by specialists would appear to clash irreparably with some fundamental canons of a society which calls itself democratic',[58] but he only does so in order to squash the idea. His clear conviction is that propaganda is necessary and inevitable in democratic societies; and that enlightened, democratic propaganda can be differentiated from the manipulative practices of totalitarian regimes. On this issue, the general consensus is that democratic society can justify and legitimate propaganda and information management on the basis of the ends to which they are applied: 'Its propaganda will be that of the common adventure for civilization, the approach of experiment and tolerance, the cooperative commonwealth. Its propaganda will not be negative; it will be positive, and affirmative of new freedoms.'[59]

But how adequate is this position? Just how distinct is information management in the cause of democracy from dictatorial propaganda and information control? If there are those, like Lasswell, for whom the princi-ple seems clear-cut, there are others who perceive a more muddy and ambiguous reality. For Francis Wilson, there is 'a narrowing range between the democratic management or manufacture of opinion and the totalitarians who carry techniques a step further in order to proclaim a new freedom for their selfless followers.'[60] And for Francis Rourke, 'it is no exaggeration to say that the possibility of controlling communications has now opened up an avenue through which the gap between totalitarian and democratic government can progressively be narrowed, as modern dicta-tors gradually substitute persuasion for coercion, and as democratic leaders acquire the ability to manufacture the consent upon which their authority is supposed to rest.'[61] Experience of the real world suggests that principles may be undermined. Democratic and totalitarian information politics may, at times, converge. The assumption, however, is that this is an excep-tional, aberrant and undesirable situation. The conviction remains that the (ideal) role of information and communications in democracies is fundamentally and essentially different from their role in totalitarian states.

It is this ideological, and even disingenuous, premise that we must

[58]H.D. Lasswell, 'The Vocation of Propagandists', p. 234.
[59]G.E. Gordon Catlin, 'Propaganda', p. 142.
[60]Francis G. Wilson, 'Public Opinion: Theory for Tomorrow', *Journal of Politics* (vol. 16, 1954), p. 611.
[61]Francis E. Rourke, *Secrecy and Publicity: Dilemmas of Democracy* (Baltimore, Johns Hopkins Press, 1961), p. vii.

question. What we would argue is that propaganda and information management in contemporary democratic societies is on a continuum with that in totalitarian regimes (distinctions are quantitative rather than qualitative). Our thesis is that, *in the nation-state of late capitalism information management is inherently totalitarian*. It is not simply that the communications and information media in democratic societies are, exceptionally and occasionally, abused or misused by powerful (dictatorial) interests. What we have is an ever more extensive information apparatus – propaganda, censorship, advertising, public relations, surveillance, etc. – through which opinion management has become not only authoritarian, but also routine and normative. Our argument is that the totalitarian aspect of this process is to be found in its increasingly systematic (totalizing), integrated and 'scientific' ambitions and tendencies. Now, we must emphasize that this argument does not presume the existence of a manipulative and conspiratorial elite of mind managers.[62] The logic of information control and management is, rather, an integral and systemic aspect of the modern nation-state. Anthony Giddens has recently advanced a very persuasive argument that information control is fundamental to, and constitutive of, the administrative unity and coherence of the nation-state: 'the administrative power generated by the nation-state could not exist without the information base that is the means of its reflexive self-regulation.' Distantly echoing the early mass society theoreticians, he attributes this necessity for coordinated information management to the complexity and territorial expansiveness of modern societies. Information and communications control are indispensable for both the cohesion and the regulation of social systems spanning such large spatial terrains. And what Giddens sees here, at the heart of administrative and bureaucratic 'efficiency', are the seeds of totalitarianism. 'Rational' and 'scientific' coordination of the nation-state – necessary to ensure its coherence and reproduction – expresses itself as control and domination. Totalitarianism, argues Giddens, 'is a tendential property of the modern state'.[63]

This tendency towards information management and control, we want now to suggest, expresses the technocratic current of the Enlightenment tradition. This is the current of rationalization, scientific management and social engineering, efficiency and expertise, that of social control: 'Enlightenment behaves towards things as a dictator towards men. He knows them in so far as he can manipulate them.'[64] It is in this technocratic philosophy of control that both totalitarian and democratic (in Lasswell's sense) systems of propaganda and information management have their *common* source. If the development of communication and information

---

[62]For an argument that does make this assumption, see C. Wright Mills, *The Power Elite* (Oxford University Press, 1956), especially ch. 13.

[63]Anthony Giddens, *The Nation-State and Violence*, (Cambridge, Polity Press, 1985), pp. 180, 295. See also pp. 302, 310.

[64]Max Horkheimer and Theodor W. Adorno, *Dialectic of Enlightenment* (London, Allen Lane, 1973), p. 9.

resources is, ideally, the prerequisite for rational public discourse in the mass society, then the process of achieving this has – historically, and perhaps even logically – encouraged the centralization and reinforcement of that state apparatus which has tended precisely to undermine rational discourse (in favour of rationalization and control). The democratic public sphere has been eroded, as Habermas suggests, both by the forces of commercialization and consumerism, and by that process of political management and manipulation which Habermas refers to as 'refeudalization'.[65] Rationality has, through the Dialectic of Enlightenment, been transformed into rationalization, technocracy and scientific social management. And propaganda and information management have, in this process, become normative and integral aspects of social control.

This political approach to propaganda raises fundamental and difficult issues about the relation between communications, information and the democratic process. Must the complexity and scale of the Great Society necessitate social engineering and opinion management (as Lippmann believed)? Is it possible to rescue a sphere of rational debate from the logic of rationalization? Can the industries and apparatuses of information control be turned to democratic ends? These questions are even more critical in the 1980s than they were for propaganda and public opinion research at the first dawn of the 'information age'. Our understanding and account of the context of information control in democratic societies suggests that there can be no simple answers to these questions.

[65] J. Habermas, *Strukturwandel*, p. 233.

Note

Indispensable is James Morgan Read's *Atrocity Propaganda 1914-1919* (New Haven, Yale U.P./London, Oxford U.P., 1941; repr. New York, Arno, 1972). For propaganda under Asquith see D.G. Wright's 'The Great War, Government Propaganda and English "Men of Letters" 1914–16', *Literature and History*, VII (1978), pp. 70–100. Sir Campbell Stuart's *Secrets of Crewe House* (London, etc., Hodder & Stoughton, 1920), is an insider's view of the 1918 phase. Post-war reaction to atrocity stories is attested by Arthur Ponsonby's *Falsehood in War-Time* (London, Allen & Unwin, 1928). The earliest scholarly treatment, Harold D. Lasswell's *Propaganda Technique in the World War* (London, Kegan Paul/New York, Knopf, 1927), shows similar tendencies. Notable in their fields are James Duane Squires's *British Propaganda at Home and in The United States From 1914 to 1917* (Cambridge, Mass., Harvard U.P., 1935), and George G. Bruntz's *Allied Propaganda and the Collapse of the German Empire in 1918* (California, Stanford U.P./London, Oxford U.P., 1938). This American dominance is no accident. The explanation surfaces in Harold Lavine and James Wechsler's *War Propaganda and the United States* (New Haven, Yale U.P., 1940) which, published on the brink of America's entry into a second European conflict, deftly analyses the propagandist deceptions practised by Britain to draw her into the first. The freshest part of Cate Haste's *Keep the Home Fires Burning* (London, Lane, 1977) is that dealing with left-wing and feminist opposition to the war.

Claud Mullins's *The Leipzig Trials* (London, Witherby, 1921) is complemented by James F. Willis's *Prologue to Nuremberg* (Westport, Conn./London, Greenwood, 1982). The captain responsible for sinking the *Llandovery Castle* had disappeared, but his lieutenants were found guilty. There was, of course, no investigation of the *Baralong* personnel for alleged war crimes.

Public Record Office material – Admiralty, Cabinet, Foreign Office, Treasury Solicitor's, War Office – appears under the standard prefixes: ADM, CAB, FO, TS, WO. Parliamentary Papers, as follows, are noted under Command numbers. *German War Trials: Report of Proceedings before the Supreme Court in Leipzig* (HMSO, 1921), Cmd 1450. *Misc. No. 1 (1916): Memorandum of the German Government in regard to Incidents Alleged to have Attended the Destruction of a German Submarine and its Crew by HM Auxiliary Cruiser 'Baralong' on August 19, 1915, and Reply of HM Government Thereto*, Cd 8144; and *Misc. No. 7 (1916): Further [Baralong] Correspondence*, Cd 8176. *Misc. No. 16 (1917): Correspondence with the German Government Regarding the Alleged Misuse of British Hospital Ships*, Cd 8692. *Misc. No. 4 (1910): Correspondence respecting the Declaration of London*, Cd 5418.

The Declaration of London sought to up-date the Declaration of Paris, 1856, on naval warfare. The former's controversial Article 49, allowing for the destruction of neutral prizes, anticipated wartime developments. Prologue to the war on hospital ships was Britain's seizure of the German *Ophelia* in October 1914, and the Prize Court's finding (probably correct but not without its dubious aspects) that the ship was being used for other than Red Cross purposes.

The considerable time spent at the Public Record Office and elsewhere was made possible by the generous assistance of the Pantyfedwen Fund, Saint David's University College.

2

'Remember the *Llandovery Castle*': Cases of Atrocity Propaganda in the First World War

Gordon Williams

Propaganda entered its modern phase with the advent of print, first of the mass media. The Emperor Maximilian I was the first to realize the capacity of print for self-projection, though censors were quickly alert to the defamatory possibilities. By the seventeenth century printed atrocity propaganda had come of age; but with the First World War it reached a scale hitherto unapproached. It was not the least significant factor that, for the first time in a European conflict, Britain was able to field a literate army.

The troops were by no means immune to hate propaganda, though they were better placed to disabuse themselves about atrocity stories than those at home. Jean Norton Cru demonstrates that *poilu* memoirists are largely unimpressed by lurid tales of outrage, and the same is true of their British counterparts.[1] Conditions, of course, were favourable to the psychopath. The Germans surely had their own versions of Lieutenant Farey, a Cold-stream Guards officer who cherished a 'Hun Skull' from which he had 'scraped off the flesh and hair'.[2] But that a child's severed hand was a favourite trophy of the German soldier must have been easily disproved.[3]

Those odd instances of aberrant behaviour are paralleled by the occasional writer who, despite front-line experience, shows a marked relish for the atrocity story. Most notable of them is Major A. Corbett-Smith, who claims to have written 'with as much reticence as possible' about the brutal side of war. He is gratified to find the following passage from his first book, *The Retreat from Mons*, to have gained particular attention in both 'Allied and neutral countries':[4] 'Hanging up in the open window of a shop, strung from a hook in the cross-beam like a joint in a butcher's shop, was the body of a little girl, five years old, perhaps. Its poor little hands had been hacked off, and through the slender body were vicious bayonet

---

[1] *Témoins* (Paris, Les Etincelles, 1929), cited by Read, *Atrocity Propaganda*, p. 29.
[2] Diary of William Brett St Leger, 18 April 1917 (Imperial War Mus.).
[3] Typical instances appear in Pierre Nothomb, *The Barbarians in Belgium* (London, Jarrold, 1915), p. 129, and Oscar Millard, *Uncensored* (London, Hale, 1937), p. 67.
[4] London, etc., Cassell, 1916, p. 170; *The Marne - and After* (London, etc., Cassell, 1917), p. 303.

stabs'. The place where this allegedly happened is not identified, but the date (26 August 1914) and circumstances point to Caudry. A similar story is given by Norman Hapgood, an American journalist, with the number of little girls hung in the shop increased to three. An investigator, finding an old woman who knew the girls and actually saw them hanging, was perforce convinced of the story's truth. Meeting the French commander in the recaptured village, however, he was told that the old woman had been crazy for years.[5]

Corbett-Smith has no intention of being disabused. He would stamp the German 'out from the world of men', proposing the genocide solution which cropped up all too often.[6] He is very influential. An hysterical book by G. Hamilton Macleod resurrects the Corbett-Smith passage as epigraph and uses a more recent press statement by the Rev. Father Bernard Vaughan as starting point for a pathological indictment of the enemy. Vaughan makes the distinction (too exclusively associated with Kipling) between Germans and human beings. It is our Christian duty, he was to urge in a lecture at His Majesty's Theatre, 'to exterminate them as we would a plague of rats'. Nor is the reverend gentleman conscious of any irony in urging the Germans' Darwinian distortions against them.[7]

It is hard to conceive how this intensity of hatred had such mass appeal – until we think of that notorious 'Gotcha' headline during the Falklands dispute, or the animus engendered between communism and capitalism. The repertoire of accusations is a familiar one. Like the Germans in 1914, the Jews of the Middle Ages were accused of child-murder, ritual crucifixions and the desecration of holy places. The same images fuelled the religious controversies produced by the Reformation. But a more immediate source for the butcher's-shop image is surely Jean Veber's painting, *La Boucherie*, exhibited at the Paris Salon in 1897. Bismarck stands at the shop entrance in butcher's apron. Hanging on display are disembowelled corpses, with the hands and feet heaped on a slab below. It reflects that French spirit of *Revanche* which was only sated by the Versailles Peace Treaty. A lithograph of *La Boucherie* was reissued in 1914, and its influence is apparent in Zislin's *La Boucherie Impériale* (1916), where Bismarck's place is taken by the Kaiser.[8]

After the incident described by Corbett-Smith, the Brigade is alleged to have seen red: 'There was no more talk of taking prisoners' (p. 171). Evidently such moods occurred periodically. One instance is described by Sir John French in his diary entry for 17 May 1915. When 700 Germans tried to surrender, some 200 were killed by German and British fire: 'I fear our men have got "blood lust" heavily upon them. The outrages committed by the Germans have stirred them *very deeply*. It is said that

[5]'Atrocities', *Harper's Weekly* (10 July 1915), p. 29.
[6]*The Marne – and After*, p. 303.
[7]*The Blight of Kultur* (London/Edinburgh, Sampson Low, Marston, 1918), pp. x–xi.
[8]Pierre Veber and Louis Lacroix, *L'oeuvre Lithographie de Jean Veber* (Paris, Floury, 1931), pl. 15. The lithograph appeared in 1899, but the Imperial War Mus. dates its print to 1914. Zislin, *Dessins de Guerre* (Paris/Nancy, Berger-Levrault, 1917), I, pl. 3.

they give very little quarter. In the condition they are in, and considering how they have been tried, it is impossible to check them!'[9] This was just days after news of the *Lusitania* sinking and of the Bryce Committee's findings had appeared in the press. In the issue of *John Bull* for 15 May, Horatio Bottomley was screaming 'NOW FOR THE VENDETTA!'. But whereas the *Lusitania's* story was treated in the British press as a piece of unparalleled barbarity, German newspapers stressed that the ship was carrying war supplies and personnel. But the latter carried scant weight with neutrals. As their own critics came to recognize, the Germans lacked finesse in balancing propaganda effects at home and abroad.

Another major miscalculation of 1915 was the shooting of Nurse Cavell. Frederick Palmer, American War Correspondent, noted that 'Its effect on the troops was electric.'[10] One Tommy wrote home, on a postcard bearing Carrey's inflammatory design of a German officer delivering the *coup de grace* to Nurse Cavell, that he saw a similar one 'pinned to a sandbag in our front line trench' as he waited to go over the top. He adds that his 'Machine Gun is named after Nurse Cavell'.

If the sinking of ostensibly peaceful vessels and the brutalizing of nurses were separately such potent propaganda-ploys, used together their value soared. Raemaekers recognized this in his cartoon on *The Sinking of the Hospital Ship 'Hesperia'*. To H. de Vere Stacpoole, who wrote the accompanying commentary, it had seemed that nothing could surpass the *Lusitania* atrocity: 'then came the sinking of the "Hesperia", a ship filled with wounded soldiers and hospital nurses.'[11] In fact, she was not a hospital ship but an Allan liner, torpedoed off the coast of Ireland on 4 September 1915. She was bound from Liverpool to Montreal and there were Canadian wounded aboard. One of these is depicted by Raemaekers being assisted from a flooded and alarmingly-tilted berth by a young nurse. In this drawing Raemaekers anticipates the shape of things after 1 February 1917, when the Germans began unrestricted submarine warfare.

This was the move which heralded the torpedoing of eight British hospital ships[12] and the advent of America into the war. Earlier, American interventionist ardour had been cooled by a demonstration that inhumanity in this conflict was by no means one-sided. This took the form of American press publicity for the *Baralong* affair. This affair, together with the sinking of the hospital ship *Llandovery Castle* – both a part of the submarine war – will take up the remainder of the discussion. Since these undoubted atrocities belong one to each side, British attitudes – which will be the centre of interest – differ profoundly in the two cases. It should be remembered that these were not minor events. At the time, and for long

[9]Gerald French, *The Life of Field-Marshal Sir John French* (London, Cassell, 1931), p. 304. The original diary is presently held at the Imperial War Mus.

[10]*Times*, 5 February 1916.

[11]*The 'Land & Water' Edition of Raemaekers' Cartoons* (London, 'Land & Water', 1916), II, p. 41.

[12]One of them, the *Lanfranc*, 'was not technically a Hospital Ship at the time, her name having been cancelled a few days earlier' (C. Brigstocke, 22 May 1917), ADM 116/1397.

after, they made a profound impression. If they, unlike the less clear-cut *Lusitania* and Cavell episodes, have been largely forgotten, that is because only such as had already made the translation into myth could survive the impact of Belsen and Auschwitz.

The *Baralong* was one of those Q-ships or decoys developed as a means of tackling the submarine problem. The submarine dominated the war at sea. Fisher, during the period between 1904 and 1910 when he was First Sea Lord, had foreseen the coming importance of the submarine and worked accordingly. His views first came to public notice on the eve of war, through letters written to *The Times* by Admiral Sir Percy Scott.[13] These letters open up the whole area of controversy surrounding the use of the submarine throughout the First World War and after. Amongst Scott's many opponents were those who hated 'any instrument which dare not come into the open, but acts by stealth, to achieve the domination of the seas'. Admiral Bacon asserted that to attack 'commerce by submarines is barbarous'. Scott's reply is magisterial: 'All war is, of course, barbarous, but in a war the purpose of the enemy is to crush his foe; to arrive at this, he will attack where his foe is most vulnerable.' Our dependance on sea-borne supplies would suggest an immediate target. No, urged Lord Sydenham, in terms which were to be of key importance in the forthcoming propaganda war; we would be protected by the fact that the submarine, of its very nature, 'cannot capture, and must destroy'. For all his naiveté, he is acknowledging something which was conveniently forgotten by wartime propagandists: actions which are here presented as a corollary of this inability to capture – actions 'hitherto . . . associated only with piracy in its blackest form' – were later presented as a matter of diabolical policy rather than necessity.

Those who, before the war, had pondered the growing significance of the submarine as offensive weapon had given scant attention to means of combatting it. The decoy-ship was one such means, its first successes coming in June and July 1915.[14] The next month another U-boat was sunk, this time by the Q-ship *Baralong*. The *Baralong*'s skipper, Lt-Commander Godfrey Herbert, had no compunction about disposing of survivors from the U-27 which he sank while she was engaged in attacking the SS *Nicosian*, loaded with army mules from America. Admiral Oliver praised Herbert for his 'skill and discretion';[15] but this was premature since he disposed of the German survivors under the eyes of the 'hard-case' muleteers,[16] several of whom were disposed to tell their story when they eventually got back to their American homeland.

[13] 5 June, 10 and 16 July 1914. Using others to promote his ideas was a characteristic Fisher ploy. He had presented his own Memorandum to the Prime Minister six months before the outbreak of war (ADM 116/3454).

[14] R.H. Gibson and M. Prendergast, *The German Submarine War 1914-1918* (London, Constable, 1931), pp. 45–8.

[15] ADM 137/385 (22 August 1915).

[16] The epithet, designed to discredit, occurs in Herbert's account, incorporated in E. Keble Chatterton, *Amazing Adventure* (London, Hurst & Blackett, 1936), p. 141.

The story broke in the *New York World* (7 October 1915), and on 14 October the *Chicago Evening American* began a five-day serialization of the event by eye-witness James J. Curran. The lurid, dime-novel style may be due to a ghosting journalist. Certainly some of the details contested by Herbert, when the Admiralty required him to prepare a point-by-point refutation, don't appear in Curran's formal affidavit.[17] But the essentials are there, and are confirmed by other deponents. They deal with the shooting of some half-dozen Germans in the water and Herbert's sending a party of marines aboard the *Nicosian* to kill five others who had sought refuge there. Four were shot while the fifth, the captain, jumped back into the water where he was riddled by rifle-fire. Of this latter point Herbert comments: 'Nothing seen of this and not believed. Taking into consideration the tissue of lies contained in the forgoing [*sic*] narrative.' But Herbert's own way with the truth seems pretty casual. According to his initial report, the Germans aboard the *Nicosian* were found dying of 'injuries they had received from lyddite shell'. In a later formal statement, he describes giving orders for the marines to 'get the first shot in. The whole affair was done in hot blood which a calmer judgement might regret.'[18] Some of what is slurred over here emerges in his account for Chatterton's book (p. 139), which tells how all were shot out of hand, including several huddled in the propellor-shaft alley. The stress on hot blood is interesting. Curran's deposition, made on 8 October, twice uses the phrase 'in cold blood'.[19] A secret memorandum to the Admiralty conveys 'Balfour's view [that] the point to be emphasized is that whatever happened on board the "Nicosian" was done in "hot blood", without authority, in fair fight against an armed enemy in possession of the ship; and should be contrasted with the deliberate shooting of the defenceless crew of E.13, stranded in a neutral's territorial waters, under definite orders from officers commanding German destroyers.'[20]

The Balfour memorandum shows the authorities' fear that this embarrassing issue would be 'raised in the House of Commons'. This fear was unrealized, the first public mention being made by Viscount Milner in the House of Lords on 8 November 1915. He was arguing the absurdity of censoring stories in the British press which had been fully aired throughout the rest of the world. Omitting the name, he instanced the *Baralong*, deploring the fact that this meant there was no chance to contradict 'this horrible calumny'.[21] Not until 5 January 1916 did it reach the British press, following the publication of Parliamentary Paper Cd 8144. The latter contained the full German complaint together with a reply by Grey, Foreign Secretary, on behalf of the Government. Herbert's denials were not used,

[17]ADM 137/385 (10 November 1915); Cd 8144, pp. 9–13.
[18]ADM 137/385 (20 August 1915; 10 November 1915).
[19]Cd 8144, p. 11; it evidently occurred in the deposition of 5 October, too, since it is picked up in the *Boston Traveler*, 8 October 1915.
[20]ADM 137/385, signed J. Masterton Smith, 26 October 1915.
[21]*Parliamentary Debates* (Lords), 5th Ser., Vol. 20, 26 October 1915–27 January 1916 (London, HMSO, 1916), col. 187 (8 November 1915).

though the testimonies of two Americans from the *Nicosian* who had joined the British Army were fed to the press. Their versions appeared first in the *Blackpool Herald* (11 January 1916) since they were stationed in that area. They contended that the shooting aboard the *Nicosian* was of wounded mules, and that their fellow Americans were for the most part disaffected New York gangsters. (Curran, the most damaging witness, was a travelling salesman from Chicago.) Officially, the Government found it unnecessary to answer the German charges. Instead, Grey resorts to heavy irony: the 'Government note with great satisfaction, though some surprise, the anxiety now expressed by the German Government that the principles of civilized warfare should be vindicated.' Along with enquiry into this incident, 'which has suddenly reminded the German Government that such principles exist', he proposes that several other incidents taking place about the same time should be investigated (pp. 16–17). These include the one referred to in the Balfour memorandum. Another is the sinking of the *Arabic* which Herbert, in his statement of 10 November, says 'was fresh in the minds' of his crew when they attacked the U-boat. The point is improved in an addition to this statement mentioning suspicions that the sinking was perpetrated by this 'same submarine, with the loss of 47 non-combatant lives.'

But well before the appearance of the Parliamentary Paper, the *Baralong* must have been a by-word amongst naval personnel in this country as well as Germany. When Lieutenant Gordon Campbell reported to the Admiralty in October 1915, he was invited to undertake special service, its nature being sufficiently indicated by reference to the *Baralong*.[22] When the German raider *Greif* was sunk (28 February 1916), one of her lieutenants, glad to be safe aboard HMS *Comus*, confided 'that he could not understand the Baralong affair being done by officers of the British Navy'.[23] On the other hand, the German press naturally professed to discover, in this affair, an essential aspect of the British character. Herbert came to be known as Mr Baralong – sometimes John Baralong, synonymous with John Bull.[24] This mode of reference might have been encouraged by suspicion of the name William McBride, by which the *Baralong's* commander was first publicly known. Curran claimed to have read a note from Herbert to the *Nicosian's* skipper signed thus, and it remained unchallenged in both the Berlin *Memorandum* and the British reply.[25] A German wrote of the *Baralong* affair that 'since the officers were not expelled from the naval officer corps, but decorated by the King of England with highest honours, it must see in these murderers

[22]*My Mystery Ships* (London, Hodder & Stoughton, 1928), p. 31.
[23]ADM 137/3620 (report by Lieut Henry Hamilton).
[24]For instance in a 6th War Loan leaflet issued by Cologne University reproduced in R. Lebeck and M. Schütte, *Propagandapostkarten I* (Dortmund, Harenberg, 1980), p. 16.
[25]November 1915, included as first part of White Book, *Der Baralong-Fall* (Berlin, Heumann, 1916); and Cd 8144. Herbert, in his rebuttal of the *Chicago Evening American's* story, denies that he used this alias; though to have done so would have been in line with the legitimate obfuscation created about the existence and function of Q-ships.

a mirror image of the whole English nation.' The same point had already been made in a cartoon by Blix, showing how 'Der Baralong-Mörder erzählt zu Windsor den Vorgang'.[26] The Germans had good reason to assume official approbation, which gained for Herbert a DSO and for Collins, leader of the boarding-party, a DSM. In addition, both had been noted for early promotion. Indeed, the words ascribed to Herbert by one witness – 'My orders are to take no prisoners' – would have been pretty well true (Cd 8144). The Admiralty not only recognized the threat of the U-boat to Britain's survival but had a rooted hatred for a weapon which challenged her sea supremacy. Long before, Admiral Wilson had viewed submarines as 'un-English', proposing to treat them in wartime 'as pirate vessels and to hang their crews'. Following the outbreak of war, the Admiralty considered court-martialling U-boat crews which had attacked merchant ships without warning; but this raised the problem of reprisals.[27] Far simpler was quietly to dispose of survivors; and Lieutenant C.A.P. Gardiner, in command of Q-ship *Lyons*, wrote to Captain Richmond that the order to take no prisoners was 'damnable'.[28]

The Germans complained of draconian measures adopted towards U-boat crews in early 1916 and returned to the issue after hearing from one of the two survivors of the *Baralong*'s second victim, U41.[29] Their wireless report told of the disinclination to take prisoners, the failure to render adequate medical assistance to the seriously wounded Oberleutnant Crompton, and obstructions to his repatriation despite his physical condition. Crompton's own version of his adventures retained these essential features, which had already become the property of the German press.[30] The British ship had not been identified as the *Baralong* since by then it went under the name of *Wyandra* and Lt-Commander A. Wilmot-Smith had replaced Herbert. But the style was unmistakable: the *Ostfriesischen Kurier* headed the story 'Ein neuer Baralong Fall'.[31] Clearly worried by this attack, the Admiralty made instant reply.[32] The initial German claim that Crompton was denied medical aid aboard the *Baralong* was rebutted by Crompton himself.[33] However, it is certainly true that the *Baralong*'s new skipper was impatient at having to take prisoners: 'unfortunately having got all the crew of the "Urbino" on board, and not knowing if they were to be trusted, had to pick them up, they could not have been left in the boat in case they should have been picked up by a neutral

[26]Hans-Erich Tzschirner, *Die Baralong-Bestialität* (Berlin, Börngräber [1917/181]), p. 12; *Simplicissimus*, 1 February 1916.
[27]Admiral Sir Reginald Bacon, *From 1900 Onward* (London, Hutchinson, 1940), p. 50; 'Treatment of the Crews of Enemy Submarines', ADM 137/2822.
[28]20 April 1915, Richmond MSS (National Maritime Mus., RIC/7/4).
[29]Cd 8176; *Times*, 7 November 1916.
[30]'*U-41*' *der zweite 'Baralong'* (Berlin, Scherl, 1917).
[31]No. 262, Suppt (7 November 1916).
[32]ADM 137/385. See *Times*, 7 November 1916.
[33]Crompton's official report, ADM 137/385.

ship.'[34] The Admiralty declared that the German accusation about 'orders that survivors of German submarines need not be rescued is an absolute lie'.[35] Further German needling in a sensitive area prompted an Admiralty pamphlet, *Does the British Navy Take Prisoners?*, which also included Smith's account of Crompton's rescue and subsequent medical attention aboard the Q-ship.[36]

It was simple enough to incense the public against the U-boat. While the *Hamburger Korrespondenz* might reasonably point out that 'It is foolish to wish to force submarine war under the rules of times which did not know submarines', a British periodical could be reproachful that sometimes U-boat personnel were still being taken prisoner.[37] For whereas the British blockade of Germany must have resulted indirectly in many civilian deaths – it has been estimated that the war killed off 700,000 in Germany through malnutrition – loss of life through U-boat activities had an immediacy which was much more emotive. It has been claimed that the successes of the British Submarine Service were achieved 'without costing one single non-combatant the loss of his or her life'.[38] But, so too, it has been noticed that 'the British had fewer targets or incentives to wage unrestricted submarine warfare.'[39] They also had luck: there is the remarkable instance of Naismith, torpedoing a crowded vessel near Constantinople. Only after the torpedo failed to explode did he observe that the people massed on deck were not troops but refugees, including many women and children.[40] Admiral Scheer was right about British hypocrisy in these matters;[41] though his censure would have carried more weight had the Germans not exhibited much the same defect over the *franc-tireur* issue. Certainly British outcries against violation of the international sea-laws sound hollow after the campaign waged a few years earlier against the ratifying of the Declaration of London. This was especially fierce in the pages of the *Standard*, which inveighed against yielding 'to other nations every essential maritime right won for this country by centuries of warfare'.[42] Indeed, in the course of the war, the Royal Navy had shed every international restriction as occasion required. When Britain protested that Sweden had altered a Hague regulation to debar submarines from its

[34] ADM 137/385: Report to Vice-Admiral Sir Charles Coke, Queenstown, 25 September 1915. The *Baralong's* log for 24 September makes no mention of the U-boat, though several words have been heavily deleted (ADM 53/34792).

[35] *Times*, 7 November 1916.

[36] See memo from Brownrigg, Admiralty's Chief Censor, to Press Bureau, 14 November 1916 (ADM 137/385). The ensuing pamphlet was printed by Darling & Son, London.

[37] *Times*, 17 May 1915; *The Great War*, ed. H.W. Wilson and J.A. Hammerton (13 vols., London, 1914–19), IX, p. 254.

[38] William Guy Carr, *Hell's Angels of the Deep* (London, Hutchinson, 1932), p. 283.

[39] Read, *Atrocity Propaganda*, p. 230.

[40] Peter Shankland and Anthony Hunter, *Dardanelles Patrol* (London, etc., Granada, 1971), pp. 117–18.

[41] Reinhard Scheer, *Germany's High Sea Fleet in the World War* (London, etc., Cassell, 1920), p. 106.

[42] 23 January 1911.

territorial waters, the Swedish Foreign Minister tartly pointed this out. The blockade of Germany itself was 'undertaken not under the rules of Blockade but under the Reprisals Orders in Council' of 11 March 1915. In April 1918 the Government was actually planning the abrogation of the Declaration of Paris as part of the peace negotiations.[43]

In truth, expediency ruled on both sides. There is apt irony in the way that the Latin tag 'Necessity knows no law' was foisted upon Bethmann-Hollweg, whilst he could describe the American Decatur's 'My country, right or wrong' as a 'proud English motto'.[44] But Britain's sea policy was a good deal less damaging as far as neutral opinion went than Germany's unrestricted submarine warfare. Resumption of the latter in February 1917 gave a renewed bitterness to the Allied propaganda war, centring on the sinking of hospital ships. Hospital ships were claimed as legitimate targets because of a widely held view amongst the enemy that they were being misused for the transport of military supplies and personnel. During the War Crimes trials at Leipzig in 1921, the court gave credence to the statement of Korvettenkapitän Saalwächter 'that throughout the German fleet [such misuse] was a matter of general belief'.[45] The combination of Red Cross emblem and armour was a favourite target of the German caricaturist.[46] And U-boat Captain Spiegel, who was well regarded by post-war British commentators for his humanity, describes seeing a clearly-marked hospital ship 'loaded from bow to stern with artillery supplies, and amongst the guns and ammunition, there was crowded an army of soldiers and horses'.[47]

Spiegel is quite likely to have seen khaki-clad figures crowding the decks of a hospital ship. The other details might have been supplied by the power of suggestion. Misuse certainly occurred. Read establishes that, as 'a matter of military economy', ambulances returning to the front often took a load of ammunition.[48] Hospital ships offered the same temptation, though what Spiegel describes would have meant an extraordinary lack of discretion. But it is precisely a lack of discretion early in the war which laid the basis for German conviction that hospital ships were being misused. Some flagrant breaches occurred, such as the use, in December 1915, of Italian hospital ships to convey pontoons to Malta; or the regular transporting of troops back to active duty after a period of convalescence.[49] But the real source of German complaints lay in a tactless habit to which

[43]ADM 137/2823 (telegram from Mr Howard, Stockholm, 1 December 1915); ADM 167/54.
[44]*Times History of the War* (22 vols., London, 1914–21), V, p. 166; *Reflections on the World War*, trans. George Young (London, Thornton Butterworth, 1920), p. 162.
[45]Cmd 1450, p. 38. Scheer, *Germany's High Sea Fleet*, p. 62, bluntly states that British hospital ships, 'under cover of the Red Cross flag, were patently used for the transport of troops'.
[46]See Karl Arnold's cartoon (unsigned), *Kriegsflugblätter* to *Liller Kriegszeitung*, II, 17 (19 September 1915).
[47]*The Adventures of the U-202* [1916], (New York, Century, 1917), p. 154.
[48]*Atrocity Propaganda*, p. 62.
[49]ADM 116/1398; W.G. Macpherson, *Official History; Medical Services General History* (4 vols., London, HMSO, 1921–24), I, p. 113.

attention was first drawn by Captain Satow of the Naval Transport Office in Port Said. This was in July 1916 and it started off a controversy which smouldered on for more than a year. The *Nevasa* and *Oxfordshire* had arrived in Port Said carrying 'such a number of RAMC men in khaki as to make it appear that they had troops on board'. The *Nevasa* looked so suspicious that she 'was actually ordered into Algiers by a French patrol'.[50] The Admiralty's Director of Transports, Graeme Thomson, conceded that 'there have been repeated allusions in the German press to the crowd of khaki-clad men on board such vessels', but insisted on the legality of carrying medical personnel as passengers. However, W.J. Evans, Director of Establishments, recognized that there are circumstances where 'things lawful may not be expedient'.[51] It was better to surrender legal rights rather than endanger the hospital ships. To the Admiralty's credit, this remained its position throughout; but it was under continual pressure from the War Office. The latter, reluctant to abandon a convenient means of transportation, was not without its barrack-room lawyers; and when they failed it borrowed the Nelson blind eye to instructions.

A vast amount of heavy gear – ambulances, prefabricated huts, tents – as well as passengers, could be shipped aboard a great liner like the *Britannic*. When she resumed her trips to Mudron on 23 September 1916, one of her passengers was Vera Brittain. By the next trip, new Admiralty regulations had come into force to the effect that henceforth hospital ships would carry only invalids, their attendants, and no stores other than those required aboard ship. Permission was given by Admiral Oliver for the *Britannic's* cargo to proceed, since arrangements had been made prior to the issuing of the instruction. But it was her load on the return trip which drew a formal complaint from Berlin on 28 January 1917.[52] The next outward journey was to prove her last, and there are indications that again she was evading the instruction.[53] (It is a tribute to the power of British propaganda that Vera Brittain had no doubt that both the *Britannic* and the *Galeka*, aboard which she completed her journey to Malta, were torpedoed when all the evidence indicates that they struck mines.)[54]

The Foreign Office's role in all this seems to have been unhelpful. Although Grey is on record as being in agreement with the Admiralty (27 September 1916), the Foreign Office had already been found 'double-tongued' (W.J. Evans's expression) on a related matter.[55] Balfour, Lloyd George's Foreign Secretary, supported the Army's practice of conveying medical personnel and stores aboard hospital ships in December 1917, despite a War Cabinet decision, the previous June, to the contrary. (Lord

[50]ADM 116/1396.
[51]*Ibid.*
[52]Cd 8692, pp. 14–19.
[53]ADM 116/1396 and 116/1398.
[54]*Testament of Youth* (London, Gollancz, 1933), pp. 297, 304.
[55]ADM 116/1396, and 116/1398. The Admiralty proposed to instruct masters of hospital ships that carrying sick officers' servants or deceased soldiers' kit was undesirable. While professing to agree, the Foreign Office had 'undesirable' changed to 'permissible.'

Derby had quickly undercut the Cabinet decision, brushing the danger to helpless troops aside in consideration of the transport space.)[56] It was the Mediterranean hospital ships which brought the most frequent protests from Berlin. As early as November 1915, complaints were made that '70 British transports have passed Gibraltar, heavily laden and painted like hospital ships, on their way to Greek waters'.[57] Publicly the Admiralty could wax indignant, choosing to miss the point by insisting that 'There are 42 British hospital ships working to and from the Mediterranean – not 70 as stated'. But privately Admiral Hamilton, Second Sea Lord, confessed to Captain Jackson, Director of Operations Division, that 'considerable laxity is creeping in'.[58] According to the German memorandum of 28 January 1917, 'The worst breach of the . . . Hague Convention' lay in the carrying of troops. This remained the chief complaint in 1918 when, with the arrival of American troops, attention had shifted to the Atlantic. Included in the official German Wireless news of 24 April 1918 was the statement that 'From papers found on American airmen who were shot down it has been proved that for their own safety many of them crossed over on hospital ships'.[59] By taking 'crossed over' to refer to the Channel rather than the Atlantic, the Admiralty was able to sweep the charge aside since 'there are no hospital ships working the cross-Channel route'. A specific allegation about the transporting of American airmen was made against the American hospital ship *Comfort*.[60]

So the scene was set for the destruction of the *Llandovery Castle*, the first hospital ship to be sunk in 1918; though the *Guildford Castle* had been attacked a few months earlier. But one more, the *Warilda*, was to be lost, and it still made potent propaganda. 'New Hospital Ship Outrage: Blinded Men Drowned', ran the *Daily Sketch* headline for 6 August 1918, on a front page which also carried news of 'Mystery Boat VCs: How they lured the U-boats to their doom'. The emphases are similar whichever side suffers. The destruction of the Austrian vessel *Elektra* gained front-page attention – 'Contempt (*Mißachtung*) for Red Cross' – with stress on the ship's having been notified as a hospital ship and marked in the prescribed way.[61] She was torpedoed without warning, whether by Italian or French was unknown;[62] and inevitable comparison was made with the *Baralong* affair. There was one fatality but also – a propagandist bonus – two nurses were seriously wounded.

What separated the *Llandovery Castle* sinking from this and all other outrages against hospital ships was Oberleutnant Patzig's efforts to leave

[56]ADM 116/1396; CAB 24/19 (GT 1329).
[57]Cd 8692, p. 3.
[58]*Times*, 22 and 23 November 1915; ADM 116/1398 (7 December 1915).
[59]*Times*, 25 April 1918.
[60]*Times*, 2 July 1918.
[61]*Neue Freie Presse* (Vienna), 19 March 1916.
[62]It was the work of a French submarine, the day after the Russian hospital ship *Portugal* was torpedoed in the Black Sea: a detail which the Austrian report neglected to mention (CAB 23/1/46, 26 January 1917).

no survivors. It is an ugly affair and newspaper reports had no need to exaggerate. *The Times* called it 'a deliberately planned outrage carried through with typical German callousness', temperately stating that there were grounds for believing that the lifeboats had been fired on.[63] Nonetheless, taken together, these true statements still manage to create a somewhat false impression. The sinking was premeditated, but the sequel was a botched attempt to cover up when suspicions of illicit activity showed themselves apparently unfounded and certainly unprovable. According to a witness at the German War Trials, several lifeboats were approached by the U-boat to allow Patzig to interrogate the occupants.[64] His attempts to establish that there had been eight American flight officers aboard is interesting in view of those recent German accusations. But, getting nowhere with this, Patzig suggested that the big explosion aft as the *Llandovery Castle* sank indicated that there was ammunition aboard. But he must have realized that the second officer's explanation about exploding boilers was more likely.[65] That the captain's boat, the only one to survive, was accosted twice for purposes of questioning, and then released, was briskly reconciled with the idea that Patzig sought to dispose of witnesses: 'the decision to get rid of the survivors was formed after the boat had finally cast adrift from the Submarine'.[66] Having made a blunder, Patzig turned to clumsy improvising, apparently without much stomach for such ruthless solutions. At least he is alleged to have confided in his chief engineer 'that he could never do it a second time'.[67] Nor, evidently, was he capable of disposing of witnesses already in his power. Aboard the submarine were two officers from the SS *Atlantian*, sunk by him two days earlier. On repatriation after the war, they were able to give testimony at a time when the German Government was still denying all knowledge of the incident.[68]

The immediate reaction of the German Government had been entirely different from that of the British following the *Baralong* disclosures. A semi-official communique was issued with, as *The Times* put it (4 July), 'imprudent haste'. The desire was to shift the blame on to a mine, preferably a British one. Nor was there a German press embargo, where the response was both agitated and inconsistent. One newspaper found it 'superfluous to reproduce Reuter's details'. Another sought to discredit them by comparison with the evidence produced in the case of the Dutch hospital ship *Koningin Regentes*, 'which was most likely torpedoed by the English themselves'. A third 'maintains that the ship was in the barred zone, and further speaks of the "audacity" of the statement that the German commander was trying to leave no trace of his deed'.[69]

[63] 2 July 1918.
[64] Cmd 1450.
[65] *Times*, 2 July 1918.
[66] ADM 1/8511/19: Foreign Office memo to Admiralty, 22 May 1919.
[67] Cmd 1450, p. 51.
[68] ADM 1/8511/19: Admiralty letter to Under-Secretary at the Foreign Office, 6 February 1920.
[69] *Times*, 5 July 1918.

A Dutch newspaper concluded that this 'repulsive crime' was not that of a man deranged by war but of one convinced that the enemy was abusing the Red Cross flag.[70] It was easy enough for the Court at Leipzig to decide that 'the 120 men in khaki [seen to] board the "Llandovery Castle" in Tilbury Docks at the beginning of December, 1916, belonged to the Medical Corps'.[71] But equally it was just such reports which helped to shape the vessel's eventual destiny. Nor is there much doubt that, in Balfour's words, Patzig was following the orders of 'some superior German authority, who alleged the presence of the flight officers'.[72] Clearly Patzig was expecting to find eight American officers aboard. He was mistaken, but (runs the War Cabinet minute) '8 Canadian medical officers were to have been on board, of whom one did not join the ship'. Another odd feature was the Wolff Bureau statement of 3 July 1918 'to the effect that Canadian, not United States, airmen had been on board'.[73] The detail about the seven, rather than eight, doctors was omitted from the otherwise full account released to the press by the Admiralty. When a question was raised in the Commons about the doctor who had been left behind through illness, there was enough imprecision in the wording for Macnamara, Parliamentary Secretary to the Admiralty, to evade it with the minimum actual lying.[74] But the story reached the Canadian newspapers. Although the survivors were supposed to be kept incommunicado, details were sent to the Toronto *Globe* of an interview with an officer of the destroyer *Lysander* which picked them up. This officer declared that the eighth doctor's passage was cancelled at the last moment, drawing the inference that the ship was attacked as a result of information deriving from Halifax, the port of departure.[75] The officer making the statement is identified – on what basis is unclear – as the ship's commander in the *Halifax Herald*, a newspaper which set up a sustained clamour for a spy-hunt in the port.[76]

The Canadian link was important. The ship, a Union-Castle liner, had been chartered by the Canadian Government to carry CEF sick and wounded to Halifax. Since this was an outward trip, there were no wounded aboard. But the medical staff was for the most part Canadian, including 14 nurses who, according to *The Times*, were all in one lifeboat.[77] Their deaths, as Andrew Macphail put it, 'profoundly moved the heart of the world'.[78] The *Kingston Standard* even suggested that peaks in the Rockies should be named after them, following the precedent of that

[70]*Times*, 3 July 1918.
[71]Cmd 1450, p. 46.
[72]TS 26/14: Balfour to Sir Walter Townley (26 October 1918).
[73]*Ibid*. The War Cabinet minute is CAB 23-7/439 (3), 2 July 1918.
[74]*Parliamentary Debates* (Commons), 5th Ser., Vol. 109, 29 July-8 August 1918 (London, HMSO, 1918), cols 1328-29 (7 August 1918).
[75]3 July 1918.
[76]5 July 1918.
[77]2 July 1918.
[78]*Official History of the Canadian Forces in the Great War: The Medical Services* (Ottawa, Acland, 1925), p. 243.

already named Mount Cavell; the mountains becoming not only a lasting monument but 'the ineffaceable scroll of shame to German savagery'.[79]

More restrained was the memorial service held at St Andrew's Church in Toronto, where the Rev. Professor J.W. Macmillan of Winnipeg preached the sermon. At the core of his message was the proposition offered so trenchantly by Connie Field's documentary film about the Second World War, *The Life and Times of Rosie the Riveter* (1980). The exigencies of war force the authorities to alter the female stereotype accordingly. But, with the peace and its different demands, women are forced back – often painfully for the individual who has developed a new self-reliance – into the old stereotype. Macmillan, with nurses filling the whole of the centre of the church, chose to warn against this very process. To offset the popular view 'that this war is going to give woman her true position in the world', he related the story of the Jews of Prague who, saving the city in an emergency, were afterwards pushed back into the Ghetto. Don't be pushed back, he urged his congregation, but 'See that this war wins a world victory for women.'[80]

That this was reported in the regular *Globe* feature 'What Women are Doing' has its own irony. Elsewhere, the same newspaper is on more orthodox ground in discussing reprisals. Sir Charles Lucas notes how the incident stimulated recruitment and, gruesomely, how it produced in the Province of Quebec, a 'more wholesome outlook on the war'.[81] But the *Globe* is chiefly concerned with the effect of the news on Canadians already in the field: 'The memory of the nurses slain by the orders of Germany's militarists will give strength and purpose to the avenging arms of Canada's sons'.[82] The premier's visit to the Western front took the message to the soldiers direct: 'The bombing of Canadian hospitals and the sinking of the Canadian hospital ship *Llandovery Castle* will never be forgotten by our troops.'[83]

The beginning of the end of the war was the August offensive. J.F.B. Livesay, semi-official historian of Canada's part in it, writes: 'the battle-cry on the morning of August 8 was, "Remember the Llandovery Castle".'[84] The code word for the Canadian Corps was 'Llandovery Castle' and 'Operational instructions for the attack . . . bore the initials "L.C."'[85] The details are valuably amplified in Charles Yale Harrison's novelistic account, of which he notes that 'everything told in this book happened'.[86] Harrison was with the 14th Royal Montreal Regiment on 8 August, when it formed part of the 3rd Canadian Infantry Brigade. He describes how

[79]*Globe*, 6 July 1918.
[80]*Globe*, 12 July 1918.
[81]*The Empire at War*, ed. Sir Charles Lucas (5 vols., London, 1921–26), II, p. 64.
[82]3 July 1918.
[83]*Globe*, 6 July 1918.
[84]*Canada's Hundred Days* (Toronto, Allen, 1919), p. 94.
[85]G.W.L. Nicholson, *Official History of the Canadian Army in the First World War* (Ottawa, Duhamel, 1962), p. 398.
[86]*Generals Die in Bed* [1930], 2nd edn (London, Douglas, 1931), p. 9.

Brigadier-General Tuxford visited the Brigade before the battle. Dispassionately, he read out the story of the *Llandovery Castle* sinking which, if Harrison's memory serves him aright, gave scant attention to facts: 'the lifeboats were sprayed by machine-gun fire as the nurses appealed in vain to the laughing men in the U-boat . . . the amputation cases went to the bottom instantly . . . they couldn't swim, poor chaps . . . the salt water added to their dying agony.' Other staff officers make their contribution: 'the battle in which we will soon be engaged will be remembered by generations still unborn as *The Battle of Llandovery Castle*'. Finally Harrison's popular CO speaks – that would be Lt-Colonel Dick Worrall: 'I'm not saying for you not to take prisoners. That's against international rules. All that I'm saying is that if you take any we'll have to feed 'em out of our rations' (pp. 228–30). Whether Harrison's final comment is artistic licence or reflects a rumour of the time is hard to say. As he is taken aboard a hospital ship – he was wounded in the foot on 8 August – he enquires from an orderly about the chances of getting torpedoed like the *Llandovery Castle*: 'The *Llandovery Castle*? . . . That was bloody murder, brother. Our officers oughta be shot for that. She was carryin' supplies and war material' (p. 248).

'L.C. Instructions No. 6' of 7 August 1918 spoke of 'thrusting the enemy back with determination'.[87] Presumably the *Llandovery Castle* propaganda was no hindrance to that objective. The savagery of the August fighting is everywhere attested, though customarily with its pendant apologetics. Livesay writes: 'the 21st Battalion in particular was little inclined to mercy after a Boche prisoner had shot down one of their officers.'[88] Coningsby Dawson, an American officer in a Canadian artillery battery, describes how a 20-year-old tank officer was found, 'stripped naked and bound to his tank', bombed to death: 'When I tell you that no prisoners were taken for the next twenty-four hours, I think you will applaud and wonder why the twenty-four hours wasn't extended. The men said they got sick of killing.'[89] It is the mood recorded in French's diary, a mood fostered to win battles at the cost of all remaining humanity.

The *Baralong* affair could prompt this mood. It was a sore picked at by German publicists through three years of war and beyond. The British had their recurrent topics, too. But the pressure which they exerted at sea furnished powerful advantages in that opportunistic kind of propaganda at which they excelled. Thus the War Cabinet agreed that the Home Secretary's speech in the Commons on the treatment of enemy aliens could be nicely sharpened by reference to the sinking of the *Llandovery Castle*, 'which engendered a state of public anger that was impossible to control'.[90] In his speech of welcome to the delegates at the Inter-Parliamentary Commercial Conference on 1 July 1918, Bonar Law applied to the *Llandovery*

[87]WO 95/3730.
[88]*Canada's Hundred Days*, p. 131.
[89]*Living Bayonets* (New York/London, Lane, 1919), p. 204.
[90]CAB 23–7/444 (11), 11 July 1918.

Castle atrocity that indiscreet phrase, *spurlos versenkt*, used by Count Luxburg, *chargé d'affaires* at Buenos Aires, in May 1917.[91] Luxburg's phrase, like Patzig's action, was a gift to the Entente propagandist. Bonar Law spices it with rhetoric from *Lusitania* days: 'A wild beast is at large. (Cheers.) There is no use arguing with it or reasoning with it. There is only one thing to do. (A voice. – "Kill it").'[92] This led straight to the heart of conference business, articulated by Sir Watson Rutherford: 'German methods in war were frequently inhuman and devilish, and those devilish and dishonest practices of *Kultur* warfare had each got its counterpart in *Kultur* trade'. In short, this was a war for world markets and the Allied countries must form a preferential trading league against Germany. Outright victory was a necessary step towards this, and the *Llandovery Castle* sinking would stiffen resolve in the face of Germany's massive peace offensive which was then, says *The Times*, 'in full swing'. Communications pouring in to the Foreign Office from British embassies throughout neutral Europe suggested that the authoritative German view of the Spring Offensive was that it had not broken the Western front deadlock but would provide a good bargaining platform.[93] Germany was ready to discuss 'Peace with honour', a catchphrase which had served Disraeli's party well during the Crimean War and later. But the Entente slogan was 'Victorious peace'.

It has been suggested that atrocity propaganda 'contributed more than any other single factor to the making of a severe peace'; that, since governments had fostered 'this propaganda, the statesmen at Paris is 1919 were largely prisoners of their own machinations'.[94] But the hard-headed ones like Bonar Law are speculators not prisoners. War and its atrocities, like propaganda in its many aspects, are counters in the game of power.

[91]Robert Lansing, *War Memoirs* (Indianapolis, NY, Bobbs-Merrill, 1935), p. 327.
[92]*Times*, 12 May 1915; *Times*, 3 July 1918.
[93]*Times*, 6 June 1918; FO 371/3223.
[94]Read, *Atrocity Propaganda*, p. viii.

Note

There is no specific work on the BBC Empire Service, although a good deal of information can be found, very widely scattered, in the first three volumes of the daunting and relatively impenetrable four-volume *The History of Broadcasting in the United Kingdom* by Asa Briggs (London, Oxford University Press, 1961, 1965, and 1970). The Briggs volumes will remain essential works of reference, but it must be remembered that Briggs wrote from the BBC's point of view (he served as a Governor for some years). He writes as an admirer of Reith who accepts Reith's objectives and self-justifications uncritically. Moreover, Briggs's focus is metropolitan and there is very little on broadcasting within the Empire, while his more accessible single-volume *The BBC, the First Fifty Years* (Oxford, Oxford University Press, 1985) contains only a brief reference to the Empire Service. The political, diplomatic and cultural context in which the Empire Service was created can be found in Philip M. Taylor, *The Projection of Britain* (Cambridge, Cambridge University Press, 1981). The projection of the Empire to the domestic audience is examined in John M. MacKenzie, ' "In Touch with the Infinite": the BBC and the Empire, 1923–53' in John M. MacKenzie, ed., *Imperialism and Popular Culture* (Manchester, Manchester University Press, 1986). Thomas G. August, in *The Selling of the Empire, British and French Imperialist Propaganda, 1890–1940* (London, Greenwood Press, 1985) has discovered (pp. 96–101) examples of Colonial Office interference in talks on the Empire and complaints about the accuracy of news items on the colonies, but these appear to relate to domestic rather than Empire broadcasting. Other publications on the BBC contain little that is relevant to the Empire Service. Technical and social aspects of broadcasting can be found in Mark Pegg, *Broadcasting and Society* (London, Croom Helm, 1983), while a series of articles by Paddy Scannel and David Cardiff deal with domestic broadcasting policies that illustrate covert propaganda techniques. These can be found in various issues of *Culture, Media, and Society* and are usefully summarized in their chapter in Bernard Waites, Tony Bennett, and Graham Martin, eds., *Popular Culture: Past and Present* (London, Croom Helm, 1982). The same authors are currently working on a social history of the BBC, but whether it will contain anything on Empire broadcasting is not known.

3

Propaganda and the BBC Empire Service, 1932–42

John M. MacKenzie

The British have always liked to portray propaganda as a foreign concept. The origins of the word in the history of the Roman Catholic Church emphasized its alien qualities while its use by the totalitarian states of Europe in the inter-war years confirmed its unacceptablity. The British preferred persuasion through publicity, the principled propagation of Anglo-Saxon truth, and they preferred to promote it by unofficial rather than official agencies. They were forced into propagandist activity only in time of war, when it was defensive in character and could be described by the much more positive word 'information'. The first great mobilization of 'information' of this sort had occurred in the First World War, but with the Armistice its machinery had been entirely dismantled.[1] It could be said that this alleged relationship of the British with propaganda has itself been one of the great successes of British propagandist activity and until recently it has been accepted by many historians.

There have now been some notable revisions of this British self-evaluation. Propaganda, though often disguised in other terminology, has been shown to have been a continuing and live issue in both British external and domestic policy. Philip Taylor has revealed the extent to which propagandist agencies designed to project Britain overseas were discussed and developed, albeit belatedly, in Britain in the 1930s.[2] Stephen Constantine has examined the diverse propagandist activities of the Empire Marketing Board (EMB) on the domestic front,[3] while students of cinema history have highlighted the unofficial and official uses of film to both positive and negative propagandist ends. In particular, Jeffrey Richards has demonstrated how effective film censorship was in ensuring that only a series of acceptable messages could be transmitted to the British public through film, protecting it, in other words, from the propaganda of

[1]Michael Sanders and Philip M. Taylor, *British Propaganda during the First World War, 1914-18* (London, Macmillan, 1982).
[2]Philip M. Taylor, *The Projection of Britain* (Cambridge, Cambridge University Press, 1981).
[3]Stephen Constantine, 'Bringing the Empire Alive, the Empire Marketing Board and Imperial Propaganda, 1926-33' in John M. MacKenzie, ed., *Imperialism and Popular Culture* (Manchester, Manchester University Press, 1986), pp. 192-231.

those whose ideas ran counter to the accepted British consensus.[4] The components of that consensus have been shown to be closely bound up with a complex of ideas, imperial, monarchical, class conciliatory and racially exclusive, that constituted British patriotism in the period.[5] This ideological cluster was promoted through the popular media of the time, not just the cinema, but also broadcasting by the monopolist BBC.[6]

The BBC was of course most active on the domestic front, but the worldwide power of broadcasting was recognized at an early stage. John Reith, who dominated the BBC for its first 15 years, saw broadcasting as a mystical force that could put both its practitioners and its listeners 'in touch with the infinite'.[7] He saw the British Empire as an international communion, an existing and practicable form of internationalism that could be given new meaning through the medium of broadcasting. From the earliest days of the BBC he envisaged the creation of an imperial short-wave broadcasting network, and was enthralled by its possibilities in bringing the democratic, freedom-loving, English-speaking peoples together, offering them the power to extend their social and political philosophies.

In his book *Broadcast over Britain* of 1924 Reith referred to the 'universality of the ether'. Broadcasting had the power to 'cast a girdle round the earth with bonds that are all the stronger because invisible', contributing to the unity of mankind and putting it in touch with 'Omnipotence'. On a more mundane level, the public affairs of the Empire could be debated within hearing of the Empire. The farthest-flung peasant could hear the statesmen of the Home Country, the Dominions and colonies. The cultural content of Reith's broadcasting prospectus was also laid out. Broadcasting was to be a 'servant of culture and culture has been called the study of perfection'. He saw a 'consolidating influence at work' in all its 'manifold phases' of 'entertainment or edification', 'enlightenment or education'. It could carry to the world 'great ceremonies of widespread interest' and convey to the furthest reaches of the colonies 'the chimes of the clock which beats the time over the mother of parliaments at the heart of the Empire'.[8] Culture, national ritual, the aural iconography of Big Ben were indeed to be the principal obsessions of the Empire Service established eight years after the publication of Reith's ideas.

Two great barriers lay in the way of the attainment of Reith's dream. One was the parsimony of the Treasury, inevitably exacerbated by the decline in Government revenues during the Depression. Propaganda by the airwaves was far too nebulous a concept for Treasury mandarins anxious

[4]Jeffrey Richards, 'The British Board of Film Censors and content control in the 1930s: images of Britain' and 'Foreign affairs', *Historical Journal of Film, Radio, and Television*, 1 (1981), pp. 95–116 and 2 (1982), pp. 39–48.
[5]John M. MacKenzie, *Propaganda and Empire* (Manchester, Manchester University Press, 1984).
[6]John M. MacKenzie, 'In touch with the Infinite, the BBC and the Empire, 1923–53' in MacKenzie, *Imperialism*, pp. 165–91.
[7]J.C.W. Reith, *Broadcast Over Britain* (London, Hodder & Stoughton, 1924), one of the chapter headings.
[8]Reith, *Broadcast*, pp. 15, 217–21.

to see practical and quantifiable returns for all expenditure. The second was the rapidly developing nationalism of the white dominions of the British Empire. Broadcasting systems in the dominions were being developed by a variety of different methods, public and private, to establish local identities, and dominion governments were as strapped for cash as that of the mother country. Reith's ideal was undoubtedly concerned primarily with a white imperial community, but it was the colonial governors of the 'dependent' territories, with their large black and brown populations, who showed greatest interest in imperial broadcasting. Bearing no electoral obligations, they could indulge in the luxury of theorizing on the dissemination of British values, consolidating the Empire through a set of aural symbols and using the medium to spread such benefits as education, hygiene, good agricultural practice. As financial autocracies they could earmark official funding without opposition, and perhaps use broadcasting to help contain the, to them, artificial elite nationalism spreading through their territories. For some of them at least, the wireless could be a powerful weapon in what Churchill later described as 'battles for the Empires of the mind'.[9]

Short-wave broadcasting with its advantage of great range had been a reality since 1924 when it had been introduced in the United States. The first European short-wave station, Eindhoven in the Netherlands, had started transmitting in 1927.[10] In the same year, an amateur radio enthusiast, Gerald Marcuse, had been licensed to broadcast on short-wave to the Empire for two hours per day, three days per week. In September 1927 an Australian programme including a song by Nellie Melba and a message from the Prime Minister of Australia had been received in Britain and re-transmitted. Two months later the Armistice Day programme had been transmitted to Australia. It had been received in other dominions too, but not in India, although the quality had been very poor. Experimental broadcasts had continued in 1928 though no news could be carried on these because Reuters would not permit it. Breakdowns at the transmitter (5SW) put all these experiments off the air in late 1928 and the demand for a full service became insistent both inside and outside the BBC.

The will to fund it was, however, absent. The idea was put to a conference of colonial governors in 1927, and three schemes were subsequently submitted to the Colonial and Dominions Offices by the BBC in 1929 and 1930.[11] They were judged too expensive, though one of them

[9]In a speech at Harvard University, September 1943.
[10]BBC Written Archives Centre, Caversham, file E4/51, 'Historical Notes'. All subsequent file numbers refer to this Archive. Material on the Empire Service can be found scattered in Asa Briggs, *The History of Broadcasting in the United Kingdom*, Vol. 1, *The Birth of Broadcasting* (London, Oxford University Press, 1961), Vol. 2, *The Golden Age of Wireless* (London, Oxford University Press, 1965), and Vol. 3, *The War of Words* (London, Oxford University Press, 1970).
[11]Papers on the BBC's relationship with the Colonial Office can be found in files E4/23–25 and E4/51.

proposed the expenditure of no more than £22,000 per annum for five years, £2,000 being set aside for news. The proddings of Reith and the interest of the Secretaries of State Ormsby Gore and Sidney Webb were to no avail, however, in the face of the developing economic crisis. Although Stephen Tallents of the EMB lobbied for Empire broadcasting at the Ottawa Conference of 1932, the BBC had already given up all hope of official support and decided to go it alone. Money was found from its own resources to build a new short-wave transmitter at Daventry to be opened on 19 December 1932 and be spectacularly inaugurated by the first Christmas broadcast of George V to the Empire. The Empire Service (ES) was launched with a tiny staff and an initial budget of no more than £100 per week.

Before examining the objectives and extent of the new venture it is necessary to establish the extent to which broadcasting already existed within the dominions and colonies of the British Empire. Services had appeared shortly after the creation of the BBC itself. The four dominions (Canada, Australia, New Zealand, and South Africa) all established their own stations in the 20s. The Indian State Broadcasting Service and a Ceylon station were open by 1926 and by 1929 there were also broadcasting systems in Kenya, Singapore and Hong Kong. Many of these were primitive affairs, broadcasting for only short periods and with very few listeners. Reith was convinced that great broadcasting opportunities existed in India and that both the India Office and the Viceroy showed a failure of vision and a lack of moral appreciation of the value of broadcasting. The founding of the BBC ES was to give a considerable fillip to the development of broadcasting services in the West Indies, Rhodesia, and other African, Asian and Pacific colonies. The existence of an ES in London brought the issue into the area of colonial policy as we shall see below. Moreover, there was a considerable traffic in BBC expertise to the Empire in the 30s. BBC personnel advised on the establishment of systems or the framing of new broadcasting constitutions in Canada, South Africa, Egypt and Newfoundland, and themselves took office in senior positions in state-run services in India and Palestine. This close cooperation was reflected in the organization of imperial broadcasting and the dissemination of programmes and news.

There were four main ways in which short-wave broadcasting could be received in the Empire. One was by the possession of private short-wave receiving sets which gave the listener the power to select whichever station he desired. The second was by re-broadcasting from a local transmitter, which permitted the use of less sophisticated receivers, reducing listener choice. The third was by rediffusion, the re-transmitting of signals from London by a line system to loudspeakers in the homes of private subscribers. The fourth, communal loud-speakers in public places or in villages, could work by either transmission or line systems. Communal broadcasting usually involved an element of compulsion, since the loudspeakers could not be switched off. The first system was universal in the dominions and India, wherever a large white population was widely dispersed. The second and third were used in the towns of colonies where a largely expatriate community of white subscribers was heavily concentrated. There were experiments in the fourth throughout the Empire, though the most prominent communal listening schemes were in India, Palestine and East Africa.

The ES never fully succeeded in identifying and analysing its audience. The practicalities of world-wide broadcasting led the BBC to divide its transmissions into zones and this approach led to a particular set of geographical divisions: Australasia, India and the Far East, the Near East, Africa, and the Americas. But from the point of view of the material to be broadcast the BBC audience divided up in quite different ways. The obvious racial distinction between white and non-white subjects of the Empire could be refined further. Among the whites were the temporary residents of the Empire, official, military and commercial, expatriates who expected to return to Britain, and settlers in the dominions and elsewhere who did not, but whose allegiance remained divided between their new territories and the wider imperial community. With this category in mind the BBC maintained records of the proportion of British- to local-born residents in each dominion. Among the non-white population of the Empire the main distinction was not among the races and the continents but between educated, English-speaking formers of opinion and the great mass of indigenous populations.

The BBC never resolved this problem. The ES hoped that it reached both categories of whites and some at least of the first group of non-whites, but in some colonies it was even hoped that BBC transmissions would reach the masses. If the whites were expected to own their own sets, it was hoped that many non-whites would listen in public places, in cafes and shops in urban areas, as well as from official sources. The objectives of broadcasting were clearly different in the case of each audience. For expatriates it was essential to keep them in touch with home, provide them with a set of nostalgic and ritual links that would offer solace in exile, a reward and consolation for service in the tropics, and maintain their awareness of the larger imperial enterprise of which they were a part. The settlers had to be reminded of a wider imperial community, had to be offered a set of symbols that would counter regional loyalties (for example, Canada's proximity to the United States) while recognizing the creation of local traditions and patriotisms. The educated indigenous population had to be weaned from dangerously premature nationalist ideas, from rival ideologies, and reminded of the superior characteristics of British culture. The greater mass of native populations had to be educated in hygiene, improved agricultural practices, literacy possibly, and convinced that their futures did not lie in following the bourgeois, sectarian nationalist leaders. The one thing that all categories had in common was the need to retain their loyalty in time of conflict, to convince them of the rectitude of British participation in and aims for a future war, to avoid civil unrest and promote recruitment. And that overriding objective was not in fact recognized until war was imminent.

Ideally, the BBC would have required services tailored to each of these groups. That was both financially and technically impractical. They varied programming to suit apparent zonal preferences but that took little account of the more significant racial and social breakdown. Moreover, audience research was conducted almost exclusively in the two white categories, particularly the expatriate one.

The ES made more strenuous efforts to assess audience reaction than domestic services.[12] There were, perhaps, two reasons for this. A short-wave system was heavily reliant upon technical information, however unsophisticated, on reception at the outer limits of its broadcasting zones. More expert judgements would come from wireless enthusiasts. Secondly, the ES was run on such a shoestring that material on the effectiveness of its programmes would be likely to play a significant part in programme planning. The ES therefore encouraged listeners to send in letters indicating the quality of reception, and such letters often also contained criticism or appreciation of specific programmes. A larger correspondence dealing solely with programme preference was carefully analysed within the BBC and presented to the weekly meetings of ES managers, with shortened versions to the BBC Governors. Questionnaires were sent out, occasionally as part of a larger research scheme, seeking responses on both reception and likes and dislikes. The Empire tours of Malcolm Frost and J.B. Clark in 1933 and 37 respectively were partly directed to the same ends.

Between the opening of the service in December 1932 and May 1933 no fewer than 500 cables, 6000 letters, and 12,000 responses to questionnaires were received. In 1934 4000 letters were received in the first quarter, but by 1935 the quantity of correspondence was declining, no doubt reflecting a reduction in the novelty value of the service. The letters, almost entirely from expatriates or settlers of British descent, continued to flow in throughout the 30s. In May 1939 an Empire Public Relations Officer was appointed within an Overseas Intelligence Department at a time when about 1750 letters were being received each quarter. The results of one more systematic piece of questionnaire research appear in the BBC Archives, but unfortunately the file is not dated.[13] This research was conducted among British exiles (it was stressed that native listeners were not involved) in three areas – India, Burma and Ceylon; British colonies in West Africa; and the Near East, Persian Gulf and Red Sea area (including Iran, Iraq and Palestine). 600 questionnaires, 200 for each area, were sent out.

The answers to these, together with the analyses of correspondence running over many years, reveal that Reith was both right and wrong in his estimation of what broadcasting could achieve. The British abroad wished constantly to be reminded that they were British; they wished to receive comforting reassurances of home, aural links that would bind them in their

[12] E4/37–39 and E4/40–41.
[13] E4/42.

far-flung outposts of the Empire. There was an insatiable demand for Big Ben and the National Anthem. More letters alluded to the symbolic chimes of Westminster than to any other feature of the ES. The National Anthem had a similar iconographic significance and there was a storm of protest when its use was suspended between the announcement of the abdication of Edward VIII and the proclamation of George VI in 1936. Programmes involving sounds and news of home were greatly appreciated, as were references by announcers to the weather in London or scenes on the way to the studio. Above all, programmes relaying national ceremonies, the great imperial rituals involving the monarchy, secured the widest audience around the world. As one departmental minute noted, nothing could beat 'the strong appeal of pageantry to listeners overseas'.[14] The King's Christmas speeches, Trooping the Colour, armistice services, and the succession of royal events of the mid-30s – the Jubilee of George V, his death and funeral soon after, the wedding of the Duke of Kent, the proclamations of Edward VIII and George VI and the Coronation of the latter – gave the BBC unrivalled opportunities to send richly aural ceremonies around the world. These broadcasts captivated not only the exiles but also the settlers in the dominions and an admiring audience in the USA. They were also used, as we shall see, to bring the power of broadcasting to indigenous peoples, although in this case it is more difficult to gauge precise audience reaction.

In all these ways Reith was right. The aural icons and the imperial rituals seem to have had, by all accounts, a spellbinding power. But Reith's ambition to carry education and culture to the Empire met with a less receptive audience. The letters and questionnaires revealed that people in the Empire, like those at home, demanded most of all variety and light music. Talks of a certain sort, particular those by famous people, were acceptable, but decidedly not those like Miss Delafield's on Victorian literature – as one audience researcher put it, something of a 'more virile nature' was required.[15] Even Sir Walford Davies's musical talks, allegedly so popular at home, encountered greater resistance in the Empire. Talks of a nostalgic vein, talks about Britain, historical features on the Empire (for example, Gordon at Khartoum or a programme on H.M. Stanley including a recording of his voice), or histories of regiments (like one on the Black Watch) were greatly admired. Serious music had a much lower rating, while religion aroused no interest at all (as low as 1 per cent of respondents to questionnaires). Some interesting variations were discovered. More serious fare was appreciated by British officials in India and West Africa, reflecting the higher social class of their origins, while much more lowbrow tastes were encountered in Australia, Canada and South Africa. Even in India, however, many listeners announced that they could do without educational or 'uplifting' fare. They wanted light entertainment to cheer up the depression of the tropics (as one correspondent put it), to relax them after the trials of the day. They did not want Empire talks which only

[14]Departmental minute, 15 September 1938, E4/34.
[15]E4/37.

reminded them of work. They also disapproved of plays which required too much concentration, particularly given the problems of interference, and they were not very keen on programmes on sheepdog trials and 'less popular games like snooker'.

The programme-makers responded, and the titles of programmes indicate the desire to inform the Empire about Britain rather than the Empire about itself. Programmes included 'Round London at Night', 'London Log', 'This is England', 'A Canadian in London' and 'Made in England'. It was a metropolitan image that was most powerfully conveyed. The ES evinced little interest in items from the regions or the Celtic fringes and material in Welsh or Gaelic was strongly disapproved of. Standard English, delivered in a slow and precise manner that was to be long associated with BBC Overseas services, was the hallmark of the ES and dialect variations or regional accents were avoided.

Reith's ethereal hopes of educating his audience were, apparently, as chimerical in the Empire as they were at home. Indeed it was the mixed, occasionally high-brow, content of the BBC, together with the comparative weakness of the signals from Daventry that drove the imperial audience to other broadcasting stations when they had the option. The surveys enquired about rival services and often received alarming results. French short-wave broadcasting was largely discounted as too weak; broadcasting from Italy and the USA was unpopular (conservative listeners in the Empire disliked jazz and other forms of popular American music, perhaps reflecting the difficulties of receiving and enjoying such music in difficult atmospheric conditions, a problem that was also a barrier to the full appreciation of classical music); but the Dutch station Eindhoven and the German Zeesen were greatly liked. Both broadcast from powerful transmitters, and both adopted the policy of transmitting an almost undiluted fare of light and light classical music together with news. As 'aural wallpaper' it ran counter to Reith's high hopes of engaging the intellects and senses of his listeners, but on days other than those of ritualistic significance it was what the imperial audience wanted. Eindhoven and Zeesen were broadcasting in English long before the BBC used foreign languages, and they posed the same threat to imperial listening that Radios Luxembourg and Normandie did to the home audience or pirate pop broadcasting in a later era. It was a threat which created disturbance but not outright alarm until war threatened in the later 30s.

Before examining the capacity of broadcasting to influence the third audience, it is necessary to survey the Colonial Office's attempts to extend broadcasting activities throughout the Empire, so that facilities might exist for the re-transmission of BBC programmes as well as local material. Soon after the inauguration of the ES the Colonial Office attempted to identify and coordinate broadcasting developments throughout the colonial Empire. The Colonial Secretary sent out circular despatches to all colonial governors in January 1933 and again in March and April 1934.[16] These

16E4/23.

consisted of a series of enquiries and suggestions. The CO wished to know about the demand for broadcasting services, the existence of or planning for colonial radio stations, the type and quality of equipment, arrangements for licensing, and whether government or private systems were favoured. It was suggested that licences should stipulate that only British equipment should be used and that news should come only from the BBC or official British sources. The despatch of April 1934 laid out the three systems available – short-wave private receivers, re-broadcasting from a colonial transmitter, and rediffusion on a line system – and enquired as to the appropriateness of each to individual colonies.

The answers revealed the diversity of systems that already existed in the Empire. Hong Kong and Ceylon possessed government broadcasting stations. Kenya, Mauritius, Fiji, Singapore and Malaya all had stations in private hands operating under licence. Government rediffusion systems existed in the Falklands, Sierra Leone and Nigeria, with a system about to be started in the Gold Coast. Private rediffusion arrangements were used in Gibraltar and Barbados. In British Guiana and British North Borneo, whites owned short-wave sets, while other colonies planned relay systems.

In February 1935 the Colonial Secretary set up a Committee on Broadcasting in the Colonies, chaired by the Earl of Plymouth (who was parliamentary under-secretary at the Foreign Office 1936–39). In May 1935 another circular despatch pointed to the importance of 1935 as the King's Jubilee year. Broadcasts of the Jubilee would create a vivid realization of the connections of the Empire and the colonies should recognize the psychological importance of being able to participate in imperial ceremonial. The Committee received evidence from most of the colonies of the Empire and found the picture to be generally a disappointing one, as information from territories as diverse as Ceylon and the Gold Coast indicated. In Ceylon the broadcasting service had been operating for 10 years. There were only 3,080 licence holders, presumably mainly in the hands of British expatriates. The licence-fee income had fallen so far behind expenditure that a cumulative deficit of more than 250,000 rupees had been built up. In the Gold Coast the rediffusion system was opened in July 1935. By the following June (when the Committee was receiving its last submissions) there were 800 subscribers, although two-thirds of these were African. They paid 10 shillings per month or three pounds per annum to have a receiver in their homes.

The Committee reported in 1936 and issued a supplement in 1939 on the suitability of wavelengths for colonial broadcasting.[17] It is interesting to compare the various drafts of the report in the BBC Archives. In early versions the word 'propaganda' was used on several occasions, but by the time it was published the word had been entirely excised. Continuing anxiety about the word emerged in many BBC documents and its use in broadcasting, particularly in the Second World War, was banned. No

[17]E4/24. Figures on the number of broadcasting licences throughout the Empire can also be found in the papers of Cecil Graves, E4/87.

reference to 'our propaganda' was permitted although the word was freely used in internal documents discussing propagandist activities. In wartime, documents headed 'propaganda points' would contain lists of information to be transmitted while avoiding reference to the actual word. The insistence on the covert approach is indeed the principal message of the Colonial Office Committee on Broadcasting.

The Report began by quoting the Colonial Secretary's despatch on the psychological importance of ceremonial occasions of high importance and continued:

> Apart from these special occasions, the Empire Service has a significance which cannot be measured in terms of entertainment value. Regular daily contact with the Home Country (and at times with other parts of the Empire) and the repeated projection on the minds of listeners overseas of British culture and ideas, and all this implies, must exert a great influence. The effect of this in the long run is perhaps the more valuable because it is neither direct nor deliberate. Its importance cannot be assessed in a positive manner. It will vary in different territories with the race and education of the listeners and according to the extent to which they are subjected to other influences whether these be foreign wireless propaganda, films or the press, and the extent also to which it can displace these influences.

When colonial governments considered expenditure, the Committee went on, considerations outside the entertainment function should be taken into account. Broadcasting was not just an instrument of entertainment for Europeans and others of similar education but an 'instrument for advanced administration', an instrument for the enlightenment and education of the more backward sections of the population and for their instruction in public health and agriculture. For these reasons, broadcasting should be under government control and the extension of communal listening schemes was strongly recommended.

This leads us to a consideration of the BBC's efforts to reach the third of our audiences, the indigenous colonial populations. It is clear in all the evidence that short-wave radio sets and rediffusion subscriptions were purchased by the intellectual and commercial elite of many territories, but reaching the mass of the population was quite another problem. The masses could not afford short-wave sets and rediffusion techniques were impracticable in far-flung village communities. The answer seemed to be communal listening in villages or in public places in towns.

In early 1935 an experiment in village broadcasting was attempted in the North West Frontier Provinces of India.[18] The Marconi Company, eager to promote broadcasting in India, gave transmitters and village sets. They produced sets that would resist heat, dust and insects and which would offer a reasonable volume at 100 yards. Sets, batteries, and installations cost 800 rupees or £60. The scheme was not a success. Programmes

[18]E4/26–32.

consisted of digests of agricultural pamphlets and were not, apparently, particularly popular. There were soon staff difficulties in re-charging and changing batteries.

In 1935 the Punjab Government set aside 43,000 rupees for the introduction of village sets. Again the scheme was not successful, the broadcast material being insufficiently entertaining to attract the villagers' attention. By 1938 there were only 100 village sets in the whole of India, 15 in Bengal and 15 in Bombay presidency, all of them positioned in the village 'chowpal' or club. The loudspeakers operated on time switches, but the villagers soon found the means of turning the sets on at all times of the day thereby swiftly running down the batteries. Whether this registered approval of the new programmes offered by All India Radio (mixing music with little dramas on health and agriculture) or a desire to restore silence as soon as possible is unclear. Certainly the Indian Government thought it unlikely that the system would develop and concluded that it was difficult to gauge the extent to which the life of the villagers could be moulded through broadcasting.

A scheme inaugurated in Palestine was regarded as more successful. An advisory committee was set up by the High Commissioner for Palestine in 1935. As a result of its report central equipment was installed and loudspeakers were supplied to halls, schools, and to 100 villages each with a population of over 1000. Broadcasts were to be in both English and Arabic with news and other material from London re-transmitted from time to time. The Palestine system was urged upon other colonies by the Secretary of State, Ormsby Gore, in 1938.

One colony that had already expressed interest was Kenya. In 1936 the *East African Standard* had urged the broadcasting of propaganda to the African reserves, qualifying its use of the word by suggesting that this could be directed not to politics but to the raising of African standards. Subsequently the Kenya Government decided to spend £250 on broadcasting of this sort in order to test African reactions. It was seen as a media experiment along the lines of the Bantu Educational Kinema Experiment in film. Major L.A. Notcutt, the Director of the latter, reported on the broadcasting scheme. He suggested that Africans were perfectly capable of using short-wave receivers, that they wanted instruction rather than entertainment, but that costs would be prohibitive and that gramophone records taken to villages would have the same effect. The Kenya scheme faded away for lack of funds.

For the rest, communal listening had taken place in a number of colonies as part of the imperial spectaculars of the 30s. In Sierra Leone the broadcasting system was inaugurated by the re-transmission of a broadcast from London on loudspeakers both inside and outside the Wilberforce Memorial Hall in Freetown. The audience, it was reported, represented every class and every age. The Governor contrived to walk into the hall at the precise moment the National Anthem was broadcast from London and the people thought it a miracle. The King's speech at the 1935 Jubilee was publicly broadcast in Georgetown, British Guiana, and the Governor duly reported on the powerful bond established with the numerous other units of the colonial Empire. No doubt such public spectaculars had a powerful novelty value, but the proportion of indigenous people actually encountering broadcasting must have been minute. Despite repeated recommendations for the extension of the idea of group listening in colonial territories the BBC recognized at the outset of the Second World War that communal broadcasting could be entirely discounted from a propaganda point of view.

The main problem in reaching the indigenous populations of colonial territories was the difficulty of language. The Ceylon system blamed its inability to extend the number of its native listeners on the lack of availability of material in the vernaculars. Only All India Radio could reach non-English speakers effectively and there were very few with sets to listen. Yet, by the war the German station at Zeesen was already broadcasting in Hindustani. When the BBC did turn to foreign-language broadcasting it started with Arabic in 1938, followed by Spanish, Portuguese, French, German, Italian, and Afrikaans. Oriental languages were not attempted until the war had begun. In 1942 when the ES became the Overseas Service, the BBC was broadcasting in 24 European languages and 21 non-European (the latter rose to 24 in 1944).

Until this immense quickening of effort took place the main priority of the BBC had been its English-language news bulletins. Indeed the prime importance of the attractiveness of other programmes lay in winning the audience for the news. As we have seen, Reuters prevented the broadcasting of news in the early experimental transmissions, but the ES was able to escape the restrictions placed upon it by the press agencies faster than had happened at home. In Britain newspapers and agencies had used their influence on government to ensure that no news was broadcast before 6.00 p.m. and that all items should come from credited news agency sources. The BBC only gradually secured the relaxation of these restrictions, fighting towards Reith's desire for 'eye-witness' reports and frequent bulletins. But no British press magnate could argue that broadcasting to the Empire would hurt his sales. Such broadcasting served a higher national purpose and was in some ways unassailable as a result. The BBC held monthly meetings with the Empire Press Union and agreed with them on the number and duration of bulletins, but these were purely informal and the Union does not seem to have been unduly concerned about broadcasting competition.[19] The fourth conference of the Union, in Australia in 1925, contained barely any mention of broadcasting, but at the fifth, in South Africa in 1935, a whole session was devoted to it.[20] The main concerns were protecting Canada from American press and broadcasting and examining the manner in which Australian newspapers had bought local commercial radio stations in order to promote their sales.

[19]E4/60–1. See also E4/35.
[20]E.P. Turner, compiler, *The Imperial Press Conference in Australia* (London, Hodder & Stoughton, 1926), and *The Fifth Imperial Press Conference (South Africa), 1935* (London, Empire Press Union, 1936).

ES news bulletins were certainly longer and fuller than domestic ones. They included commercial information and 'market notes' that would not have been broadcast at home at that time. Various parts of the Empire clamoured for such information, illustrating the importance of commodity prices to the imperial economy. The significance of such material was increasingly appreciated in the later 30s. The Colonial Office asked for the daily broadcasting of cocoa prices to West Africa. The ES was also permitted to be more relaxed in the naming of products and of companies than the BBC could be at home. By the war the ES was being asked to stress British achievements through the 'made in Britain' approach. At the same time the Dominions Office asked that the BBC should use the ES to collect information on emigration to be broadcast at home. This no doubt reflected growing anxiety about the rapid decline in the proportion of the populations of the dominions that were British-born.

An examination of some of the broadcasts that the ES regarded as having greatest significance reveals the durability of the Reith formulas of the 20s. Royal nostalgia, imperial achievements and responsibilities, remained the watchwords. An examination of the scripts and contents of the programmes which surveyed the events of each year (for example 'Highlights of 1935') reveals the extent to which the BBC pursued its approach of 'no controversy'.[21] In the 1935 programme Hitler was mentioned only in the context of disarmament, and positively at that. The Italian invasion of Abyssinia, which had originally figured quite prominently in the script – including a speech of Haile Selassie on his country's continuing fight for freedom – was whittled down to a brief extract of a speech of Sir Samuel Hoare at the League of Nations. Even an extract of a speech by Eden on the anachronism of war was excluded. The programme concentrated on the safe royal and sporting events, with the launching of ocean liners a perennial favourite. The best the ES could do with Vita Sackville-West was to ask her to record her memories of the Coronation of George V.[22] After the King's death Arthur Bryant wrote the script for a programme on his life.[23] It laid great stress on the Delhi Durbar and other imperial rituals and was designed to 'capitalize on the Empire-wide loyalty' to the King. An allegedly libellous passage (possibly on the General Strike) was excised (and no record of it remains), as were all other mentions of industrial and social discontents at home or nationalist reactions abroad. Kiplingesque sentiments (including a speech by Kipling at the St George's Day Dinner of 1935) were repeatedly used. The presence of imperial figures at the Jubilee of 1935 and the Coronation of George VI in 1937 provided opportunities for a series of talks on the Responsibilities of Empire, but none was of a critical nature and all had to avoid controversial issues.[24] Smuts spoke of the great improvement in race relations in South

[21]E5/29.
[22]E5/46.
[23]E4/40.
[24]E4/12; E4/80; E4/84.

Africa (meaning relations between Briton and Boer) in the very year that the residual African franchise was abolished. Lord Snell for the Labour Party spoke of his party's 'realization of the immense value of a closely knit Empire on a basis which, in essentials, is not different from that recognized by other parties'. At one point the BBC decreed that the broadcasting of speeches from luncheons and banquets was particularly valuable and this was done for the departures and arrivals of Lords Willingdon and Linlithgow when the latter took over the Viceroyalty of India from the former.[25] In 1937 the Director of the ES objected to a discussion programme with the title 'The Way to Peace' which consisted of statements and counter-statements.[26] Selective listening he felt, could lead to misleading impressions.

In the careful avoidance of controversy the immense rites of passage of an imperial family were given great prominence.[27] The funerals of First World War 'heroes' like Jellicoe and Beatty and the wedding of the Duke of Kent gave rise to several programmes surrounding the ceremonies themselves.

If the Britain conveyed to the Empire was a safe consensual one, featuring mainly royal rituals, sporting events, nostalgia, liner launchings, and the platitudinous pronouncements of politicians, very little effort was made to interpret the Empire to Britain. The annual Christmas surveys of the Empire that preceded the monarch's Christmas broadcast for most of the 30s incorporated a series of colonial stereotypes, as I have shown elsewhere.[28] Only once was there a genuine effort to produce a programme illustrative of local culture elsewhere in the Empire. This was a programme from Bombay in 1933 featuring Indian music, descriptions of Bombay street scenes and the like.[29] It was heard in Britain, Canada, Australia, the USA, Denmark and Czeckoslovakia, though, interestingly, the broadcasting services of Rhodesia and South Africa declined to take it. Programmes like 'Empire Magazine' attempted some exchange items, but generally the BBC was devoted to the transmission of a very particular set of aural images of Britain. The British-centred character of the ES was perfectly symbolized on the BBC's Christmas card in 1936. This consisted of a world projection by MacDonald Gill with Daventry at the centre transmitting to the world. It bore the message 'The searchlights of broadcasting now play over the Empire for more than 17 hours of each day and night' and announced the opening of new transmitters in the spring of 1937 (ready for the Coronation) which would be 'bringing all Dominions and Colonies, and many of the King's subjects outside the Empire, into closer touch with Britain and with each other'.[30] The image of the searchlight illuminating the Empire reflects some of the idealistic hopes of the service.

In fact the limitations of Empire broadcasting were identified by two ES

[25]Departmental minute, 30 January, 1936, E4/33.
[26]Departmental Minute, 5 May, 1938, E4/34.
[27]E4/38; E5/18; E4/86.
[28]MacKenzie, 'In touch', pp. 182–3.
[29]E4/85; E4/12.
[30]A copy of this Christmas card can be found in E4/51.

officials on extensive tours in 1933 and 1937. On the first occasion, Malcolm Frost, a young employee of the BBC who became responsible for the marketing of 'bottled' programmes, was sent around the world to assess the influence of the new service.[31] *World Radio*, waxing lyrical, saw his visit as designed to 'forge the first real link in that long chain which will serve as a new and strong bond between the Empire and the Mother Country', a chain connecting farmers in Cape Province, planters in Assam and Ceylon, and missionaries in the North-West Territories of Canada.[32] Frost did indeed concentrate on the white expatriate audience and was specifically instructed not to trouble himself with vernacular village broadcasting in India (which was clearly already being discussed at that time). In many places he discovered reception to be very poor and ruffled the feathers of the BBC engineers by his criticisms of technical quality. In 1937, the more senior J. Beresford Clark, by that time head of the ES, travelled even more extensively, but he tended to move from Government House to Government House hearing the views only of more senior expatriates.[33] Not surprisingly they immensely appreciated BBC output relating to the Coronation, annual ceremonies and patriotic programming. Even so, Clark repeatedly reported on the great popularity of the German and Dutch stations. People in New Zealand, for example, appreciated the informal manner of announcing and the constant flow of music and news that emanated from them. They, and others like them, seemed to have little desire to engage with the mixed cultural fare offered by the BBC, with the possible exception of the great imperial ceremonies. In India, Clark discovered that the Indian press was very sceptical of the BBC's claim to be free of propaganda. But there was little change in broadcasting policy in the years before the war.

Given the low levels of BBC funding, the conservatism of BBC approaches, and their apparent inability to respond to competition or criticism, the response of the BBC to the needs of impending and actual war from 1939 is perhaps all the more remarkable. The transformation in instructions on news broadcasting from early 1939 is striking. As well as the great expansion of language broadcasting detailed above, the BBC news was to be geared to specific propaganda ends. In February 1939 during the Russo-Finnish war, New Zealand listeners had to be reminded of the wickedness of the Soviet Union which had 'abandoned the principles of Marx and Lenin for imperialist aggression'.[34] (The image of the Soviet Union changed swiftly after the Nazi invasion.) Australia had to be

[31]The recording of programmes to be despatched for local broadcasting in the Empire was an important technical development pioneered in the ES; the more sophisticated dominions services could also record London transmissions direct and re-broadcast them on their own wavelengths, which created much larger audiences for the national rituals. Documents on Frost's tour are in E4/44-50.

[32]*World Radio*, 25 November, 1932.

[33]E4/13-22.

[34]E4/61 and Empire Weekly Programme Meeting, 28 October, 1941 and 28 May, 1942, E4/43.

informed of the world strategic picture as it affected that Dominion. Britain had to be presented as the very centre of the war, 'not a quiet outpost'. Production achievements, fighting spirit, heroes and individual achievements had to be emphasized. The word 'native' was banned in references to the dependent Empire, announcers had to be aware of issues, especially the seeming paradox of an autocratic Empire fighting for democracy.[35] An Empire Intelligence unit was established at the Ministry of Information and the BBC under distinguished academics.

The new sensitivities at the BBC led to the banning of a programme on Cecil Rhodes.[36] One on Clive had to be carefully considered in the light of Indian susceptibilities. A lengthy programme on Christopher Columbus clearly signalled the importance of the Atlantic partnership. Yet even in wartime the popularity of the stream of music (including light classics) emitted by German and Japanese stations was noted. As the activities of George Orwell in the Indian Section of the new Overseas Service reveal, the BBC was still wedded to a combination of news, emphasis on distinctively British traditions, and varied cultural, particularly literary, fare. Orwell's interests in promoting talks, discussions and features reveal the old didactic ambitions of the BBC still at work.[37]

The exigencies of the war demonstrated, however, that the main propagandist thrust had to be directed not so much to the Empire as to the Americans, the Latin Americans and Europeans. At the exact moment when more vigorous propagandist efforts became possible with extensive government funding the searchlight was, in proportionate terms at least, removed from the Empire. In 1942, a mere 10 years after its foundation, the ES succumbed to this new reality. It was re-named in turn the Overseas Forces, the Overseas, and the World service, a reorganization within the BBC that reflected changing circumstances in Britain's world situation. Maintaining the cultural and political unity of the Empire, however much Churchill might huff and puff, was no longer a prime British objective. The ES had been, in the classic British tradition, too little, too late. Returning to our analysis of its audience, it barely reached indigenous populations at all. (Ironically enough, broadcasting was probably to be more influential in the spreading of nationalist ideas after the war.) It had little effect on dominions' nationalism, though the great imperial rituals do seem to have struck chords with dominion populations and with an American audience, no doubt reflecting the emphasis of feature films and newsreels in the contemporary cinema. (The BBC was often astonished at the size and interest of the American audience and took care to refer to 'short-wave' rather than 'Empire' service to American correspondents.) The greatest success of the ES was perhaps in acting as a solace to the expatriate community maintaining their morale and their loyalty in the difficult decade of the 30s.

[35]E4/40.
[36]Empire Weekly Programme Meeting, 12 November, 1940 and 3 December 1940, E4/43.
[37]W.J. West, ed., *Orwell, the War Broadcasts* and *Orwell, the War Commentaries* (London, Duckworth/BBC, 1985).

The ES certainly illustrated the reluctance of the British to indulge in official propaganda, a reluctance born principally of parsimony. But, as on the domestic scene, unofficial agencies took up the challenge. The BBC, like many such agencies, denied propagandist intent, but the careful selection of material, particularly the emphasis on nostalgia, monarchy, heroic achievements and patriotic ritual, and the avoidance of controversy or critical comment has, in retrospect, the appearance of propaganda, if not always particularly effective propaganda. Moreover, once the agency was in place, Government was only too anxious to use it, as the recommendations on emigration and commodity prices make clear. But the approach to the use of the word 'propaganda' was the most revealing characteristic of the period. Banned from official publications and from broadcasting, it was nonetheless used in private internal documents. Since the dividing line between a selection of the truth and untruth is such a fine one, propaganda needs to be covert. Yet it was perhaps the doubts and anxieties about the word that led to the practice of the actual activity – at least before the outbreak of war – being relatively ineffectual. The BBC's propaganda set out to promote a set of institutions and values that were seen as distinctively British. In its studied avoidance of what it defined as controversy and polemic, the BBC clung to a particularly anodine form of persuasion.

Note

1. *Primary Sources*. The main text discussed in the essay is available in a short but serviceable edition by D.M. MacDowell, *Gorgias: Encomium of Helen, edited with Introduction, Notes and Translation* (Bristol, Bristol Classical Press, 1982). Unfortunately the only comprehensive edition of the (somewhat fragmentary) remains of the Sophists is in Italian (M. Untersteiner, *I Sofisti*, Florence 1961–2) but they are all (including Gorgias) translated in R.K. Sprague, ed. *The Older Sophists* (South Carolina, Columbia University Press, 1972). Early Greek Philosophers are collected in *Die Fragmente der Vorsokratiker*, ed. H. Diels and W. Kranz, (6th edn. Zurich, Weidmann, 1966 [3 vols]), and translated in K. Freeman, *Ancilla to the Presocratic Philosophers* (Oxford, Blackwell, 1971). Thucydides and Plato are available in accurate Penguin Classics translations with good notes (for the latter, see especially *The last days of Socrates*, tr. H. Tredennick, 1954, but continually reprinted). Greek drama is also available in Penguin Classics, of variable quality (Aeschylus and Sophocles excellent and Aristophanes outstanding). More consistently good are the Chicago translations of Greek Tragedy, ed. D. Grene and R. Lattimore, 9 vols., 1953–9 (also continually reprinted). A selection of Hippocratic medicine is conveniently available in G.E.R. Lloyd ed., *Hippocratic Writings*, (London, Penguin, repr. 1986). Greek oratory has not hitherto been easily accessible, but we now have M. Edwards and S. Usher, *Greek Orators I: Antiphon and Lysias, edited with Introduction, Notes and Translation* (London, Aris & Philips, 1985), with more volumes to come.

2. *Secondary Sources*. Rhetoric in fifth-century Athens has been treated under the 'origins of . . .' rubric in the introductory chapters of many general studies of ancient rhetoric, of which G. Kennedy, *The Art of Persuasion in Greece* (Princeton, NJ, Princeton University Press, 1963), is the fullest. However, the present essay takes its inspiration from a number of recent studies which, from different angles, treat verbal persuasion as a phenomenon which represents a vital link between different political and cultural areas in a specifically fifth century BC context. See especially: G. Kerferd, *The Sophistic Movement* (Cambridge, Cambridge University Press, 1981) [the epistemological and ethical implications of increasing linguistic consciousness]; G.E.R. Lloyd, *Magic, Reason and Experience: Studies in the origin and development of Greek Science* (Cambridge, Cambridge University Press, 1979) [the subordination of scientific and philosophical ideas to the social circumstances of adversarial debate]; R. Buxton, *Persuasion in Greek Tragedy* (Cambridge, Cambridge University Press, 1982) [role of persuasion in drama as a reflection of social development]. Discussion of fifth-century Athens as 'oral' or 'face to face' society in, e.g., E.A. Havelock, *The Liberal Temper in Greek Politics* (London, Macmillan, 1957), and more recently from a specifically political angle in M.I. Finley, 'Athenian Demagogues' in *Studies in Ancient Greek Society*, pp. 1–25, (London, Routledge & Kegan Paul, 1974). The emphasis on language and communication in recent studies (which clearly owes much to recent developments in modern literary theory) is clearly demonstrated in S. Goldhill, *Reading Greek Tragedy* (Cambridge, Cambridge University Press 1986), a book which, while regrettably appearing too late for use in the present essay, opens up many avenues of further investigation.

4

Speech, the Mighty Ruler: Persuasion and Power in Democratic Athens

Chris Emlyn-Jones

But if speech was the persuader and deceiver of her *psyche*, it is not hard to make a defence against that too, and to dismiss the accusation thus. Speech is a mighty ruler. With the smallest and most invisible body it accomplishes the most god-like deeds; for it can put a stop to fear, banish sorrow, create joy and increase pity.

Gorgias, Encomium of Helen, 8

This celebration of the power of speech is taken from a display oration (*epideixis*) composed at about the end of the fifth century BC, in which the renowned Sicilian orator Gorgias seeks to praise Helen of Troy, or rather to defend her from censure traditionally incurred for deserting her husband Menelaos and eloping with Paris. The formal structure of a eulogy (*encomion*), with which the work begins, lightly masks the real subject, to which Gorgias swiftly turns – a short quasi-legal defence which aims to free Helen from any responsibility for her actions. Gorgias suggests four possible causes of her elopment: she was subject to the will of the gods, seized by force, persuaded by speech or captivated by love. With argumentative sleight-of-hand, Gorgias tries to plant in his audience's mind the conviction that these four causes exhaust all conceivable possibilities; since in each case, he maintains, Helen was faced by *force majeure*, she cannot be held responsible for her actions, or, as Gorgias puts it at the start of the defence proper (Section 5), he will state the causes '. . . which made it *reasonable* for Helen's voyage to Troy to occur' (the Greek for 'reasonable', an important persuasive word in Greek legal language, matches the English in combining the idea of logical probability and adherence to an ethical norm).

The occasion on which the *Helen* was delivered is not known, but the declamatory style (of which the introductory quotation gives some idea) suggests a public performance before a large audience on a ceremonial occasion. We assume this took place at Athens; this is probable but by no means certain, as Gorgias, in common with other celebrated public speakers, travelled extensively in the Greek world, living on the high fees charged for teaching his rhetorical skill to aspiring pupils.

In blaming the gods or the irresistible power of love for Helen's action, Gorgias is drawing on ideas which would have been familiar to an audience steeped in a common cultural heritage. However, in contrast to the elaboration of traditional themes, the central third of Gorgias' speech (Sections 8–14) stands out sharply as a new idea, an exploration of the power of verbal persuasion. That speech has absolute power to control the emotions is argued with reference to poetry (the Greek word *poiesis* includes, and perhaps in this context principally denotes, drama) and magical incantations, which cause the *psyche* to react violently (*psyche* – see introductory quotation – is difficult to define precisely in modern terms; in the fifth century BC, it denotes the individual principally as a centre of emotion, and desire). Helen is no more able to resist persuasive speech than if she were subject to physical force: 'For her reason was driven out by [verbal] persuasion; and indeed, persuasion, though it does not have the appearance of compulsion, has the same power' (Section 12).[1] Gorgias concludes his study of verbal persuasion thus: 'The power of the word has the same relation to the ordering of the *psyche* as the ordering of medicines has to the constitution of bodies. For just as different medicines draw out different humours from the body, and some prevent illness but others stop life, so, too, with speeches (words); some cause sorrow, some cause pleasure, some frighten, some make their audience bold, others drug and bewitch the *psyche* with an evil persuasion' (Section 14). Gorgias here reflects a current interest in medical practice associated with the anonymous scientific treatises assembled under the collective name of the Hippocratic Corpus. Yet he is not just displaying his erudition, but introducing a conception vital to his argument. Despite the simile form, which points to simple analogy, the final 'drug' and 'bewitch' reflect a conception in which the physiological and the psychological do not exist as distinct processes; moreover, Gorgias is using this confusion in order to get his audience to believe that persuasion works physically like medicine; Helen is as helpless under verbal persuasion as under a powerful drug, and for the same reason – that it acts irresistibly on the structure of the *psyche*.[2] 'Persuasion . . . moulds the *psyche* in the way it wishes' (Section 13). Is 'moulds' simply a metaphor here?[3] A speaker of modern English would assume so, but the Greek word has strong concrete associations: e.g. in moulding bronze sculpture and stamping coins (we derive 'type' from it); the advanced psychology of Gorgias' time (e.g. that of the Atomists) postulated a thoroughgoing materialist model of sensation and its relation to the *psyche*, in which the passivity and receptivity of the latter were

[1]The text here is very corrupt; I translate the restoration of D.M. MacDowell, *Gorgias: Encomium of Helen*, p. 39 (for details, see bibliographical note with which this article begins).
[2]On the assimilation of physiological and psychological models here, see C.P. Segal, 'Gorgias and the psychology of the logos', *Harvard Studies in Classical Philology*, 66 (1962), pp. 99–155 (p. 104ff.)
[3]So, MacDowell, *Helen*, note on Section 13.

emphasized.[4] Once again, Gorgias is using fashionable scientific theories for his own purpose.

The *Helen* has been awarded its place in the history of rhetoric as the earliest attempt at a theoretical discussion of the psychology of verbal persuasion and its author was in later centuries justly revered as one of the earliest exponents of an art which, as Rhetoric, dominated Graeco-Roman society for a thousand years, permeated later European culture, and still has great influence in the context of modern theories of communication.[5]

Yet, despite the apparent cultural continuity, Gorgias' ideas about the psychology of persuasion and moral responsibility seem curiously alien to the modern mind. We are familiar with persuasive techniques deployed to cause people to act against their better judgement; in certain circumstances, for example under the application of bodily or mental stress, and with certain groups of people, for example the very young or elderly, we might regard moral responsibility as removed from the argument, or rather, assigned to the persuaders. Yet Gorgias' argument seems to presuppose a model of totally conditioned human behaviour in which nobody, or very few, can ever resist verbal persuasion. This extreme view, according to which almost nobody is ever morally responsible for anything, has, needless to say, serious shortcomings both from a philosophical and psychological standpoint.

Philosophically, Gorgias seems unaware of a distinction, first made explicit by Aristotle, between causal and evaluative responsibility: persuasive words may have been the *cause* of Helen's action but the *responsibility* for succumbing or resisting lay with her.[6] In other words, something may have prompted what she did, but we still believe that she was capable of acting otherwise. Turning to psychology, there appears to be a confusion between persuasion as a technique which appeals to, and indeed relies on, the exercise of reason and persuasion as something which by-passes or even 'drives out' (Section 12, see above p. 56) the rational in us in order to appeal directly to the emotions. In *Helen*, the *psyche* is essentially passive; it 'suffers' in reaction to external stimulus; the persuader invariably 'compels' (e.g. Section 12). Here Gorgias relies on, and is to some extent the victim of, rhetorical polarization which, in its cruder forms, offers simple antithesis as 'explanation' and ignores anything between the extremes of black and white; in this case, the persuader's 'compulsion' must be answered by the victim's 'suffering'. The limitations of genre and technique prevent a less polarized and psychologically more complicated explanation.

Yet there is something more fundamentally wrong with Gorgias' theory of persuasion; the form of his defence belies the content, as its ultimate

---

[4]See W.K.C. Guthrie, *A History of Greek Philosophy* (Vol. II, Cambridge, Cambridge University Press, 1962), pp. 442–65.
[5]See especially *The New Rhetoric. A Treatise in Argumentation* by Ch. Perelman and L. Olbrechts-Tyteca, (London, U. of Notre Dame Press, 1958).
[6]Aristotle, *Nichomachean Ethics*, Book 3, 1106 b 10ff. On the distinction, see J. Barnes, *The Presocratic Philosophers* (London, Routledge & Kegan Paul, rev. edn. 1982), pp. 525–30.

success surely depends upon the audience being capable of appreciating his logical skill, of evaluating his arguments *critically*, or, in other words, not being passive sufferers of persuasive technique. Or perhaps we should take a traditional route out of this dilemma and cite Section 13, in which Gorgias depicts professional orators moulding minds in rhetorical contests '. . . in which one speech delights and persuades a large crowd because it is written with skill but not spoken with truth'. Perhaps we should see Gorgias as one of these professional showmen. Support for this view has been found in the final sentences of the *Helen*, where Gorgias states that he has composed the speech partly as an amusement (*paignion*) for himself – the verbal equivalent of the '. . . twinkle in the eye as he reveals in the very last word that he regards the whole paradoxical composition as a game'.[7] Seen in these terms *Helen* is less a philosophical or psychological treatise than a defence, and a defence of a type which gained notoriety in later fifth-century Athens, an exercise in making 'the weaker case the stronger', an activity attributed to many rhetoricians and teachers, known collectively as Sophists.

Game or not, what relevance has the treatise to an estimate of the role of verbal persuasion in fifth-century Athenian society? At first sight, very little. To take only one example: Athenian law (which to a large extent reflected popular consensus) was even less accommodating than ours to 'diminished responsibility'; roughly speaking 'madness' was felt to be a result of 'badness' and so worthy of moral censure.[8] The Athenians, one might assume, must have thought even less of the case for Helen than we do. Yet, to expose the central argument about persuasion as eccentric is not to dismiss the whole speech. The fact that the argument exonerating Helen could be deployed in a large gathering suggests that, on some level or other, Gorgias' performance carried conviction. Moreover, the very existence of an (apparently popular) institution of public verbal display and of a group of people professionally involved in it raises important questions about the general nature of verbal persuasion in late fifth-century Athens. It is to the broader political and cultural issues that we now turn.

If Gorgias' treatment of the 'word' (*logos*) is idiosyncratic, the choice of subject is not. At this time Greece still retained many of the characteristics of the oral society it had once been. The rise of the independent city-state (*polis*), had served, if anything, to magnify the importance of verbal eloquence in political and social life. A gradual decline in the arbitrary power of a noble class was accompanied by a corresponding rise in the degree to which political affairs were a subject of public discussion between members of an increasingly broad spectrum of the population.

In Athens, this process was taken further when, in the fifth century BC, the avenue of political power was opened to large numbers of the city's inhabitants. The ultimate political authority was the Assembly, a body to

---

[7]MacDowell, *Helen*, note on Section 21.
[8]See K.J. Dover, *Greek Popular Morality in the time of Plato and Aristotle* (Oxford, Blackwell, 1974), p. 148.

which all adult male citizens belonged and in which they were entitled to vote. Moreover, the deliberate restriction of executive magistracies to short-term posts filled by process of lot from among the citizen body ensured that the power to make and, more pointedly in the present context, to debate major political decisions remained with the Assembly. And the debate was oral; in Athens, where basic literacy was probably commoner than elsewhere, and important for specific specialized activities, for example, commercial transactions and the keeping of public records (which would include the recording of political decisions), the primary medium of political, social and cultural life was still the spoken word.

The result was a political arena of spontaneity and directness unique in history. The comparative fluidity of political alignments, with the possibility of swift change of decision on major issues and penalties for those who were subsequently decreed to have given 'bad advice', meant that one of the keys to continued success and power was verbal eloquence. This need was not confined to the Assembly. The judicial system worked on a similar principle. Cases were tried by large jury panels of citizens selected by lot, whose task it was, undirected by specialists, to assess the evidence and deliver verdict and sentence. While, unlike in most modern judicial processes, those directly involved had to plead their cases personally, professionals were available to give advice and often to write their speeches for them. The survival of a large number of forensic speeches from the fifth and fourth centuries BC as well as rhetorical models of speeches for teaching purposes, provides overwhelming evidence for the skill of these 'logographers' as they were called, and, incidentally, demonstrates that, for the jury, the question of guilt or innocence often came a poor second in importance to the creation of a plausible moral character for the defendant which involved the ability to sway the audience and appeal to its basic values and instincts.[9] Once again, we are not all that far from the *Helen*: it is no coincidence that Gorgias chooses a legal framework for his *Encomium*. His attempt to removal moral responsibility from the 'suffering' Helen would, despite the somewhat intellectual context, have had a familiar ring to an audience accustomed to sitting on a jury and deliberating on a verdict.

An important cultural institution, closely, if unexpectedly, related to Assembly and lawcourt is the Athenian tragic and comic theatre. Gorgias' description of poetry as 'speech with metre' (Section 9) looks, at first sight, like a special plea for drama as a sub-species of rhetoric, as unconvincing as his argument for the power of verbal persuasion. Yet, it needs to be noted that the dramatic performances at the major Athenian religious festival of the God Dionysos were performed in competition, the result of which was decided by a jury drawn from the citizen body. The plots of Greek tragedies, though mythical in form, reflect in their details many of the contemporary issues and debates of the *polis* – and these are often, to our

9See especially S. Humphreys, 'Law as discourse' and 'Social relations on stage', in *History and Anthropology*, (1985), p. 241–54 and 313–69.

eyes, surprisingly controversial. This, and the physical setting – a mass audience (up to 14,000) seated in the theatre of Dionysos on the southern slope of the Athenian Acropolis – relate the theatre closely, in civic terms, to the more obviously political institutions of Assembly and Law Courts. This may help to explain the degree to which verbal persuasion features in Greek tragedy, either implicitly or in formal debate. The short but climactic exchange in which Clytemnestra 'persuades' (or better, seduces) Agamemnon into entering his palace treading on precious crimson tapestries (Aeschylus, *Agamemnon*, 931–49) would have been savoured by the audience quite as much as the more formally arranged debates, e.g. that of Helen and Hecuba the mother of Paris, amid the smouldering ruins of Troy in Euripides' *Trojan Women*; or the bitter accusation and counter-accusation of Jason and Medea in Euripides' *Medea*.[10] In comedy, a more overtly political genre, the *parabasis* (the point in the play at which the dramatist, in the guise of the Chorus, 'stepped forward' to address the audience on a current political topic) allowed full scope for argumentative skill.

Were all these in essence so different in social terms from the setting of the *Helen*? A particular piece of evidence clarifies in a very specific way our understanding of Gorgias' relationship to the Athenian *polis*. It is recorded that Gorgias led an embassy to Athens in 427 BC from his home town of Leontini in Sicily, and rendered the Athenians spellbound by the cleverness and intricate novelty of his speech.[11] His main task, in which he succeeded, was to win over the Athenians (who had recently begun a major and protracted war with their main rival in the Greek world, Sparta) to the idea of an alliance with anti-Spartan elements in Sicily, and to persuade them to send help. The details of Gorgias' performance on this occasion are unknown; the contemporary historian Thucydides, who records the appeal without mentioning Gorgias, suggests that the Athenians in being persuaded had an underlying strategic motive of their own.[12] Yet the very presence of a professional orator and teacher of rhetoric in a political capacity before the Athenian Assembly suggests a more central role for Gorgias in the *polis* than we might otherwise have been inclined to credit. Such a prominent political role for a Sophist may have been unique, although Gorgias' fellow Sophists are known to have had great influence: for example, his older contemporary Protagoras, who was a close friend and confidante of the important statesman, Pericles, and was appointed to draw up a code of laws for the new Athenian colony at Thurii in Italy in 444 BC; and Antiphon, chief organizer of an anti-democratic coup in Athens in 411 BC celebrated by Thucydides for his cleverness behind the scenes.[13] In practice, most of the Sophists, as non-Athenians (Antiphon may have been

---

[10]On the persuasion of Agamemnon, see P. Easterling 'Presentation of character in Aeschylus', *Greece and Rome*, 20 (1973) 3–19, and in general, R.G.A. Buxton, *Persuasion in Greek Tragedy* (Cambridge, Cambridge University Press, 1982).
[11]Diodorus Siculus 12, 53.
[12]Thucydides, 3, 86.
[13]Thucydides, 8, 68.

an exception), would have been unable normally to address the Assembly; yet, although we have no direct evidence that any prominent politicians in the late fifth century were pupils of the Sophists, the central importance of the teaching of persuasive speaking in the Sophists' curriculum testifies to their social, if not direct political, importance.[14]

In Greek images of cultural development, verbal persuasion was often seen as in direct opposition to violence as a means of settling disputes. In this opposition Greeks naturally saw themselves, in direct contrast with 'barbarians' (non-Greeks), as on the side of persuasion, and, among Greeks, the Athenians contrasted themselves with others in the same way.[15] Pericles, in his 'Funeral Speech' recorded by Thucydides, (for the year 430 BC), celebrates the Athenian willingness to submit political decisions to discussion, in contrast to neighbouring city-states, and by implication, Sparta, Athens' chief enemy in the Peloponnesian war.[16] In the evolutionary schema which forms one aspect of the latter part of Aeschylus' *Oresteia* trilogy (produced in 458 BC), the attempt to establish Orestes guilty or innocent of the murder of his mother, Clytemnestra, takes the form of a judicial trial in which persuasion (*peitho*) wins over force (*bia*) – an idea which is linked by implication to the emergent Athenian democratic constitution.

The word *logos*, translated variously, e.g. 'word', 'story', 'speech', 'account', can also be translated 'reason' or 'argument'. This latter range of meanings acquired new significance during the sixth and early fifth century BC, when used to describe the theories of emergent rational speculation about the origins and nature of the Universe, which the Greeks developed in conscious opposition to the traditional mythological stories of their ancestors in Greece, and of peoples further east in Egypt and Babylonia. *Logos* was associated with attempts to get at the incontrovertible truth of matters – a truth which was, in theory at least, attainable by the application of reason in logical argument, the nature of which would, again in theory, carry its own persuasive force; yet one of the consequences of this uncompromising position was a greater recognition of potential separation of language and reality or, as George Kerferd has tellingly put it, 'a fairly fundamental change towards a society in which what people thought and said was beginning to be more important than what was actually the case.'[17]

A popular picture of the Sophists as concerned to teach pupils the manipulation of situations by means of illegitimate verbal persuasion is conveyed by Aristophanes, the comic dramatist, in his play *The Clouds* (originally produced 423 BC; we have the revised version, composed between 420 and 417). Aristophanes chooses the philosopher Socrates,

---

[14]For cogent arguments against a specific teacher–pupil relationship between Sophists and prominent politicians, see W.R. Connor, *The New Politicians of Fifth-Century Athens* (Princeton, Princeton University Press, 1971), p. 166 n. 54.
[15]See Buxton, *Persuasion*, p. 58 ff.
[16]Thucydides, 2, 40.
[17]*The Sophistic Movement*, p. 78 (for details, see bibliographical note).

whom he associates with the Sophists, as his chief target and represents him as the rascally head of a school engaged in esoteric meteorological speculation and logically suspect arguments which, in comically exaggerated form, can be used by the main character, Strepsiades, to cheat his creditors. A more serious and extended examination of the relations between language and reality can be found in Thucydides, in whose historical analysis the contrast between *logos* (what is said, alleged, appears to be the case) and *ergon* (the facts, what really is the case) is used in a more constructive way to try to uncover the real significance of historical events.

Thucydides frequently uses speeches (allegedly delivered by politicians in a variety of political and civic contexts) as a commentary on events; his customary arrangement of these in pairs, while following the outward form of contrasted *logoi*, actually transcends rhetorical 'compulsion', by offering choice in the interpretation of events and moral and social viewpoint.[18]

In these speeches, Thucydides occasionally allows his speakers to reflect directly on the role of persuasive speech in political affairs; for example in the debate in the Athenian Assembly over the fate of the inhabitants of the island of Mytilene, which in 427 BC revolted from the Athenian alliance and was subsequently recaptured.

The opposing speakers both reflect on *logos*: Kleon, who advocates punitive measures against the Mytileneans, accuses the Assembly of being more like an audience at a Sophist's display than a responsible political gathering: they judge facts not by their own senses but by speeches that they hear.[19] This criticism of the Assembly as being, in a sense, the prisoners of rhetoric, is highly cynical; Thucydides gives Kleon himself a highly rhetorically contrived speech. Kleon's opponent Diodotos, whose more moderate policy is eventually adopted, reflects, in clear reference back to Kleon's speech, on the problems attendant on not knowing whom to believe if 'a good proposal honestly put forward is just as suspect as something thoroughly bad, and the result is that just as the speaker who advocates some monstrous measure has to win over the people by deceiving them, so also a man with good advice to give has to tell lies if he expects to be believed.'[20] This 'oversubtlety', as Thucydides makes Diodotos call it in the following sentence (using an extremely rare Greek word), reminds us that Thucydides is probably not recording faithfully an Assembly speech (we have unfortunately no direct record of any of these), but using the occasion to express his own disquiet at some aspects of verbal persuasion in Athenian politics – a disquiet which has at least part of its origin in the author's aristocratic background and inherently low estimate of the political judgement of the average Assembly voter.[21] We are left with a question not dissimilar to that asked of Gorgias' *Helen*: how do these

[18]See, esp. A. Parry, *Logos and Ergon in Thucydides* (New York, Arno, rev. edn 1981).
[19]Thucydides, 3, 38.
[20]Thucydides, 3, 43, 1–2, tr. R. Warner.
[21]Such estimates are frequent in Thucydides, e.g. 2.65, 7.14, 8, 1.

theoretical speculations relate to the actual world of Athenian political persuasion?

To return for a moment to Gorgias: in Section 1 of the *Helen*, Gorgias states that 'the adornment of *psyche* is wisdom'; yet an indication of the *psyche* as having any autonomous power of reflection and moral choice (see above p. 57) is just what is missing from Gorgias' account of the psychological process in *Helen*. The *psyche* receives impressions and reacts emotionally. The immediacy and absence of reflection with which Gorgias associates this process is emphasized by a consideration of his account of reaction to visual images. In an attempt to exonerate Helen from blame because she was a victim of love (*eros*), he depicts the *psyche* as being moulded in its character (or 'habits') by what the individual sees, to the extent that a fearful vision alarms the sight which in turn 'agitates the *psyche*, so that often people flee in panic from imminent danger as if it were present. For powerful is the neglect of the law implanted through fear caused by their vision, which, when it comes, causes them to disregard the honour awarded for obeying the law and the good which arises from acting justly . . . so much does fear extinguish and drive out thought' (Sections 16, 17). This idea is clearly intended to reinforce the earlier discussion of verbal persuasion in Section 9–10, whose 'speech with metre' and magical incantations are said to have the same direct effect upon the *psyche*.

Does this theory of the *psyche* as essentially passive recipient of verbal persuasion have any wider significance? Suspicion of special pleading on Gorgias' part is reinforced by the recognition that any actively reflective role for the *psyche* would destroy his argument at its base by introducing the possibility of Helen's voluntary rejection of the persuasive influence, leading her to the assumption of moral responsibility and so, blame. Yet, this very possibility takes us back to the point made earlier (p. 58), that the argument eliminating responsibility was clearly intended to carry conviction with (or at least, impress) a large audience. Are there any elements in Gorgias' psychological view which can be related to the more general cultural framework?

The idea of the *psyche* as material, being acted upon like the body under the influence of drugs (*Helen*, Section 14) does reflect in many respects ancient Greek psychology. As suggested earlier (p. 56) a precise definition of *psyche* is impossible, since the Greek term does not correspond to 'soul', 'mind' (as MacDowell misleadingly translates throughout the *Helen*[22]) or even 'psyche' (although this last term is perhaps nearest, for all its post-Freudian associations). In Homer, the *psyche* was an inner 'breath' which left the body at death to inhabit the Underworld as an insubstantial shadow of the living individual. In early philosophical speculation (sixth and early fifth centuries BC) the association with air was extended in order to relate the individual *psyche* to the ultimate constituents of a living universe. Psychic activity was seen in physical terms, for example, in the early fifth century BC philosopher Herakleitos, a 'dry' or a 'wet' *psyche* was

[22]MacDowell, *Helen*, (see above n. 1).

related to the presence or absence of intelligence.[23] Later in the century, parody in *The Clouds* of Aristophanes suggests that in intellectual circles, *psyche* was associated with radical notions of the connection between air and intellectual activity. Yet the uncompromisingly materialist philosophy of Atomism not only claimed to establish the corporeality of all things, including the *psyche*, but also emphasized the passive and reactive role of the *psyche* in the process of sensation.[24] The later fifth century BC was a period of transition in theories of the psychology of sensation and knowledge, ending in the fundamental dichotomy of body and *psyche* in the philosophy of Plato (fourth century), and the much greater independence assumed by the latter. Nevertheless, for fifth and fourth century Athenian non-philosophical and non-scientific writers (and we need to remember that the range of our evidence for the ideas of 'ordinary people' is very limited),[25] the *psyche* was the seat of non-intellectual states such as courage, passion, pity, anxiety.[26] We can, perhaps, conclude that in his emphasis on the emotionally reactive *pysche*, Gorgias was, for his own purposes, exploiting an idea which would nevertheless have seemed unexceptionable to the majority of his audience, whose unquestioned assumptions on the subject would probably have reflected an amalgam of traditional beliefs and popular distortions of more radical theories.

A further indication of the absence of a clearly developed idea of an independently functioning power of reflection and choice in the psychology of the individual is the close link in the Greek mind between persuasion and seduction. Strong evidence for the popular view is the traditional association in religious cult of the Greek goddess *Peitho* (Persuasion) with Aphrodite, the goddess of love.[27] The link between possession by sexual desire and persuasion clearly goes deep; yet seduction of a non-erotic nature was seen as analogous. 'Casting a spell on the audience' rated far higher than truth as a criterion of success for the story tellers in Homer's *Odyssey*;[28] later, in the fifth century, the prominent Athenian statesman, Pericles, according to the comic dramatist Eupolis, had a similar effect: 'a kind of persuasion lived in his lips. He cast a spell on us. He was the only orator who left his sting behind in his audience.'[29] Once again we are not entirely in the realm of metaphor. The persuasive speaker in fifth-century Athens, consciously removed from his poetic forebears in one respect, nevertheless saw it as part of his function to enchant the audience by appealing directly to their emotions as the poets

[23]E.g. Herakleitos, fragment 118 (Diels-Kranz, Vol. 1, p. 177, transl. Freeman, *Ancilla to the Presocratic Philosophers*, p. 42, for details, see bibliographical note).
[24]On sensation and thought in Greek Atomism, see Guthrie, *History of Greek Philosophy*, pp. 438–54.
[25]On this point, see the remarks of Dover, *Greek Popular Morality*, 1ff.
[26]See E.R. Dodds, *The Greeks and the Irrational* (Berkeley and Los Angeles, 1951), p. 139.
[27]See esp. Buxton, *Persuasion*, p. 31ff.
[28]See my discussion in 'True and Lying Tales in the Odyssey', *Greece and Rome*, 33 no. 1 (1986) pp. 1–10.
[29]Eupolis, fragment 94 (transl. J Ferguson in *Political and Social Life in the Great Age of Athens* (London, Ward Lock Educational/Open University Press, 1978), p. 228).

had done.[30] It is not fortuitous that the heroine of Euripides' drama, *Medea*, combines a persuasive tongue with a witch's power to use drugs and magic tricks, both of which cause destruction. The possession of both types of gift earned Medea the epithet *deinos* (clever, powerful, marvellous, strange, frightening) which also had currency as an epithet describing a persuasive speaker, i.e. someone who produced an effect which was both powerful and not explicable on an entirely rational level. Evidence from fifth century forensic oratory (in many respects the best evidence we have for the beliefs of ordinary people) reveals that a standard adversarial formula was to attribute to one's opponents and deny for oneself the ability to be 'clever at speaking' (*deinos legein*).[31] It was this epithet which, according to Diodorus (see above n. 11) was applied to Gorgias' performance before the Athenian Assembly in 427 BC.

We have looked so far at speech in two aspects, both of which were suggested by the *Helen*: firstly its role as a form of persuasion independent of truth (if such may be held to exist) or 'the facts'; and secondly as a quasi-medical force which acts irresistably on the *psyche*. The central concept which links together these two aspects of verbal persuasion is *power*. It is the power of the orator to construct his own 'reality'. It is also the power of the active persuader to lead the passive victim whichever way he chooses. This power seemed strange and unaccountable to the Greeks in that it is not associated with physical size or large numbers but achieves its massive effects from almost nothing. As the fourth century BC writer, Xenophon, comments: 'The man who dares to use force needs no small number of allies, but he who can persuade needs no one.'[32] The solitary persuader possesses the 'mighty ruler', *logos* (where the implication of the Greek *dynastes* [= ruler] is power *without* accountability).

The implications of this position were drawn out by Plato in his philosophical dialogue, *Gorgias*, written in the early fourth century BC (when the orator may have still been alive). Under questioning from the chief participant, the philosopher Socrates, Gorgias explains his profession in terms of the power it confers to rule one's fellow citizens; Plato makes him take the matter further: 'By means of this power, you will have as your slaves the doctor and the physical trainer; the money-maker will turn out to be making money not for himself but for someone else – for you, since you have the power to speak and persuade the mass of people.'[33]

Plato is, for his own purposes, making his characters draw out implications which are not necessarily relevant to our immediate subject ('Socrates' is not the historical Socrates nor 'Gorgias' the historical Gorgias). Yet the idea of verbal persuasion as, in some way, subordinating to itself other professional activities in the late fifth century BC, has recently been suggested in a full and wide-ranging study of the origins and

[30]See J. de Romilly, *Magic and Rhetoric in Ancient Greece* (Cambridge, Mass., Harvard University Press, 1975), pp. 16–22.
[31]See Antiphon II, 2, 3 (for details, see bibliographical note).
[32]Xenophon, *Memorabilia* I, 2, 11.
[33]Plato, *Gorgias*, 452e.

development of Greek science by Geoffrey Lloyd.[34]

Taking in particular the body of medical treatises known as the Hippocratic Corpus (a number of which date from the relevant period) Lloyd has demonstrated that much of the medical theory contained in them owes its polemical tone and dogmatism to the influence of rhetoric – the tendency, in a competitive situation, to subordinate strictly scientific questions to the need to 'present [one's] own thesis in as favourable light as possible. It was not his [i.e. the Hippocratic doctor's] responsibility to scrutinize, let alone draw attention to, the weakness of his own case with the same keenness with which he probed those of his opponents.'[35] The subordination of a variety of scientific subjects to the technique of persuasion goes some way to explain the educational programme of the Sophists, in which a very wide variety of subjects was offered, but with the chief emphasis on equipping pupils with the persuasive means to succeed, in politics and elsewhere. The prevailing ethos has been discussed and effectively summed up by J.P. Vernant: 'For the Greeks of the fifth century BC, acting meant influencing men, overcoming them, dominating them.'[36] This assumption is in fact embedded in the Greek language: *peithomai* means both 'I am persuaded' and 'I obey'.

This emphasis upon power takes us to a central paradox: verbal persuasion grew up with and flourished under the conditions of open debate associated with Athenian democracy; at the same time its working and effects were seen by some theoretical writers to imply absolute power for the persuader, whether for good or ill. It will be immediately obvious that this paradox, in which a medium regarded by its practitioners as highly despotic, exists within, and indeed derives its sustenance from, a political and social system strongly opposed to despotism, underlies the other apparent contradiction which has run through our discussion so far: the use of the forms and the profession of the purpose of rational argument to subvert or by-pass reason. The key question is how far this paradox is a product of the minds of such writers as Gorgias and Thucydides and how far it can be related to the social and cultural situation in fifth-century Athens.

There is one piece of evidence which suggests that the link perceived between democracy and rhetoric extended beyond the Sophists' circle; during the oligarchic coup at the end of the Peloponnesian War in 404–3 BC, known popularly afterwards as the rule of the 'Thirty Tyrants', the teaching of rhetoric was banned by edict,[37] though on what grounds we do not know, and we should be wary of following Thucydides and Gorgias in

[34]G.E.R. Lloyd, *Magic, Reason and Experience: Studies in the origin and development of Greek Science*. esp. pp. 86–102 (for details see bibliographical note).

[35]Lloyd (see previous note) p. 98.

[36]J.P. Vernant, 'Some remarks on the Forms and Limitations of Technological Thought among the Greeks', in *Myth and Thought among the Greeks* (London, Routledge & Kegan Paul, 1983), p. 301.

[37]Xenophon, *Memorabilia*, I, 2, 31.

their anti-democratic assumption that the 'ignorant mass' was easier to hoodwink than a small group of oligarchs.[38] More informative is Pericles' assertion (Thucydides' account of the Funeral Speech, see above p. 61) of the importance of political debate as a characteristic of Athenian democracy, seen in the context of the emphasis, in the speech as a whole, on the cultural dominance of Athens over Sparta and other Greek city-states.

It is at this point, I think, that what we know of the historical picture leads to the decisive rejection of the more extreme implications of Gorgias' argument. Protagoras claims, in Plato's dialogue of that name, that his teaching would make a pupil 'most powerful in word and deed in the affairs of the city'.[39] There is no evidence that, in practice, this power, taught by the Sophists, was absolute or often led to the mass seduction which Gorgias implies. Competitive oratory was heard, both in Assembly and law court, and choices were made, on principled or pragmatic grounds, between opposing arguments, and decisions were made. Yet, it is equally clear that Athenians were as aware as we are of the irrational, and even frightening elements in persuasive oratory – the tendency for *peitho* (persuasion) to turn into its apparent opposite, force (*bia*). Protagoras, who enjoyed the protection of Pericles during the heyday of Athenian democracy, is associated with teaching students to make 'the weaker case the stronger' (see above p. 58) a skill at which Athenians could laugh knowingly when parodied in the comic theatre by Aristophanes (*Clouds* 112) but which became inevitably associated with an attitude to moral values exemplified, according to Thucydides, by the Athenians in their debate with the beseiged inhabitants of the small island of Melos: absolute moral standards are to be replaced by expediency and inexpediency as a yardstick by which arguments are assessed; force becomes its own justification.[40]

The degree to which political controversy was associated with attitudes to verbal persuasion is illustrated by the case of Socrates. In his famous speech at his trial of 399 BC on a charge of corrupting the youth of Athens by teaching doctrines which subverted traditional religious and political beliefs, Socrates, according to Plato in his *Apology*, emphasized his dissociation from both the regime of the Thirty Tyrants (the oligarchic junta which had prevailed for a short time at the end of the Peloponnesian war) and the subsequent, restored democracy which had brought him to trial. He did this by explicitly rejecting the conventional rhetoric of verbal persuasion in favour of a defence which made no concessions to anybody. In his highly ironic introduction, he sums up the whole fifth century tradition of verbal persuasion and his critical attitude to it:

I have no idea, men of Athens, how my accusers have affected you; for my part, I almost forgot my own identity, they were so persuasive. And

---

[38]For Thucydides, see refs at n. 21. For Gorgias, see ref. to effect of a (false) persuasive speech on a 'large mob' at *Helen* Section 13.

[39]Plato, *Protagoras*, 318e.

[40]Thucydides, 5, 85–113.

yet there is hardly a word of truth in what they said. Of the many lies they told, one in particular amazed me – when they said you must beware of being deceived by me because I am a clever speaker (*deinos legein*). This I thought the most brazen aspect of their conduct, their lack of shame at soon being effectively refuted, when I show that I am not in the least clever at speaking, unless, of course, they call a clever speaker someone who speaks the truth. If that is what they say, then I'm prepared to agree that I am an orator, but not in their fashion.

Plato, *Apology*, 17 a–b.

This opening address to the jury, including the statutory disclaimer of elequence, is, on the surface, composed in the conventional rhetorical tradition. Yet it was – and the jury, if Plato is reporting Socrates faithfully, must have immediately realized it was – a parody of the conventions. Socrates swiftly makes it clear that he is not interested in playing rhetorical games with conventional argument or fine phrases, but is stating the truth as he sees it.

There are obviously deeper levels of irony in this speech; Plato is an accomplished stylist, and Socrates does not speak with 'the words which happen to occur to me'. Yet the rejection of the conventional means of persuasion also represents a decisive turning-point in the development of intellectual attitudes; whether or not Plato reports Socrates faithfully in the *Apology*, the explicit association of persuasion exclusively with truth, and the assumption that truth has its own persuasive power irrespective of the manner of presentation or the power and skill of the opposition, was developed by Plato in his early philosophical dialogues, and especially in the *Gorgias*. In this major attack on verbal persuasion as practised in the late fifth and early fourth centuries BC, the choice of Gorgias as a representative of oratory is not fortuitous. Plato systematically rejects claims on behalf of the orators that they benefit society, or, indeed, have power to do anything at all, since their art of verbal persuasion is based not on knowledge but merely belief. In a later dialogue, *Phaedrus*, Plato partly rehabilitated oratory, but only as a technique of persuading people of the validity of independently established philosophical truths.

The transition from Gorgias and the Sophists to Plato has been described by Ch. Perelman as a change from an 'audience-centred' rhetoric to a 'truth-centred' approach to argumentation, the latter being a characteristic of the rationalist tendency in ancient and modern philosophy.[41] This is true of the intellectual tradition, but harder to establish in a broader social and cultural framework, in which, strange as it may seem from our perspective, Plato was a marginal figure. The cultural continuity from fifth to fourth-century Greece was much greater than a reading of the Sophists and Plato might lead us to believe. Indeed the fourth century saw the activity of the greatest Greek orator, Demosthenes, in whose speeches the 'audience-centred' theory and practice of several generations of Athenian orators had its culmination.

[41] In *The New Rhetoric* (see above n. 5).

Towards the end of the century, the philosopher Aristotle, in his *Rhetoric*, laid the foundations for centuries of treatises aimed at the training of statesmen and lawyers in the later Greek and, soon, the Roman world. Yet, this was a world in which the independent city-state and the democratic Assembly, while enjoying a semblance of local autonomy, had given way to other more powerful forces, served by the 'vir bonus dicendi peritus' (the good man skilled in oratory) who represented an acceptable and durable compromise between Gorgias and Plato.

The homage constantly paid by the Graeco-Roman oratorical tradition to its fifth century BC origins can be seen as an aspect of the reverence shown by later Greeks and Romans to all aspects of Classical Athenian culture (a nostalgic reminiscence which has its origins as early as the fourth century BC). Yet, the resulting emphasis on continuity, which has had a decisive effect upon the way in which modern scholarship views the origins of rhetoric, has obscured for us the unique contribution of Athenian orators and teachers of the late fifth century to the study of verbal persuasion. Never again in the Ancient World were the psychological and epistemological premisses upon which persuasive techniques are based so thoroughly and unequivocally questioned.[42]

[42]I would like to thank my friend and colleague Lorna Hardwick for helpful criticism of an earlier draft of this essay.

Note

The study of attitudes and attitude change has traditionally occupied a central position in social psychological research. Undergraduate textbooks on social psychology typically devote a chapter to this topic (see, for example, Tedeschi, Lindskold and Rosenfeld, 1985;[1] Deux and Wrightsman, 1984; Worchel and Cooper, 1983; Baron and Byrne, 1984) and major scholarly reviews of the published research in this field appear regularly in the psychological journals (see, for example, Eagly and Himmelfarb, 1978; Cialdini, Petty and Cacioppo, 1981; Cooper and Croyle, 1984; Eagly and Chaiken, 1984). The fact that Cooper and Croyle (1984), in reviewing contributions to the major journals over a three-year period, found it necessary to refer to some 150 sources in the academic literature suggests that this area of research continues to thrive in contemporary social psychology.

Many social psychologists have turned to the methodology of the natural sciences to guide them in their approach to attitude research. In this approach, predictions concerning attitude change are made on the basis of the investigator's theoretical ideas and these hypotheses are then put to the test empirically (this may involve the design of a suitable experiment). The data yielded in this kind of investigation are typically quantitative in nature and are normally subjected to statistical analysis in order to determine whether or not the results of the study support the theoretical hypothesis. Whilst this approach has been severely criticized (see, for example, Harré and Secord, 1972), it continues to dominate work in this area. In this chapter I shall focus on one of the theories which has been particularly influential in this area of research: the Fishbeinian model of intention (see Fishbein and Ajzen, 1975). I shall do this at the expense of providing a general introduction to a wide range of attitude theories; for this the reader may consult one of the texts or review articles cited above.

Because quantitative techniques for attitude measurement abound in research carried out in connection with the Fishbeinian model of intention, I shall provide some general remarks on this topic. I shall keep the discussion of attitude measurement to a minimum; my aim will be to provide the reader with an orientation to the quantitative approach which, on the one hand, will serve as an introduction to the Fishbeinian model and, on the other hand, will support arguments presented later in the chapter when I offer an alternative interpretation of this model.

I would like to thank Dr Deborah Thomas, Sunderland Polytechnic, for her helpful comments on an earlier draft of this chapter.

·

[1]Because of the large number of references to the relevant literature, works are referred to by author and date and listed alphabetically at the end of the chapter.

5

Making People Offers they can't Refuse: A Social Psychological Analysis of Attitude Change.

John L. Smith

Introduction: The measurement of attitudes as an exercise in semantic mapping

Quantitative techniques typically demand that the research participant respond to a series of questionnaire items relating to the attitude topic in question. The investigator is then able to produce a score which is taken to be indicative of the respondent's attitude. I shall start, therefore, by considering how a person's thoughts or feelings (which are most naturally expressed in ordinary language) can be given a numerical representation. I am not, here, primarily concerned with the question of how accurately this may be done or with how much faith should be placed in such measurements; I merely wish to provide an orientation to the way this process may be construed.

I would like to suggest that, for the purposes of the present chapter, this process be construed as an exercise in mapping the person's attitude onto a graphical model of semantic space (see Palmer, 1976, p. 71 or Clark and Clark, 1977, for a discussion of the field theory of semantics and Leech, 1981, for a general treatment of the topic). Let us consider a typical questionnaire item which uses the 'semantic differential' format (developed by Osgood, Suci and Tannenbaum, 1957). The question might be concerned with the person's evaluation of a particular brand of washing powder, nuclear missiles, or whatever:

I think Bloggo's washing powder is:
bad: —————:—————:—————:—————:—————:—————:—————:good
　　　extremely　quite　slightly　neither　slightly　quite　extremely

This item may be regarded as a map of semantic space, provided by the social scientist, and as such (at least in Western culture in the twentieth century) could be seen as an extension of what de Saussure refers to as the ideographic system of writing (de Saussure, 1966, p. 25). The questionnaire item, as map, pin-points the location of the value words 'good' and 'bad' as polar opposites and charts the semantic distance between them with markers drawn from a series of secondary words, such as, 'extremely', 'quite', etc. The respondent is then requested to indicate where on the map the signifier of the attitude object (e.g. Bloggo's washing powder) should be positioned and this is usually done by marking the map with a tick or a cross. Let us suppose that a respondent marks the map in the following manner:

I think Bloggo's washing powder is:

bad: ———— : ———— : ———— : ———— : ———— : —✔— : ———— :good
      extremely   quite   slightly   neither   slightly   quite   extremely

The above map may be read as a symbolic expression of the person's attitude and taken to be equivalent to the following statement in plain English: 'I think Bloggo's washing powder is quite good'.

The investigator may then use a scoring key as a set of coordinates, rather like longitude or latitude, which will enable the respondent's 'position' to be specified unambiguously, in short-hand form. With the scoring key presented below, the score of '+2', in this example, may also be read as being equivalent to the statement:

'I think Bloggo's washing powder is quite good'.

$$-3 \qquad -2 \qquad -1 \qquad 0 \qquad +1 \qquad +2 \qquad +3$$

bad: ———— : ———— : ———— : ———— : ———— : —✔— : ———— :good
      extremely   quite   slightly   neither   slightly   quite   extremely

Perhaps I should say that this way of looking at attitude measurement is best suited to techniques which employ similar graphic designs in their questionnaires to the one illustrated here. I have focused on this particular graphical form because it is frequently used by researchers investigating hypotheses derived from the Fishbeinian model of intention (see the Appendix in Ajzen and Fishbein, 1980, for example).

The Fishbeinian model of intention

The Fishbeinian model of intention (see Fishbein and Ajzen, 1975) predicts whether or not a person will intend to do something on the basis of two factors: attitudes and social expectations. The attitude component of this model is concerned with the person's evaluation of the consequences which are likely to flow from the act in question; the component dealing with social expectations is concerned with the person's perception of what other people think he or she ought to do in the situation and takes account of the person's motivation to conform to such expectations. This model addresses behaviour indirectly through the concept of intention and the assumption is made that, other things being equal, people will generally do what they intend to do. It is usual for the symbolic expression of this model to take the form of a simple algebraic equation (see Appendix 1 for the formal version of this equation):

Attitude + Subjective Norm = Intention

Values are computed for the two predictor variables (Attitude and Subjective Norm) from data obtained using a questionnaire technique similar in principle to the one described in the previous section. These values combine to yield a predicted value for intention and this may then be checked against a direct measure of intention, also obtained by questionnaire. I shall briefly indicate how these data are obtained and how the appropriate values are derived for inclusion in the equation. For illustrative purposes, I shall consider the case of Mary who, we may imagine, is contemplating strike action over a pay dispute. Where appropriate, I have included a suitable scoring key, for the reader's benefit.

Intention
Ajzen and Fishbein (1980, Appendix A) provide the following questionnaire format for use in connection with the measurement of behavioural intention:

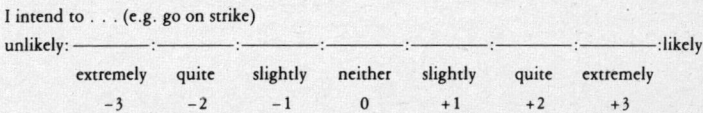

I intend to . . . (e.g. go on strike)

unlikely:							:likely
	extremely	quite	slightly	neither	slightly	quite	extremely
	-3	-2	-1	0	+1	+2	+3

The attitude component
The person may be aware of various consequences which are likely to flow from his or her action, should the intention to act be put into effect. For each of these consequences two things are taken into account by this component:

1 The person's evaluation of the consequence (symbolized by the letter 'e').
2 The person's belief as to how likely it is that the consequence will, indeed, flow from the intended action (symbolized by the letter 'b').

For illustrative purposes, let us consider the consequence that Mary may obtain higher wages as a result of this action:

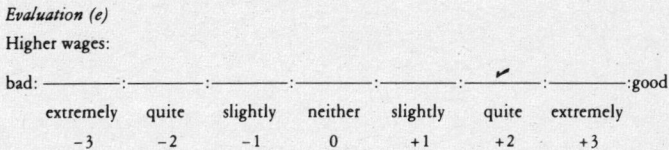

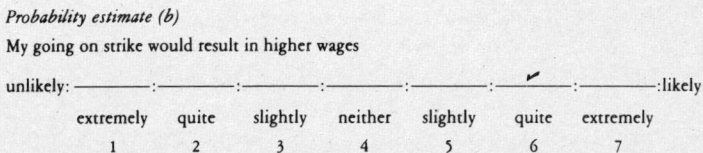

Evaluation (e)
Higher wages:

bad:						✓	:good
	extremely	quite	slightly	neither	slightly	quite	extremely
	-3	-2	-1	0	+1	+2	+3

Probability estimate (b)
My going on strike would result in higher wages

unlikely:						✓	:likely
	extremely	quite	slightly	neither	slightly	quite	extremely
	1	2	3	4	5	6	7

Given a modicum of flexibility in semantic mapping, Mary's evaluation score (e = +2), when coupled with her probability estimate (b = 6), may be regarded as equivalent to the following composite statement: 'I think it would be quite good to have higher wages and it's quite likely that my going on strike would result in higher wages.'

In Fishbein's model the two scores are multiplied together before being added into the attitude component. So in this case, a score of ' +12' (+2) × 6 would be the contribution with regard to this particular consequence. Other consequences (for example, the possibility of being made redundant) would be measured and added into the attitude component in a similar fashion.

The subjective norm component (social expectations)

The person may be aware of various social expectations which other people or social groups may have as to whether he or she ought (or ought not) to act in the manner being considered. Of course, the person may (or may not) be motivated to comply with these social expectations. Both of these considerations are taken into account by the Subjective Norm component of the Fishbeinian equation:

1 The belief that others hold a particular expectation as to how the person should act (symbolized by the letter 'b').
2 The person's motivation to comply with the other's expectations (symbolized by the letter 'm').

Returning to the illustration of Mary's strike action, the following items would address the social expectations of her co-workers, for example:

Social expectation (b)
'My co-workers think I should go on strike'

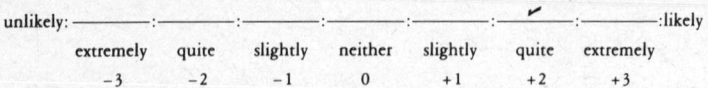

unlikely:	:	:	:	:	✔ :	:likely
extremely	quite	slightly	neither	slightly	quite	extremely
−3	−2	−1	0	+1	+2	+3

Motivation to conform (m)
'Generally speaking, I want to do what my co-workers think I should do.'

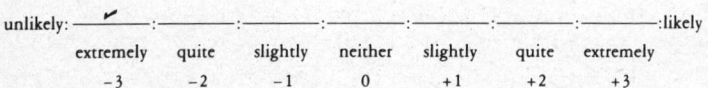

unlikely: ✔	:	:	:	:	:	:likely
extremely	quite	slightly	neither	slightly	quite	extremely
−3	−2	−1	0	+1	+2	+3

Mary's social expectation (b = +2), together with her motivation to conform (m = −3) could thus be mapped onto the following composite statement in plain English:

'I think it's quite likely that my co-workers think that I should go on strike but it is extremely unlikely that I shall want to do what they think I should do.'

If more flexibility in mapping is allowed, a less precise form of this statement could be produced which, perhaps, would be more likely to occur in the context of a conversation in everyday life. For example: 'My mates think I should go on strike – they can get lost!'

In the Fishbeinian model, the numerical value of the normative belief (b) is multiplied by the numerical value of the motivation to comply (m), for each of the social expectations involved. Thus, for Mary's co-workers, a score of ' – 6' (– 3) × (+ 2) would be contributed by this item. Any other relevant social expectations (e.g. her husband's expectations) would be added in in a similar fashion.

Let us imagine that Mary's scores were as follows:

Attitude:			*Subjective Norm*		
Higher wages	=	+12	Co-workers	=	– 6
Redundancy	=	– 6	Husband	=	+2
Total	=	+6	Total	=	– 4

By feeding the values of the Attitude and Subjective Norm components into the Fishbeinian equation we can arrive at a predicted value for the person's Intention:

Attitude + Subjective Norm = Intention
  (+6)   +   (–4)   =   +2

In this illustration, Intention takes a positive value (+ 2) and so the model would predict that Mary would intend to go on strike.

Fishbein and Ajzen (1975, p. 310), reviewing some 13 different studies, report that the evidence strongly supports the theory, showing that the two predictors (attitude and subjective norm) offer high correlations with behavioural intentions.

An alternative interpretation

I have already indicated that questionnaire items may be mapped onto statements in plain English, although this must sometimes be done in a fairly flexible fashion. I wish to explore this idea further by generating a conversation about a possible action in which question–answer pairs should be regarded as equivalent to the sort of statements we have already met and, as such, it will be assumed that they may be expressed symbolically using the conventional algebra of the Fishbeinian equation. I shall refer to conversations of this type as *clusters of accounts*.

In theory, it should be possible to generate a cluster of accounts where the symbolic representation produces a balanced Fishbeinian equation. But, more interestingly, we may also generate a cluster of accounts whose symbolic representation produces an unbalanced Fishbeinian equation. The following conversation provides an illustration of this latter possibility:

Interviewer: 'Do you think that going on strike will get you a wage increase?'

Interviewee: 'Yes, definitely. And I really like the idea of having more money.' (High probability [b] coupled with positive evaluation [e] yields a *positive* item for the *attitude* component).

Interviewer: 'What does your wife think you ought to do?'

Interviewee: 'She thinks I should go on strike. Generally speaking, I want to do what my family thinks I should do, and this is no exception.' (Positive social norm [b] coupled with a positive motivation to comply [m] yields a *positive* item for the *subjective norm* component).

Interviewer: 'Well, what do you intend to do? Will you go on strike or not?'

Interviewee: 'No, I'm not going on strike.' (*Intention* takes a *negative* value)

Interviewer: 'Well, is there anything else that's relevant to this issue that we haven't talked about?'

Interviewee: 'No, that's everything'.

I have included the final exchange to provide closure to the cluster and to dispense with the possibility that there may be some 'hidden' reason which the interviewee has not disclosed. Taken as it is, the cluster produces an unbalanced Fishbeinian equation, as follows:

Attitude +	Subjective Norm	≠ Intention
(positive)	(positive)	(negative)

There is something odd about the above cluster: it simply doesn't make sense. In a previous publication (Smith, 1982) I have suggested that the Fishbeinian equation may be regarded as a rule governing the intelligibility of a cluster of statements (such as the one given above). Looked at this way, the Fishbeinian equation expresses a synchronic relation between statements concerning intention, attitude and subjective norms. It may be useful to think in terms of a structural hierarchy of intelligibility, adopting the *word* as the basic unit at the lowest level. For the purposes of the present analysis, this would yield the following three levels:

1 CLUSTER
2 ACCOUNT (equivalent to the SENTENCE)
3 WORD

It is assumed that rules exist which govern the way words may be combined to produce an intelligible account in the form of a sentence, although any detailed discussion of such rules lies beyond the scope of this chapter. However, just as rules may exist which govern the way in which words may be combined to form an intelligible account in the form of a sentence, so may the Fishbeinian equation be regarded as a rule governing the way accounts may be combined to form an intelligible cluster. It should perhaps be noted that the order in which accounts are presented in a given cluster is of no importance in terms of this rule, whereas the order with which words are combined to produce an intelligible sentence can be of central importance.

In terms of semantic mapping, an agent's location in semantic space may be pin-pointed directly by a statement which reveals his or her behavioural intention. One could regard the Fishbeinian model as a series of instructions which would enable the behavioural intention to be pin-pointed on the basis of the information contained in the subsidiary items measuring attitude and subjective norms. In other words, the model allows behavioural intention to be plotted indirectly and the location so obtained may then be compared with the direct position. The Fishbeinian model may therefore be regarded as being equivalent to a rule which says that the agent can't be in two places at once on such a map.

Whether or not being in two places on a semantic map causes problems in the everyday world of the agent's social interaction will depend very much on the situation in which this ambiguity becomes manifest. Lalljee *et al*. (1984) offer an interesting critique of the traditional conceptualiza-tion of attitude as a learned predisposition to respond in a consistently favourable or unfavourable manner with respect to a given object (cf. Fish-bein and Ajzen, 1975, p. 6). They resist the implications of this stance: that attitudes are enduring internal affective or evaluative predispositions which have a causal influence on behaviour. Instead, they propose that attitudes be conceived of as communicative acts which imply evaluations of a class of objects, persons or events. This leads them to construe the avowal of attitudes in terms of self-presentation (see Goffman, 1959). Speech is therefore not regarded as a source of information about internal realities such as attitudes. Rather, making an attitude statement is seen as a lin-guistic device which results in a particular impression being created on a particular social occasion. Lalljee *et al*. (1984) point out that the expression of attitude may fruitfully be regarded as a way of achieving things, and, as such, the theory of speech acts and of conversational implicature (they refer to Austin, 1962; Grice, 1957, 1975; Searle, 1975) may be of relevance to attitude theory.

Following Lalljee *et al*. (1984), the problems of being in two places at once on a semantic map could become manifest at the level of impression management, with implications for the agent's personal identity. Some of my previous research *indirectly* supports the idea that the attributional consequences of breaking the Fishbeinian rule could be serious. For example, when I presented subjects with extracts from the transcripts of (imaginary) interviews between doctors and patients, I fould that the patients were judged to be more irrational, in the psychiatric sense, the more the clusters of accounts deviated from a balanced Fishbeinian equation. However, I do not wish to suggest that people will automatically avoid the production of unintelligible clusters in order to protect their identity. Some individuals may do all they can to avoid negative attribu-tions (e.g. attributions of insanity) but others may be prepared to live with them. Warren (1985), for example, suggests that giving up self-hatred will be experienced by a masochist as a loss, if it is the linchpin of his or her personality.

As a predictive model of behaviour, Fishbein's theory assumes human nature to be rational and provides a specification as to how the relevant calculations might be made. The limitations of this approach are high-lighted in Warren's (1985) explanation of psychological masochism, since she sees pain as an essential part of the masochist's identity. The clusters of accounts which a masochist might produce in connection with his or her masochistic behaviour would doubtless be in transgression of the Fish-beinian rule of intelligibility. However, Warren argues that the desire to remain a masochist is understandable because one prefers to be oneself, even if being oneself does involve pain and suffering.

Fishbein, in attempting to predict behaviour from attitudes, reaches out for a causal explanation of behaviour and thus by-passes the concept of agency. However, the position changes if the concept of identity is admitted as an important part of attitude theory. Schlenker (1982) sees identity as a theory (or schema) that is constructed about how one is and should be perceived, regarded and treated in social life. Schlenker goes on to say that individuals may have a range of schemata pertaining to specific situations, audiences and behaviours, organized to some degree under the rubric of the larger theory of identity which is, in turn, embedded in an even larger theory called the self-concept. He suggests that explanations of conduct are proffered to oneself and/or to others when behaviour appears to violate standards in ways that threaten one's identity or when some ambiguity exists about the relevance of the event for one's identity. Such explanations may well involve the production of clusters of accounts similar to those I have referred to in relation to the Fishbeinian model of intention. Schlenker (1982, p. 203) argues that it is only when people are responsible for an event that they are answerable or accountable for it in the sense that they can be condemned or praised: 'Responsibility is the adhesive that links an actor to an event and attaches the deserved sanctions to the actor.'

People can only be regarded as responsible for what they do if they are also regarded as human agents, i.e. as the efficient causes of their own actions (see Harré and Secord, 1972). In sum, when the concept of identity is admitted into attitude theory, the concept of agency comes with it.

Harré's understanding of the self-concept is not dissimilar to Schlenker's. He suggests that the 'sense of self' is: 'that which, as Doris Lessing has put it, is "kept burning behind our many roles" ' (Harré, 1983, p. 78).

Instead of adopting the conventional duality between mind and body, Harré (1983) introduces a duality between persons and selves. In this, persons appear as locations for speech acts, they are more like places than things, and can be pointed to using proper names and personal pronouns; they are thus identifiable by public criteria. Selves are psychological indi-viduals, manifested in the unified organization of perceptions, feelings and beliefs. Harré, like Schlenker, sees the self as a concept and not as an empirically given entity. He draws an analogy with the concept of gravity, in order to illustrate this point: 'Just as I can ascribe properties to the gravitational field without experience of it, so too I can ascribe properties to myself without an empirical acquaintance with my "inner being". Persons are indexed (indicated) as speakers; selves are referred to as organizing principles of the psychological unities that confer subjective individuality' (Harré, 1983, p. 80).

Harré states the basic thesis of his work as follows: 'Animate beings are persons if they are in possession of a theory – a theory about themselves. It is a theory in terms of which a being orders, partitions and reflects on its own experience and becomes capable of self-intervention and control' (Harré, 1983, p. 93).

This theory of self, Harré suggests, derives from the way the concept of person is used in the public-collective talk produced by folk belonging to a given linguistic community. 'It (the self) is a theoretical concept whose source analogue is the socially defined and sustained concept of 'person' that is favoured in the society under study and is embodied in the grammatical forms of public speech appropriate to talk about persons. Our personal being is created by our coming to believe a theory of self based on our society's working conception of a person' (Harré, 1983, p. 26).

I now wish to consider the Fishbeinian model, as a rule for intelligibility, in the light of this.

Insofar as the empirical evidence reflects the linguistic practices of the Western, English-speaking linguistic community (and one may have reservations about this), the Fishbeinian rule may be regarded as articulating one small facet of the self-concept which is widely shared amongst members of that community. The subject of all statements present in what I have called a cluster of accounts will always be a person who can be located in the array of persons in Harré's primary psychological structure. The Fishbeinian rule covers the sort of talk that persons in this community may produce when reflecting on their experience in relation to past or future actions. Talk which transgresses the Fishbeinian rule may be regarded as a failure, if it is deemed to be unintelligible. An unintelligible cluster of accounts could, in some circumstances, be taken as evidence that the individual had not grasped this facet of the theory of self. This could be a serious state of affairs, since, following Harré's argument, it is possession of such a theory that entitles individuals to the status of personhood, as opposed to that of merely 'being animate'. In particular, the individual's ability to act as an effective agent, within the criteria of the local linguistic community, may be called into question.

Given the above, if someone is put in the position of 'being in possession' of an unintelligible cluster of accounts, he or she may well feel that it is in his or her interest to do something which will effectively restore intelligibility to the cluster, in order to maintain an acceptable identity. In terms of the Fishbeinian model, this could involve changing the contents of the cluster so that its representation results in a balanced equation; such change could occur with respect to attitudes, subjective norms or the intention. From this point of view, *persuasive communication could be regarded as an attempt to place the recipient in the invidious position of being in possession of an unintelligible cluster of accounts*. To use the language of the movies, the recipient is given an offer she or he can't refuse. To refuse the offer would be to run the risk of appearing not to have grasped an important facet of the theory of self and this would be tantamount to relinquishing one's claim to the status of personhood. I propose to explore these ideas further by developing an analysis of a therapeutic technique, known as 'behaviour modification', and, in so doing, I hope to provide an illustration of how my conceptual framework may be deployed in practice. I have chosen behaviour modification since it is a technique which explicitly aims to modify behaviour, and I take this to be the ultimate goal of all persuasive communication.

An analysis of Behaviour Modification

According to Kazdin (1981), an important development in contemporary behaviour modification is the *token economy*. Token economies work best in institutional settings (psychiatric hospitals, schools, homes for delinquents, etc.) where it is possible to arrange for a system of rewards (and sometimes punishments) to be made contingent on the occurrence of precisely specified, desirable behaviours (or, in the case of punishments, undesirable behaviours). The behaviour therapist sees the situation in terms of stimulus–response theory and the principles of instrumental conditioning will often inform the therapeutic strategy to be adopted. In other words, it is assumed that stimuli come to elicit particular responses because those responses have, for a given client, been reinforced in the past. Behaviour may be changed, therefore, by reinforcing only that behaviour which is regarded as desirable; in this way new stimulus–response patterns are acquired and the client's behaviour is thus 'modified'. Kazdin describes the implementation of a simple token economy as follows: 'Essentially three ingredients are needed, including a token or medium of exchange, back-up reinforcers, and a set of rules that describe the interrelationships between behaviours and token earnings and between tokens and back-up reinforcers' (Kazdin, 1981, p. 60).

Kazdin goes on to explain that tokens may consist of poker chips, cards, points, marks, stars, and so on. Tokens, within the closed institution, are therefore equivalent in function to money. The tokens, once acquired, may be exchanged for consumables, privileges, etc. (these are the 'back-up reinforcers'). The rules of the system will specify how many tokens are needed to purchase any given back-up reinforcer. The range of back-up reinforcers on offer may be wide and varied and include such items as food, clothes, cosmetics, real money, free-time, access to TV/radio/record players, etc. The effectiveness of a back-up reinforcer is largely determined by how much the client wants it. Finally, clear rules are specified which describe how and when tokens may be earned (or, in some schemes, lost). Kazdin provides the following illustration of a token economy:

> As an example, Nelson and Cone (1979) used a token economy with 16 psychiatric patients on a locked ward. Both psychotic and mentally retarded patients were included in the sample. These patients were on a locked ward because of episodes of aggressive behaviour and attempts to

escape from the hospital. The purpose of the programme was to alter behaviours in four general categories: general hygiene, personal management, work on the ward and social skills. Within each of these categories, several specific behaviours were identified. For example, social skills included behaviours such as verbally greeting staff, answering questions about the current hospital environment and participating in group discussions. Behaviours that were included in each category were observed directly on the ward. Each behaviour was associated with a value in terms of tokens (coloured tickets) that would be delivered contingent upon its performance. (Kazdin, 1981, pp. 61–2)

In the above scheme, a 'store' was made available to the patients, so that they could exchange their tokens for beverages, sweets, cigarettes, etc. and sometimes the patients could exchange their tokens for small amounts of real money, to be spent on shopping trips in the local community. Apparently the project was a success, with staff indicating improvements in several general areas such as social competence, interest, neatness and decrements in patient irritability.

A concise summary of the evolution of this technique may be found in Davey (1981, p. 190). As mentioned above, it is grounded in the behaviourist school of psychology and its principles derive primarily from work with animals, especially rats and pigeons! Outlining the rationale behind this approach, Davey makes the following comment:

Firstly, the writings of behaviourists J.B. Watson and later B.F. Skinner (1953) were to stress a belief in the continuity of psychological mechanisms between non-human animals and man. If conditioning principles had been established with animals then – since man was only quantitatively rather than qualitatively different from animals in his learning abilities – these principles should apply to humans. (Davey, 1981, pp. 190–1)

Thus both the concept of agency and the concept of person are alien to the behaviour therapist's way of thinking. We may note that it is agency and the possession of a theory in the form of the self-concept that, according to Harré (see above), distinguishes persons from animate beings in general. The two perspectives are therefore diametrically and fundamentally opposed to one another. I propose to accept the general descriptions of social behaviour occurring within token economy episodes, as recounted by the behaviour therapists (see above example from Kazdin). However, by offering an interpretation which draws on the concepts embedded in the opposing paradigm, I hope to show that what goes on within the social episodes of the token economy schemes may be construed in a very different light.

Let us start by considering the target behaviours in a token economy scheme. These behaviours must be described in some detail to the client, if the rules relating to the contingencies of reinforcement are to be clearly understood. If a verbal description of a target behaviour is available, then, presumably, the opportunity exists for the client to formulate an intention to act accordingly (or not, as the case may be). If this is the case, then the Fishbeinian model should be directly applicable to the therapeutic situation (although, to my knowledge this situation has not hitherto been examined from the perspective of attitude theory). If the Fishbeinian model is admitted as relevant, then so too must the conceptual framework which I have developed earlier in this chapter. I therefore seek to analyse the token economy situation in terms of the impact of reinforcement on existing clusters of accounts and their symbolic expressions in the form of Fishbeinian equations.

The position may be simplified by considering the state of affairs which may exist before the introduction of a token economy scheme with regard to a particular client and a specific target behaviour. At this stage, the client will either be behaving in an undesirable fashion or not doing something that he or she ought to be doing; I shall use the term 'target behaviour' to refer to either of these alternatives. For any given target behaviour we may consider the state of the relevant Fishbeinian equation (whether or not the rule for intelligibility has been transgressed) and the relation between the currently held intention and current behaviour. This gives rise to the four categories represented in Figure 5.1. On the one hand, the Fishbeinian equation may be balanced or unbalanced (a positive attitude, a positive subjective norm component and a negative intention would be an example of an unbalanced equation thus transgressing the rule of intelligibility). On the other hand, the way a person behaves may or may not square with their intention (a mismatch between behaviour and intention would occur, for example, when someone intends to do something but does not, in point of fact, do it). I shall comment briefly on all four possibilities generated by Figure 5.1 before singling out the first category for a more detailed consideration.

Figure 5.1.   Classification scheme for action in terms of intelligibility and the match between intention and behaviour

Fishbeinian equation	Intention/behaviour relation Matched	Mismatched
Balanced	1 Unproblematic	2 Agency problems (e.g. akrasia)
Unbalanced	3 Problems at the level of identity schemata or self-concept	4 Superficially unproblematic for behaviour therapist, otherwise – messy!

Category 1: Equation balances – behaviour matches intention.
In my view, it is only cases falling within this category that can be adequately dealt with by behaviour modification, given the array of concepts available to the therapist committed to this theoretical perspective. By way of illustration, I will consider the hypothetical case of a client whom I will call George. George does *not* greet the hospital staff in a friendly fashion and has no intention of doing so. Let us assume that this negative intention

is supported by a balanced Fishbeinian equation. Perhaps the relevant cluster of accounts contains items indicating that he doesn't actually like the hospital staff and that his fellow inmates would take a dim view of it if he did start chatting to them in a friendly fashion! The therapist's task will be to force a change of intention upon George, possibly by upsetting the existing state of balance in the Fishbeinian equation. If successful, George will mend his ways and behave appropriately. I shall return to a further discussion of cases falling within this category after commenting briefly on the other three categories.

Category 2: Equation balances – mismatch between intention and behaviour

Cases falling within this category involve the failure to act. If this failure cannot be accounted for, then one might be tempted to regard the person as akratic. If the difficulty is seen as a problem of agency, then it is difficult to see how a behaviour therapist could begin to talk about it since the concept of agency is alien to the discourse of behaviourism. One could, of course, look to Harré's analysis of agency (see Harré, 1983, Ch. 7) for an approach to the problem but this would be to relinquish the behaviourist framework.

Category 3: Unbalanced equation – behaviour matches intention.

Here, the problem is not that the person's behaviour is discrepant with intention but that the relevant cluster of accounts will be unintelligible. I have already indicated that an individual in this situation may be faced with problems in terms of his or her identity and, more seriously, the individual's claim to the status of personhood may be called into question. Behaviour therapy can hardly be expected to deal with this situation, since it recognizes no qualitative difference between persons and animate beings, in this respect.

Category 4: Unbalanced equation – mismatch between behaviour and intention.

This is rather a messy situation. For the behaviourist, it is the behaviour which counts. This could give rise to the therapist assuming that the situation is unproblematic if the client is, in point of fact, behaving in a desirable fashion. On the other hand, if the client is behaving in an undesirable fashion, the behaviourist might well confuse the situation with the first category (see above) where intention and behaviour match and the Fishbeinian equation balances. I shall now return to a more detailed analysis of cases falling into the first category, since it is these that I believe to be optimally suitable for modification in token economy schemes.

Let us return to the illustration of George who will not greet staff in a friendly fashion. The behaviour therapist, by making reinforcement contingent on this behaviour, links an additional consequence to the intention under consideration. A subjective estimate of the probability that tokens will be acquired, together with an evaluation of the back-up reinforcers which may be obtained in exchange for the tokens, may thus be fed into the attitude component of the Fishbeinian equation. At the same time, the existing cluster of accounts may be expanded to include statements concerning this contingent reinforcement. For example, if George is a cigarette smoker and tokens can be exchanged for cigarettes, then the therapist will have introduced the acquisition of cigarettes as a possible consequence into George's cluster of accounts. If this new consequence is highly evaluated, the effect may be to throw the existing Fishbeinian equation into a state of imbalance, since the new positive item feeds into the attitude component. The patient will then be saddled with an unintelligible cluster of accounts; one way to restore intelligibility will be to change the intention. George may come to feel that, in the world of the token economy scheme, it would make sense to spend some time chatting to the staff, if only to secure his supply of cigarettes! If all goes well, then, the change in the cluster of accounts leads to a change in intention which is accompanied by a change of behaviour; the case thus remains in Category 1 of my classification (see Figure 5.1), which I regard as unproblematic. It is possible that things may not work out so well and that the case could slip into one of the other categories (2–3 in Figure 5.1). For example, if the change in intention was not paralleled by a change in behaviour, there would be a mismatch between intention and behaviour. But I have already suggested that behaviour modification is ill-equipped to deal with such cases.

In order for a token economy scheme to work, the behaviour therapist must have the power to enforce the token contingencies and, also, must have sufficient control over the supply of reinforcers. It is not surprising, therefore, to find that these schemes work best in closed institutions. Psychiatric patients may be denied the right and the opportunity to obtain the back-up reinforcers from other sources. It goes without saying that the patient must not be allowed to use conventional money and any wealth or assets accumulated in the form of savings from a previous period outside the institution must be frozen. Put simply in terms of our hypothetical illustration, George must not be allowed to cash a cheque at his bank which would enable him to go to a shop in the ordinary way and buy a packet of cigarettes, or whatever took his fancy.

We may note that as the behaviour therapist loses power and control, the efficacy of this therapeutic technique is likely to diminish. It is not surprising, for example, to learn from Kazdin (1981, p. 68) that token reinforcement has been used relatively infrequently as an outpatient treatment for adults; presumably, little control can be maintained over an adult who is still able to enjoy the comparative freedom of life in the wider community. However, the therapist's domain of control can be extended by recruiting suitable agents such as psychiatric aides, parents, teachers and others (Kazdin, 1981, p. 70). Kazdin, when talking about the training of these secondary agents, discusses some procedures which have been used which themselves amount to token schemes (i.e. the secondary agents are reinforced with tokens for correctly implementing the primary token economy scheme). The issue of power becomes transparent in the following quotation:

> Usually, it is more difficult to control and deliver reinforcers for behaviour change agents than it is to deliver them to their clients. For example, it is difficult to provide reinforcers to hospital aides or teachers because some of the events that they highly value (e.g. extra vacations, wages or privileges at work) are not easily applied on a contingent basis because of practical constraints. (Kazdin, 1981, p. 71)

Hospital workers are protected by powerful trades unions whose primary purpose is to prevent the exploitation of their members in matters relating to conditions of employment, such a wages, vacations and privileges at work. Psychiatric patients, prisoners and schoolchildren (to name three social groups from which token economy clients are often drawn) are not protected in this way; they are politically impotent by comparison.

The power relation between client and therapist may be of crucial importance should a conflict arise over the intelligibility of the client's behaviour. One way in which this could, in principle, happen is if the client denied the validity of admitting the reinforcing side-effects into the existing clusters of accounts. It could be argued that the contingent reinforcements do not flow naturally from the actions covered by the token economy scheme; for example, when one greets someone in everyday life, beyond the hospital walls, one is not usually given coloured tickets and told that they may be swapped for cigarettes or access to a TV later in the day! It is possible, therefore, that the client's cluster of accounts could differ from the therapist's in important ways. The client's cluster of accounts may exclude any reference to arbitrary reinforcements and would therefore contain the opposite intention to the therapist's (which *would* contain reference to the reinforcing consequences). From the client's point of view the behaviour is intelligible; from the therapist's point of view the client's behaviour appears unintelligible and, incidentally, counts as a failure of the token economy scheme to bring about the desired change in behaviour. In this sense, I would like to consider the failure of a token economy scheme as a conflict concerning the intelligibility of the client's behaviour. This opens up the possibility of extending the social psychological analysis into the domain of critical sociology where questions of meaning may be discussed in terms of power in society:

> Power is expressed in the capabilities of actors to make certain 'accounts count' and to enact or resist sanctioning processes; but these capabilities draw upon modes of domination structured into social systems. (Giddens, 1979, p. 83)

Given my earlier comments on the power relationship between client and therapist, I suggest that it is the therapist's account which is likely to count in such situations. If this is so, then it may be of interest to consider what institutionalized sanctioning processes may be brought into play.

Although obviously regarded as therapeutic by the psychiatric establishment, the administration of electric shocks (ECT) or powerful psychotropic drugs could be regarded in this light. Whilst I do not intend to pursue this controversial and speculative idea in any depth here, Schrag's (1978) aggressive critique of such practices does suggest that a case could be developed along these lines (although, with regard to ECT, it would, perhaps, be prudent to take note of more measured discussions of the topic, such as that provided by Clare, 1976). I am not, I hasten to add, wishing to imply that psychiatrists and behaviour therapists are a bunch of Frankensteinian gangsters but I do wish to draw attention to the theoretical possibility suggested by the analysis presented in this chapter: the justification for interference with a person's physiology may be unwarranted where it is underpinned by an assessment of intelligibility which draws upon the modes of domination structured into social systems, such as our psychiatric institutions.

Concluding remarks

Attitude change continues to be an important area of research in social psychology, with the prevailing methodology being that of the traditional 'scientific' paradigm. However, the traditional paradigm has, over the past 10 to 15 years, been subjected to a sustained critical attack (see Harré and Secord, 1972; Harré, Clarke and de Carlo, 1985, for example). More specifically, a critique of traditional attitude research has been made from the perspective of the 'new' paradigm in social psychology by Lalljee, Brown and Ginsburg (1984). In this chapter I have described one of the more influential theories of the traditional paradigm and have provided an alternative interpretation of it from the perspective of the 'new' paradigm. My approach has not been to challenge or cast doubt on the empirical findings of traditional research projects but to suggest that these findings may be understood in a way that is quite different from the way they would normally be interpreted within the traditional framework. Similarly, my approach has not been to challenge the efficacy of the token economy but to interpret this therapeutic practice from a 'new' paradigm perspective.

Limitations of space have prevented me from attempting a broader analysis of persuasive communication; I have not, for example, dealt with advertising or propaganda campaigns. However, I see no reason why the conceptual framework developed in this chapter should not be extended to apply to these broader concerns at some future date. An obvious starting point would be the analysis of campaigns in which a conscious attempt has been made to generate persuasive appeals on the basis of the Fishbeinian model. Ajzen and Fishbein (1980, pp. 153–65) devote a section of their book to a discussion of the use of attitude theory in marketing research, and a specific example of the application of this model to the design of persuasive appeals is provided by Hoogstraten *et al.* (1985) in a study which monitored attempts to stimulate demand for dental care in the Netherlands. My point is that if marketing and media campaigns can be discussed from the perspective of the Fishbeinian model, then it should be relatively simple to provide an analysis based on the alternative interpretation of that model, which I have developed in this chapter. The reason for doing this would be to raise a range of issues and questions which would not normally be addressed if the standpoint of the traditional paradigm in social psychology were to be adopted.

The Fishbeinian model, located in the traditional positivist paradigm, supports a conception of the individual as a somewhat soulless machine whose intentions are determined by weighing the relevant pros and cons. One of the consequences of subjecting this model to an interpretation from the perspective of the 'new' paradigm is to restore the concepts of person, self, identity and agency to the human being. This should facilitate integration between attitude change research dealing with the detailed analysis of the intelligibility of particular clusters of accounts for specific individuals, on the one hand, and studies concerned with broader questions of media influence, on the other. Gender stereotyping in the media, for example, may be construed as the presentation of 'off-the-peg' identities for biological males and females and whether or not a given account is admitted into a cluster as legitimate by a given individual may depend upon the extent to which that individual accepts the stereotypic gender identity. In other words, it is hoped that the new approach to attitude change research developed in this chapter might act as a bridge, enabling the broader studies of media contents to be grounded at the level of individual autobiography.

Appendix

Formal statement of the Fishbeinian model of intention (see Fishbein & Ajzen, 1975).

The theory may be stated in the form of the following equation:

$$B \sim I = (A)w_1 + (SN)w_2$$

Where

B = Behaviour in question

I = Intention to perform behaviour B

A = Attitude towards performing behaviour B

SN = Subjective norm regarding the performance of behaviour B

w_1 and w_2 are empirically determined weights

The attitude component A may be further defined as follows:

$$A = \sum_{i=1}^{N} b_i e_i$$

Where

b = the belief that performing behaviour B leads to a particular consequence or outcome (i)

e = the person's evaluation of the outcome (i)

n = the number of beliefs concerning outcome(s) of behaviour B
i = a particular consequence or outcome
The subjective norm component SN may be further defined as follows:

$$SN = \sum_{n=1}^{N} b_i m_i$$

Where
b = the person's belief that a particular reference person or group (i) thinks that he/she should or should not perform behaviour B
m = the person's motivation to comply with referent (i)
n = the number of normative beliefs relevant to behaviour B
i = a particular normative belief

References

Ajzen I. and Fishbein M., *Understanding Attitudes and Predicting Social Behaviour* (Englewood Cliffs, NJ, Prentice Hall, 1980).
Austin J.L., *How to do things with Words* (Oxford, Oxford University Press, 1962).
Baron R.A. and Byrne D., *Social Psychology: Understanding Human Interaction* (Boston, Allyn & Bacon, 1984).
Cialdini R.B., Petty R.E. and Cacioppo J.T., 'Attitudes and Attitude Change', *Annual Review of Psychology*, XXXII (1981), 357–404.
Clare A., *Psychiatry in Dissent: Controversial Issues in Thought and Practice* (London, Tavistock Publications, 1976).
Clark H.H. and Clark E.V., *Psychology and Language: an Introduction to Psycholinguistics* (New York, Harcourt Brace Jovanovich, 1977).
Cooper J. and Croyle R.T., 'Attitudes and Attitude Change', *Annual Review of Psychology*, XXXV (1984), 395–426.
Davey G., *Applications of Conditioning Theory*, ed. G. Davey (London, Methuen, 1981).
Deux K. and Wrightsman L.S., *Social Psychology in the 80s*, 4th edn. (Monterey, Cal., Brooks/Cole Publishing Co., 1984).
Eagly A.H. and Chaiken S., 'Cognitive Theories of Persuasion', *Advances in Experimental Psychology* XVII (1984), 267–359.
Eagly A.H. and Himmelfarb S., 'Attitudes and Opinions', *Annual Review of Psychology*, XXIX (1978), 517–54.
Fishbein M. and Ajzen I., *Belief Attitude, Intention and Behaviour: an Introduction to Theory and Research* (Reading, Mass., Addison-Wesley, 1975).
Giddens A., *Central Problems in Social Theory: Action, Structure and Contradiction in Social Analysis* (London, Macmillan Press, 1979).
Goffman E., *The Presentation of Self in Everyday Life* (New York, Doubleday, 1959).
Grice H.P., Meaning, *Philosophical Review*, LXVI (1957), 377–88.
——. 'Logic and Conversation', in P. Cole and J.L. Morgan, *Syntax and*

Semantics Vol. 3 (New York, Academic Press, 1975).

Harré R., *Personal Being* (Oxford, Blackwell, 1983).

Harré R., Clarke D. and De Carlo N., *Motives and Mechanisms: an Introduction to the Psychology of Action* (London, Methuen, 1985).

Harré R. and Secord P.F., *The Explanation of Social Behaviour* (Oxford, Blackwell, 1972).

Hoogstraten J., De Haan W. and Ter Horst G., 'Stimulating the Demand for Dental Care: an Application of Ajzen and Fishbein's Theory of Reasoned Action', *European Journal of Social Psychology*, XV (1985) 401–14.

Kazdin A.E., 'The Token Economy', in Davey G., *Applications of Conditioning Theory* (London, Methuen, 1981), 59–80.

Lalljee M., Brown L.B. and Ginsburg G.P., 'Attitudes: Disposition, Behaviour or Evaluation?', *British Journal of Social Psychology*, XXIII (1984) 233–44.

Leech G., *Semantics* (Harmondsworth, Penguin, 1981).

Nelson G.L. and Cone J.D., 'Multiple-baseline Analysis of a Token Economy for Psychiatric Inpatients', *Journal of Applied Behaviour Analysis*, XII (1979) 255–71.

Osgood C.E., Succi G.J. and Tannenbaum P.H., *The Measurement of Meaning*, (Urbana, University of Illinois Press, 2nd edn, 1967).

Palmer F.R., *Semantics: a New Outline*, (Cambridge, Cambridge University Press, 1976).

de Saussure F., Translated by W. Baskin, *Course in General Linguistics* (New York, McGraw-Hill Book Co., 1966).

Schlenker B.R., 'Translating Actions into Attitudes: an Identity-analytic Approach to the Explanation of Social Conduct', *Advances in Experimental Social Psychology*, XV (1982), 193–247.

Schrag P., *Mind Control* (London, Marion Boyars, 1978).

Skinner B.F., *Science and Human Behaviour* (New York, Macmillan, 1953).

Searle J., 'Indirect Speech Acts', in Cole P. and Morgan J.L., eds, *Syntax and Semantics* Vol. 3, (New York, Academic Press, 1975).

Smith J.L., 'A Structuralist Interpretation of the Fishbeinian Model of Intention', *Journal for the Theory of Social Behaviour*, XII (1982), 29–46.

Tedeschi J.T., Lindskold S. and Rosenfeld P., *Introduction to Social Psychology* (New York, West Publishing Co., 1985).

Warren V.L., 'Explaining Masochism', *Journal for the Theory of Social Behaviour*, XV (1985), 103–29.

Worchel S. and Cooper J., *Understanding Social Psychology, 3rd ed*, (Homewood, Ill., The Dorsey Press, 1983).

Note

In the linguistic literature, aspects of persuasion have attracted immense interest, especially in recent years when linguists have increasingly directed their attention to the use and function of language, i.e. to pragmatic issues. Still, book-length studies of persuasion are scarce, and the topic is typically dealt with in an indirect manner, as a by-product of discussions of other points the particular linguist happens to be interested in – either more general, or more specific ones: say, advertising, or the use and distribution of particular words or constructions in different types of discourse. The first set of publications below is of this general linguistic kind: they do not address persuasion as such, but their findings are nevertheless important for the study of the language of persuasion, too.

Penelope Brown and Stephen C. Levinson, 'Universals in Language Usage: Politeness Phenomena', in *Questions and Politeness: Strategies in Social Interaction*, ed. Esther N. Goody (Cambridge, Cambridge University Press, 1978).

Wallace L. Chafe, 'Integration and Involvement in Speaking, Writing, and Oral Literature', in *Spoken and Written Language. Exploring Orality and Literacy*, ed. Deborah Tannen (Norwood, NJ, Ablex, 1982).

Charles J. Fillmore, *Santa Cruz Lectures on Deixis* (Bloomington, Indiana University Linguistics Club, 1975).

H. Paul Grice, 'Logic and Conversation', in *Syntax and Semantics 3. Speech Acts*, eds. Peter Cole and Jerry L. Morgan (New York, Academic Press, 1975).

Geoffrey N. Leech, *Principles of Pragmatics* (London, Longman, 1983).

Stephen C. Levinson, *Pragmatics* (Cambridge, Cambridge University Press, 1983).

John Lyons, *Semantics*, vols. 1–2 (Cambridge, Cambridge University Press, 1977).

Jan-Ola Östman, *You Know: A Discourse-Functional Approach* (Amsterdam, John Benjamins, 1981).

Robin Tolmach Lakoff, 'Questionable Answers and Answerable Questions' in *Issues in Linguistics*, eds. Braj B. Kachru, *et al.* (Urbana, University of Illinois Press, 1973).

——, 'Remarks on this and that', in *Proceedings of the Tenth Regional Meeting of the Chicago Linguistic Society*, eds. Michael W. LaGaly, *et al.* (Chicago, Ill., Chicago Linguistic Society, 1974).

——, 'Stylistic Strategies within a Grammar of Style', in *Annals New York Academy of Sciences*, 1979.

The second set of publications deals more specifically with linguistic manifestations of persuasion. The list is very selective: not only does it include only fairly recent studies, but in its diversity it also tries to give a hint of the different ways in which persuasion can be approached linguistically.

Gloria Italiano Anzilotti, 'Searching for Linguistic Universals through Contrastive Analysis', in *Cross-Language Analysis and Second Language Acquisition*, vol 2, ed. Kari Sajavaara (University of Jyväskylä, Department of English, 1983).

Erwin P. Bettinghaus, *Persuasive Communication* (New York, Holt, Rinehart & Winston, 1968; 3rd ed. 1980).

Michael Burgoon and Erwin P. Bettinghaus, 'Persuasive Message Strategies,' in *Persuasion: New Directions in Theory and Research*, eds. Michael E. Roloff and Gerald R. Miller (Beverly Hills, Sage, 1980).

Susan Ervin-Tripp, 'Ask and it shall be given unto you: Children's Requests', *Georgetown University Round Table on Languages and Linguistics*, 1982.

Mohan R. Limaye, 'The Syntax of Persuasion: Two Business Letters of Requests', *Journal of Business Communication* 20:2, 1983.

G. Peeters, 'Implications of a Relativistic Evaluating-Meaning Concept for Persuasive Communication', *Revue de Phonetique Appliquee* 57, 1981.

Donald L. Rubin, 'Adapting Syntax in Writing to Varying Audiences as a Function of Age and Social Cognitive Ability', *Journal of Child Language* 9:2, 1982.

John Sherblom and N.L. Reinsch Jr, 'Persuasive Intent as a Determinant of Phonemic Choice', *Journal of Psycholinguistic Research* 10:6, 1981.

——, 'Stylistic Concomitants of Persuasion in Conversations', *Communication Quarterly* 29:1, 1981.

Robin Tolmach Lakoff, 'Persuasive Discourse and Ordinary Conversation, with Examples from Advertising', *Georgetown University Round Table on Languages and Linguistics*, 1981.

Edwin Webb, 'The Rhetoric of Education', *The Use of English* 32:3, 1981.

6

Pragmatic Markers of Persuasion

Jan-Ola Östman

Introduction

The aim of this paper is to argue against the prevalent view that persuasive language does not in itself constitute a register, or style of speech. According to that view, *anything* can be persuasive language, all depending on the particular situation at hand and the interactants' background real-world knowledge. Consequently, in that view, there can be no linguistic markers of persuasion.

But a particular situation, and interactants' background knowledge are also reflected in a linguistic message, and thus, a priori, it should not be inconceivable to talk about markers of persuasion in a particular discourse. In order to be able to deal with persuasion as a particular style of language, however, it is not enough to look solely at the overt formal characteristics of a text or a discourse. The analyst – and, consequently, the interactants in a particular situation – also needs to take note of linguistic aspects in the domain of pragmatics. I would even argue that we need to take a *particular* view of pragmatics in order to be able to deal satisfactorily with the language of persuasion. The view I am referring to has been dealt with in some detail in my doctoral dissertation,[1] and will be summarized briefly in the next section.

I also want to make a further point with my discussion. In opposition to the general feeling within the mainstream of linguistics today, I want to show that literary works – although they are in the first instance works of art – can well be used as reliable data for linguistic studies. And I will argue below that in some cases, as in the present one, a literary work of art can be thought of as even better data than a surreptitiously recorded conversation or monologue. In my analysis of the language of persuasion I have used James Clavell's *The Children's Story* as my primary source for examples. ·

[1] Jan-Ola Östman, *Pragmatics as Implicitness. An Analysis of Question Particles in Solf Swedish, with Implications for the Study of Passive Clauses and the Language of Persuasion.* Unpublished PhD dissertation, University of California, Berkeley, 1986. (Available through University Microfilms International.)

The three parameters of implicit pragmatics

Pragmatics is the study of language (form and content) in relation to language users, who are part of a culture, who have specific psychological make-ups and sociological backgrounds, and whose (communicative) acts are to be seen in relation to the particular contexts in which they are performed.

In my work on pragmatics I have come to regard it as particularly important that a distinction is drawn between explicit and implicit aspects of language.[2] A useful rule of thumb for distinguishing between the explicit and the implicit in a message is that if you can be held responsible for what you have said (or done) – ultimately, in a court of law – then you have said it (or done it) explicitly. Thus, if I say to you, *You're a s-o-b!*, you can take me to court. I have explicitly said something for which I can be charged with slander. However, if I say *You're just like my mother!*, it will be much more difficult for you to prove to a jury that this is necessarily an offence. In the latter case, then, I offend you implicitly. Thus, an implicit linguistic choice is a linguistic choice that the speaker in principle can deny that he or she has made. The speaker is not (or does not think that he or she is) to be held responsible for such a choice.

When a speaker wants to persuade another person openly, he or she can do this explicitly, and the analysis of such overt persuasion can be done in straightforward semantic terms. Explicit persuasion needs no markers, since both participants are aware of what is going on. But for a discourse to be an instance of explicit persuasion, *both* interlocutors have to agree on the persuasive means to be used. If speaker *i* relies solely on means of logical deduction in his/her argumentation, and speaker *j* uses a combination of logical and religious argumentation, then to the extent that the religious means that speaker *j* uses are effective (especially if speaker *i* is not aware that any but logical means are used), to that extent the persuasion by speaker *j* of speaker *i* is simultaneously carried out on an implicit level. Whereas most aspects of explicit pragmatics can be dealt with in traditional semantic terms, implicit aspects are expressible in terms of the three pragmatic parameters of Coherence, Politeness and Involvement.

A speaker tends to conform to, and be Coherent with, what is expected of him/her in the community. The notion of Coherence is most directly related to culture, and it is structurally manifested for instance in textual cohesion, as a reflection of, say, norms for telling a story in a particular culture. The parameter of Politeness has interaction in focus. The speaker has to take his/her addressee or audience into account. The parameter has a supermaxim of 'Avoid Confrontation!' as its most noticeable manifestation – in our culture. Finally, the parameter of Involvement has the speaker him/herself and his/her attitudes, feelings, even prejudices, in focus.

These three areas of human behaviour are connected in three different ways. First, they are interrelated and interdependent. Secondly, all three

---

[2] A detailed discussion of this distinction is to be found in Östman, *Pragmatics*.

are communicated implicitly. And thirdly, speakers' utterances are simultaneously anchored to each of these three parameters. In *Pragmatics as Implicitness* I have developed the Level Analysis as a device in terms of which the pragmatic anchoring of utterances to these parameters can be depicted.

In this chapter I will illustrate how the three parameters can be made use of in an analysis of persuasive language. The analysis starts out from persuasive discourse as a type of language, and investigates how this type manifests itself linguistically: what kind of pragmatic markers of Coherence, Politeness and Involvement are there in persuasive language? I will not so much argue for the necessity of the Coherence–Politeness–Involvement framework in order to point to some new facts that only this framework can handle. Rather, I will show how what we know about the language of persuasion can be given a coherent frame of reference if we utilize the insights that recourse to the pragmatic parameters can offer. And in this sense, of course, I will claim that an analysis of this discourse type not only can, but needs to, refer to the pragmatic parameters, and, moreover, that the analytic use of these parameters in turn can help to define that discourse.

Linguistics and persuasion

From a linguistic point of view, persuasive discourse is interesting for a number of reasons. First, persuasion has not been dealt with extensively in the linguistic literature, although it is probably fair to say that all interactions – except perhaps pure small-talk conversations – have *some* element of persuasion in them. (We can also note that pragmatics has recently been connected with aspects of rhetoric,[3] and rhetoric of course is traditionally understood as the use of language for persuasive purposes. Even though pragmaticists today do not stress the persuasive aspect of rhetoric, the connection is still there.)

Secondly, persuasion is not a speech act on a par with, say, promising or requesting. For one thing, a persuasive sentence cannot be analysed in terms of a performative statement of the form (1).

(1) I persuade you that S

I will argue below that this is precisely due to the inherent implicitness of prototypical persuasion and persuasive discourse.

Thirdly, one common view of persuasion is that *any* discourse or element of discourse *can* have a persuasive effect, but that there are no specific features of persuasion in language, and therefore no persuasive discourse to be treated as a separate type of discourse. There are at least two issues involved here. First, even though it is customary to think of persuasion only in terms of whether a piece of discourse has a persuasive effect or not, I will not here restrict myself to this view. Rather, I see persuasive language in the

---

[3]Cf., e.g., Geoffrey Leech's *Principles of Pragmatics*.

first instance as a manifestation of a speaker's persuasive intention. And secondly, it is indeed true that there is no *one* linguistic feature that can be talked about as a particular marker of persuasion in English. But the reason for this is precisely the implicit way a speaker's persuasive intent has to manifest itself in persuasive language. However, if we do not view the concept 'persuasive discourse' in terms of necessary and sufficient conditions, but instead give it a prototype characterization, then we will also be able to find prototypical markers of persuasive discourse. Persuasive discourse exists as a discourse type, and an adherence to the three pragmatic parameters can help define and characterize this discourse type. In general, persuasion is not like metaphors and irony which 'can acquire conventional indicators and structural correlates',[4] but it is more like the implicitness of allusions, where the communication of an allusion rests solely on hints.[5]

The Children's Story as linguistic data

The kind of persuasive discourse that I will be concerned with in this paper is implicit persuasion. My hypothesis is that there exist linguistic means (e.g. words and structures) that can be regarded as markers of implicit persuasion. We cannot expect to find any particular marker, or set of markers, that would always and unambiguously indicate that the speaker wants to persuade his/her addressee or audience. Such a marker – if it existed – would effectively destroy the whole enterprise of attempting to carry out implicit persuasion. We can, however, discover bundles of markers, or combinations of words and structures that together indicate (at least to the analyst) that a piece of discourse is persuasive in nature.

Since a thorough analysis of all the potential words and constructions that might serve a persuasive purpose is probably an impossible task – and certainly outside the scope of this chapter – I will here illustrate implicit persuasion with an analysis of some of the linguistic aspects of a persuasive text, namely of James Clavell's *The Children's Story* (Sevenoaks, Hodder & Stoughton, Coronet 1983; first published 1963). In particular, I will show how the aspects of Coherence, Politeness and Involvement are drawn on in this text for the purpose of (implicit) persuasion.

The Children's Story might not be considered a good representative of ordinary persuasive discourse. And, strictly speaking, my analysis is of an 'ideology' of persuasive discourse, rather than of a 'reality'. But ideologies, like prejudices, are based on some – albeit stereotypical – connection with reality. From this, there are two possible lines of argumentation. We can either say that Clavell's perception of persuasion represents people's stereotypical attitudes about what persuasive discourse looks like, and we can thus treat Clavell's perception of it as a framework in the same way as

[4]Stephen Levinson, *Pragmatics*, p. 165. Cf. also Penelope Brown and Stephen Levinson, 'Universals in language usage: politeness phenomena', pp. 267ff.
[5]On allusion, cf. Claes Shaar, 'Vertical Context systems', in *Style and Text*, ed. Håkan Ringbom (Åbo Akademi/Stockholm, Skriptor, 1975); and 'Linear Sequence, Spatial Structure, Complex Sign, and Vertical Context System', *Poetics* 7:4, 1978.

Grice's Cooperative Principle[6] forms a frame of reference: as something that is not normally adhered to in everyday face-to-face interaction, but which is a norm for such behaviour. The second alternative, and the one that I am inclined to follow, takes the opposite line of argumentation, and says that this story depicts basic principles of persuasion, and *because* it is a story about the persuasion of children (a summary of the plot is given below), the manifestations of persuasive strategies and methods are shown, and can be seen, much more clearly here, than in, say, *Mein Kampf*, or Nixon's Checkers Speech and Watergate Speech. Furthermore, it seems unlikely that a strict separation of ideology and reality is in practice possible when doing pragmatics. (Although in theory, of course, such a separation is important and possible.)

Another reason why a literary text like Clavell's story is to be preferred to a piece of ordinary conversation is that the analyst does not have to rely solely on his/her own interpretation of the text. The author – by being omniscient – not only gives the reader/analyst an insight into what the persuader intended, but also into how this intention was perceived, whether it was effective or not. The story – as a story – is a coherent piece of persuasive discourse, which ties together manifestations of persuasion from different levels. The characters of the story not only have their own ideas and attitudes, and attempt to exert their power when possible, they are also part of a larger whole – the story – which is controlled by Clavell himself. Thus, the effects of all the three parameters can be seen clearer here than in an ordinary conversation, where the analyst him/herself might be one of the interlocutors, and might thus not have all perspectives so clearly at hand.

The plot of the story

The Children's Story is a story about the 25 minutes during which a classroom of seven-year-olds is politically converted into accepting an enemy force. A foreign power has invaded the US, and all over the country representatives of this power have been given the task to show how good and friendly, in fact, how much better, the state of affairs is now that the foreign power is in charge, in comparison to the situation people had been living in before.

In the school class of the story there are two main forces, on the one hand there is the New Teacher, and on the other hand there is Johnny, whose father has been very active in the resistance movement, and who is the only pupil who overtly objects to being converted. The story is ultimately about how the New Teacher manages to persuade Johnny into accepting the enemy.

At the discourse level, the story is an instance of persuasive discourse in its most simple and straightforward fashion: the New Teacher's persuasive discourse is directed toward children of the age of seven. Although Clavell

[6]H. Paul Grice, 'Logic and Conversation'.

is the omniscient writer, the story is often told, and the situation experienced, from the point of view of the children.

Manifestations of coherence-establishing strategies

Linguistically, 'Coherence is defined as that principle of pragmatics which deals with how the choice of a linguistic element contributes to establishing . . . the function . . . of a discourse . . . as a whole.'[7] In this section I will give some examples of how the parameter of Coherence is drawn on in Clavell's story.

Persuasion does not take place only at the verbal level. When attempting to influence somebody, it is of great help if you also look influential – where your particular looks and behaviour, of course, have to be synchronized with the purpose at hand, and the group or individual toward which persuasion is directed.

When the New Teacher enters the classroom for the first time, she immediately succeeds in making a positive impression on the children. And *that* is the first prerequisite of effective persuasion:[8]

> (2) The children gasped. They had expected an ogre or giant or beast or witch or monster. . . . But instead of a monster, a beautiful young girl stood in the doorway. Her clothes were neat and clean, all olive green – even her shoes. But most important, she wore a lovely smile, and when she spoke, she spoke without the trace of an accent.

In the next couple of pages, the New Teacher is given even more positive attributes: her perfume was clean, fresh and young, she smelled youth and cleanness; she spoke gently and radiantly, she sat down on the floor 'as gracefully as an angel'.

In fact, not only did everything in her behaviour show that she took good care of herself (clean, fresh), but also that she cared about her audience. If a person has an established authority, his/her way of dressing might not make a difference with respect to his/her credibility and power, but if – as in this case – the New Teacher had all reason to believe that her authority would be questioned, her way of dressing would at least not make them question that authority even more. We have to remember also that to a seven-year-old, sparkling clothes are apt to arouse more positive feelings than they would in adults. But in the adult world, too, dress and behaviour are important for creating a positive first impression. If you come to a meeting in a shabby dress, you not only give a bad impression of yourself, your behaviour is also most likely interpreted by your interlocutor as being negatively directed against him/her, i.e. as being offensive. (In this case

---

[7] Östman, *Pragmatics*, p. 184.

[8] The Coronet edition has no page numbers. In fact, the graphic channel is very dominant, and well handled, in the sense that it parallels the development of, and activities in, the story. It has blank pages, and half-filled pages, where this is called for – to give the appropriate effect.

the impression that the New Teacher's appearance communicates of caring for her audience is not sincere. We learn that from the omniscient writer. But potential ambiguity is enough at the level of implicit pragmatics.)

In addition to her dress, cleanliness and youth, the New Teacher had also learned everybody's names, and she had found out that it was Mary's birthday today. In other words, she (succeeds in giving the impression that she) regards the children as people and as individuals.

The New Teacher's non-verbal behaviour is most effective in the initial stage of her persuasive task. It creates the important first impression. (This is also paralleled in Clavell's treatment of the subject. There is much less stress on the New Teacher's non-verbal actions in the latter part of the book.) The non-verbal dimension is a very implicit one. You may notice that somebody is clean, but you might not directly associate your positive evaluation of that person with his/her cleanliness. This association takes place on an implicit, unconscious level.

Apart from the non-verbal cues, the New Teacher also uses a number of other devices to make the children see not only the Coherence of the enemy's framework, but also its positive sides. In particular, she uses metaphorical expressions, and draws parallels between the new and the old systems.

The New Teacher's comparisons of the new situation (manifested in herself) with the previous situation (manifested in their old teacher, Miss Worden, and in their parents) turn out to be a particularly effective Coherence strategy. The purpose of the New Teacher's comparisons are, of course, obvious (to the reader, but perhaps not to the children), but comparisons have to be made very implicitly if they are to serve the purposes of persuasion. Her strategy is to be as logical and commonsensical as possible – using the seven-year-old's idea of common sense to her advantage – and lead the children into a situation where they cannot but draw the conclusions she wants them to draw. An example follows. The New Teacher says:

(3) a. Well, before we start our lesson, perhaps there are some questions you want me to answer.

Her use of *well* here almost says that she is not so inclined to answer them;[9] i.e. she just wants them to get the principle clear.

(3) b. Ask me anything you like. That's only fair, isn't it, if I ask you questions.

'Fairness' is stressed here, as all through the story – and it is used here, as elsewhere, ambiguously between its technical and its 'children's' sense. If the New Teacher is fair, and she represents the conquerors, then *they* must all be 'fair', she wants to imply.

Mary then says:

(4) We never get to ask our real teacher *any* questions.

[9]Cf. Robin Tolmach Lakoff, 'Questionable Answers and Answerable Questions'.

Notice that Mary uses the present tense; and she talks about Miss Worden as their real teacher. So, at this point the children have not yet accepted the New Teacher completely.

(3) c. You can always ask me anything. That's the fair way. The new way. Try me.

'Fairness' and 'newness' are presented together, to implicitly indicate that they equal one another. It is also implicitly directed toward Mary's statement. This is the 'now', and the New Teacher is their real teacher.

Manifestations of the use of different interactive strategies

'Politeness is defined as that principle of pragmatics which deals with how the choice of a linguistic element contributes to establishing . . . the social relation between speaker and addressee/audience.'[10] In my explication of Politeness, I have taken Robin Tolmach Lakoff's strategies[11] as my starting point. The basic principle here is that communicative interaction is seen as a choice among three basic strategies, those of Distance (which imputes authority), Deference (the speaker gives the addressee options and power, and does not impose), and Camaraderie (the speaker and the addressee are equal in every sense). Although I argue in *Pragmatics as Implicitness* that interaction in modern Western society rarely takes recourse to either Distance or Camaraderie, I will retain the terms here as forming a convenient frame of reference for Politeness. I have also found it necessary to make a distinction between Formal and Informal Deference, the former being sanctioned by your society's rules of etiquette, whereas using the latter strategy you simply see to it that you do not create any offence. Thus, whenever you want to communicate with somebody, you start by choosing the strategy of Politeness you find most appropriate. Oversimplifying, we can see these strategies as a hierarchy of more-and-less Politeness – where 'Politeness' is a technical term, covering aspects of communicative interaction.

> Distance
> Formal Deference
> Informal Deference
> Camaraderie

The New Teacher is in an extremely dominant position. Not only is she the teacher, she is also a representative of the invaders. Thus, she *could* use a very power-ridden Distance strategy to convert the children. She *could* threaten them, she *could* even use physical force to make them do as she wants. To a certain extent she also uses her status as a teacher and therefore a power-ridden strategy when she makes the kind of comparisons exemplified in the previous section. However, overtly these comparisons do not

[10]Östman, *Pragmatics*, pp. 189–90.
[11]Robin Tolmach Lakoff, 'Stylistic Strategies within a Grammar of Style'.

appeal to feelings, but are in the format that a teacher *as* teacher would be expected to use to inform her pupils.

But it is not enough to make the children obey. She also wants to make them *think* the way she does. If they, the invaders, manage to convert the children, then at least they will not have any problems with the next adult generation. And in order to reach this goal, she knows that she will be much more effective if she uses a strategy that is closer to Camaraderie than to Distance Politeness.

In this particular case, the use of Deference strategies would be difficult, since the children *know* they do not have the power. Thus, they do not have to act *as if* they did not have power; and for the New Teacher to pretend that they do have power would be paradoxical in light of her status. But as we shall see below, she occasionally – and very effectively – reverts to Deference strategies, too.

However, what the New Teacher does is not to choose to follow either the Distance or the Camaraderie strategy. Instead, she chooses to keep *both* these strategies within reach. In fact, part of the reason why her persuasion becomes so effective is that she knows how to alternate between the two strategies. Again, one example will have to suffice.

The New Teacher cannot use a Distance strategy even when she talks to Miss Worden at the beginning of the story (and Miss Worden surely knows her situation and status in relation to that of the New Teacher):

(5) a. Hello, Miss Worden.
    b. I'm taking over your class now.
    c. You are to go to the principal's office.

Miss Worden asks why, and is very upset and afraid.

(5) d. He just wants to talk to you, Miss Worden.

'The New Teacher said gently.'

(5) e. You really must take better care of yourself.
    f. You shouldn't be so upset.

Here the New Teacher obviously *could* have used a Distance strategy. And she also does so to a certain extent: (5b) is a direct statement, instead of something like 'Please don't feel bad, but I have to take over your class now', or some form of 'I'm sorry, but I have to . . .'. Utterance (5c) is also quite direct, but she could have said, 'Go to the principal's office straight away!' Instead she mitigates her statement and her use of the BE + *to* INF construction suggests that this has been decided on by somebody else: some 'unknown' entity.[12] She, the New Teacher, is not herself responsible. It is simply something that has to happen.

A similar implicit reference to something decided on beforehand is

---

[12]Cf., e.g., Randolph Quirk and Sidney Greenbaum, *A University Grammar of English* (London, Longman, 1973; third edition 1975). Stephen Levinson (*Pragmatics*, pp. 72–3) also notes that the expression *You are to X* encodes that the source of the instruction is not equivalent to the speaker, and it gives the speaker authority.

made by using a form of *shall* in (5f). Frank Palmer[13] has suggested that *one* semantico-pragmatic aspect of the English modals is that *will, can, must* and *dare* are subject-oriented: *John will come* means that the subject, John, has the power to decide about his comings and goings; whereas *shall, may, ought* and *need* are discourse-oriented: *John shall come* implies that somebody else has decided for him, and that he himself cannot influence his coming. In (5f) the New Teacher could have said 'You must not be so upset'. By using *should*, she does not appeal to Miss Worden, but to something like general rules of etiquette. On the other hand, the New Teacher uses the subject-oriented *must* in (5e), implicitly indicating that it is her own fault: Miss Worden herself has the power to take care of herself – but she has not done so.

Why, then, does the New Teacher not use a straight Distance strategy toward Miss Worden? The answer is obvious: because of the children. She cannot give them an impression of her being 'bad' or 'cruel' to *any*one. Note also Clavell's masterly indication of this two-edged situation in the phrase 'The New Teacher said gently.'

In (5a) *Hello* is for the children – she does not say 'How do you do'. In (5d) she uses the pragmatic particle *just* to indicate to the children the unimportance of going to see the principal, but at the same time *just* is an indication to Miss Worden that the situation could be extremely serious for her: she knows, or should know, that the expression *X just wants to . . .* is a standard way of indicating the seriousness of a situation. In (5e) she uses the pragmatic particle *really* to show Involvement. But combined with *must*, her way of expressing this is almost as if she spoke to a child: *You really must.* And in (5f) she uses the same strategy: *You shouldn't be.* We can imagine her raised finger, the slight horizontal back-and-forth movement of her head, and the smacking sound from her mouth.

Thus, at the same time as she talks to Miss Worden, her addressee, she simultaneously chooses her words and expressions to make an impact on the children, her audience. And this, of course, is something that we frequently see in political speeches: the person who asks an impertinent question cannot easily be persuaded, so the best strategy for the politician is to concentrate his/her efforts on persuading the other people in the audience, for instance by belittling or reinterpreting the questioner's point.

In general, then, we note that persuasive discourse is very different from ordinary discourse: whereas in an ordinary interaction with somebody you do not know too well, you tend to start out with a Formal Deference strategy,[14] and work your way toward Informal Deference or even Camaraderie, in persuasive discourse you start out on either side – or on both sides simultaneously – of (Formal and Informal) Deference in the Politeness hierarchy (cf. above), and work your way towards the middle.

[13]Frank R. Palmer, *The English Verb* (London, Longman, 1974; second edition of *A Linguistic Study of the English Verb*, 1965).
[14]Cf. also Ron Scollon and Suzanne B.K. Scollon, *Narrative, Literacy and Face in Interethnic Communication*. (Norwood, NJ, Ablex, 1981).

Markers of involvement

Involvement is defined as 'that principle of pragmatics which deals with how the choice of a linguistic element contributes to expressing the speaker's feelings, attitudes and prejudices toward the topic of discourse, the situation and/or the addressee.'[15]

One very striking feature indicating Involvement all through the story is the New Teacher's use of an abundance of pragmatic particles in her persuasive discourse. With these she mitigates and qualifies her speech acts, and indicates her (insincere?) Involvement in the situation, and in the welfare of the children. She uses *just* to belittle a fact, tag questions to appeal to her audience and create a feeling of Deference, and *really* to express her intense feelings. Other particles she often reverts to are *well, of course, just because* and *after all*.[16]

But except for the use of different pragmatic particles, there are also other kinds of markers of Involvement in persuasive language. Here I will just deal with a small selection from Clavell's story. Clavell uses both explicit and implicit markers of Involvement.

The three examples below contain clear instances of explicit indications of attitudes:

(6) That's very good, Mary. Very, very good.
(7) Yes it *is* a pretty [flag].
(8) Yes, Johnny, you're quite right. You're a very, very wise boy.

The interesting thing is that all three examples come from situations where the New Teacher simply cannot be too pleased.

Utterance (6) is a response to the fact that Mary *does* know what *pledge* means. The New Teacher wants to argue that they should not say things they do not understand. Fortunately for the New Teacher, no one knows what *allegiance* means. Example (7) is said in reference to the

[15]Östman, *Pragmatics*, p. 200.
[16]Some other important particles for persuasive discourse include

- *why* to suggest something obvious (cf. Robin Tolmach Lakoff, 'Questionable Answers and Answerable Questions');
- *anyway* to suggest that what has just preceded is of little importance, a digression: let us now get on to the important issues (or back to the main line of the story; cf. Jan-Ola Östman, *You know: A Discourse-Functional Approach*);
- *you know* to imply that something is settled and accepted although it is not (cf. Östman, *op. cit.*);
- introductory *so* and *then* to indicate that the speaker is allowed to draw the inference that follows: *so* because of what he or she hears or perceives, *then* because of what the interlocutor has just said (cf. Levinson, *Pragmatics*).

Some further important devices include

- the switch from *this* to *that* to indicate emotional distance, and from *that* to *this* to show empathy (cf. Levinson, *Pragmatics* (p. 81), Robin Tolmach Lakoff, 'Remarks on this and that', Charles J. Fillmore, *Santa Cruz Lectures on Deixis*, and John Lyons, *Semantics*); and
- the use of nominalized constituents to introduce an (unwarranted) presupposition (cf. Wallace Chafe, 'Integration and Involvement in Speaking, Writing, and Oral Literature').

stars-and-stripes, and her statement can – at best – be taken as ironical: the flag, after all, is *the* sign that stands for the conquered nation. Example (8), finally, is said in a situation where the children are supposed to keep their eyes closed while they pray to Our Leader for candy, but Johnny peeks, and sees that it is not Our Leader that puts candy on everyone's desk, but the New Teacher herself.

These examples suggest quite strongly that the use of *explicit* expressions of (especially positive) attitudes in persuasive discourse is a mark of *insincerity*. But for children at age seven, the New Teacher's explicit expression of positive attitudes in this manner is taken as a sign of her appreciation. The explicitly expressed positive appreciation is, however, a conventional aspect of school-teaching. That is, *as pupils* the children need appreciation when they are right. However, for the New Teacher, the children have a dual role of being pupils and persuadees, and in their latter role, the children do not fare well when they behave in a manner that produces the New Teacher's responses in (6–8). Adults would be more alert and suspicious than children when hearing too much explicit expressions of positive Involvement from somebody they do not know very well.

Above, I mentioned the use of different pragmatic particles as implicitly marking also Involvement in persuasive discourse. Some further examples of implicit markers of Involvement in the New Teacher's speeches in Clavell's story are given below.

The use of children's vocabulary helps to enforce her 'we' relationship with the children. She communicates that even though she is a teacher, she is willing to use small kids' words like *tummy*. Other words with the same effect include *daddy*, *fine* (in the expression 'a fine man riding a fine horse') and *fair*.

Another construction typical of children's discourse is *I wish* as used by the New Teacher in the following example.

(9) I wish I could have a piece of it [= the flag]. If it's so important, I think we should all have a piece of it. Don't you.

Notice again the concretization: if something is important, then one should want it. And she manages to get the children to accept cutting up their flag into little pieces. Notice also that the appeal here (the tag *don't you*) is not a question. In other words, she is not prosodically giving the children the option to disagree, even if verbally she seems to be doing just that.

A final example involves strengthening a phrase with words like *lovely*, which are characteristic both of 'women's language'[17] and of children's discourse. And thus, since she uses it as a woman, the subtleness with which it

[17]Note that 'women's language' is not only used by women, and it is not to be seen as anything necessarily negative. For a brief and recent overview of women's language, including notes relevant for persuasion studies, see Mary G. McEdwards, 'Women's Language: a Positive View', *The English Journal*, 74:3, 1985.

can be interpreted as coming closer to children's language is very uncon-scious and implicit.

(10) Oh yes, I have a lovely surprise for you. You're all going to stay overnight with us. We have a lovely room and beds and lots of food, and we'll all tell stories and have such a lovely time.

Notice the expressions *I have a . . . surprise for you*, *We have lots of food*, and *We'll all tell stories*, which all appeal to the kinds of things children like.

All these cases of indicating implicit Involvement are closely connected to the Politeness strategy of Camaraderie. The New Teacher uses the register of the group she wants to convert in order to show her solidarity with that group. But it is not a matter of first establishing rapport, and *then* trying to persuade the victim(s). You have to do both at the same time: the more effort you need to put down in being persuasive, the more frequently you have to use indicators of rapport in your discourse.

The goal achieved

As I said in the beginning of this analysis, *The Children's Story* is not really about how the New Teacher persuades a whole class; it is rather the story of persuading Johnny. We do not know much about Johnny, so maybe it is too much to interpret his position as that of a leader. But it is with him the New Teacher has problems, and she also knows that when and if she manages to persuade him, that is the end of her ordeal.

The first step for Johnny toward getting persuaded comes after the New Teacher has talked about fear. Her argumentation here is in many respects similar to the argumentation that Johnny's father has previously used to him. Johnny's father had said:

(11) Don't be afraid, Johnny. If you fear too much, you'll be dead even though you're alive.

The New Teacher says:

(12) Fear is something that comes from the inside, from your tummies, and good strong children like you have to put food in your tummies. Not fear.

Clavell writes:

(13) Johnny hated her even though he knew she was right about fear.

Thus, Johnny's journey towards getting persuaded starts with the New Teacher showing him what she has in common with his father (perhaps unconsciously; but as a Coherence strategy Clavell uses it effectively).

Johnny is not easily persuaded, however, and when nothing else seems to work on him, the New Teacher resorts to the traditional method of 'if you can't beat them, join them'. Or, in this case: 'have them join you'. Johnny gets special treatment, he gets a better position than his friends – he gets promoted in society (i.e. in the classroom). The New Teacher says:

>   (14) And because Johnny was especially clever, I think we should make him monitor for the whole week, don't you?

'Johnny decided that he liked his teacher very much. Because she told the truth. Because she was right about fear. Because she was right about God.' But we all know what the real reason was: because she made him monitor for the whole week.

In general, then, on the basis of the analysis offered here, we can see that there are two ways to deal with obstinate people: either – as in Johnny's case – give them special favours, and they will let themselves be persuaded; or – as in the case of Johnny's father – put them to 'school' and use more direct and explicit means of persuasion.

Conclusion

My analysis of Clavell's *The Children's Story* is, of course, only a partial analysis. Because of the medium in which the text is transmitted, I have been forced to leave prosody out of my account; there are also, of course, grammatical constructions and turns of phrases that should have been dealt with more in detail. As an example, note the implication of the use of *allow* in the following sentence: 'the New Teacher opened the window and allowed them to throw it [= the flagpole] into the playground'.

On pp. 94–5, I justified using this kind of story as it is a prime example of how persuasion works in a simplified context. Relatively speaking (and I have indicated in my analysis what this means), however, the strategies used in the story by the New Teacher to the children are the same as those that would be used in ordinary persuasive discourse, and the *type* of linguistic manifestations of persuasive discourse directed toward adults will also turn out to be very similar to those we have found in this story.

What, then, are the verbal devices we use in persuasion, and what are the cues that the addressee should be aware of in order to realize that he or she is the target of an effort at persuasion? As I argued on page 92, in more explicit instances of persuasion this is not a problem. As a manifestation of a Distance strategy, even the use of direct commands by the persuader is permissible – not to mention physical power.

In general, as we saw, there is no *one* marker of persuasion, nor does there exist a predetermined set of markers that are by definition persuasive. In fact, such a situation would be counter to the whole essence of persuasion. If, as I have argued, persuasion – especially Deference persuasion – is implicit, then the unmarked situation would be an *avoidance* of markers – especially explicit markers – that might indicate that you are in the process of persuading somebody. If you make your purpose *too* obvious and explicit, your actions and yourself might well be interpreted as being pretentious, which might easily lead to an interpretation of you as somebody not to be taken seriously.

But, as this analysis has shown, even though we might not be able to separate out any specific markers of persuasion, there are still verbal features in persuasive discourse that implicitly indicate the persuasive purpose of a persuader. And *because* no such persuasive marker can be extracted, the analysis I have presented, and the framework within which the analysis is presented, is crucial for an understanding of how persuasive discourse works.

Coherence shows up in the general purpose of persuasive discourse. Persuasion involves an attempt by Speaker A to alter the coherent framework *i* in which Speaker B lives and acts, into becoming more like the coherent framework *j* that Speaker A lives in. Political, moral and religious persuasion is often directed not to one person at a time, but to the whole of a society, a particular group in the society, or a culture as a whole, against a prevailing tradition. The goal is to introduce new, or simply different, values as being more rewarding than those that the people in that culture live by today. In this very broad sense, persuasion draws on the implicit aspect of Coherence.

The use of different Politeness strategies turned out to be very significant. Persuasive discourse seems to use the whole scale of interactive strategies, and what is particularly significant for persuasion is the *shift* of strategies in one and the same persuasion. Robin Tolmach Lakoff's argument[18] that Distance and Camaraderie strategies can never be adhered to simultaneously, will not hold for persuasive discourse. In persuasive discourse these strategies not only *can* be used simultaneously, they *have to* be used in that manner: the switch from one to the other is typical of this type of discourse. (The reason being, of course, that as persuader you do not always have to be sincere on all levels: the end justifies the means.)

Persuasion also draws on the parameter of Involvement. But note that the explicit use of attitudinal expressions in persuasive discourse tends to be a sign of insincerity. If you attempt to change somebody's beliefs and values, you best succeed by appealing to that person's feelings: his/her emotions, attitudes, even prejudices. Or, if that person has no prejudices (!), you can attempt to create prejudices for him/her, in order to persuade him/her of the opposite.

[18]*Language and Woman's Place* (New York, Harper & Row: Harper Colophon, 1975).

Note

Despite the fact that parody manifests itself in a variety of cultural forms (a fact which should not surprise us since any artistic or behavioural mode which is available to humankind can also be adopted by the parodist), most studies tend to treat it as if it were an exclusively literary phenomenon. The reasons for this are understandable: literature is a less fugitive, more easily analysable form than, for instance, a comic 'turn' in a television show, and arguably of more significance. Nevertheless, as I shall be contending later on, such studies do obscure the fact that parody is a ubiquitous activity and may just as easily be seen in graffiti on a wall or in the face of a saloon-bar raconteur as in the more rarefied forms of the mock-heroic. But this bibliography must perforce restrict itself to works which deal with purely literary parody. The best known of the early anthologies of parodies was by Jerrold and Leonard,[1] and is in effect an act of homage to those poetic labours of the nineteenth century which mark the golden age of the art in English literature; but for a truly eclectic choice of both poetry and prose the best anthology is still Dwight Macdonald's,[2] which appeared in 1961. Its bonus is Macdonald's own discussion of the subject, which is lively, provocative and free of that scholastic pomposity which is itself cause for parody. A selection which includes many recent parodies has been made by Simon Brett,[3] but it perhaps relies overmuch on the fruits of the *New Statesman*'s weekend competitions, and although in his introductory discussion Brett starts a few good theoretical hares he chases none of them.

Since it has been generally (though not unanimously) regarded as a subdivision of satire, most critical discussions of parody have occurred within general treatments of satire, among the more illuminating of which have been Gilbert Highet's[4] and Matthew Hodgart's.[5] Both these critics have usefully emphasized the broadly cultural as distinct from purely literary ambit of satire, and Hodgart also observes that there is a sense in which all satire is parodic. Two other studies of satire whose accounts of parody are not less illuminating for their brevity are Arthur Pollard's[6] and John Jump's,[7] and there are also insights in D.C. Muecke's magnificent, painstaking book on irony[8] and Wayne Booth's racy, more argumentative discussion of the same subject.[9]

Among specialized studies of parody two seminal essays must be noted. The achievement of these – 'Parody as Criticism' by J.G. Riewald[10] and 'The Aesthetics of Parody' by G.D. Kiremidjian[11] – has been to promote intense interest in parody both as a mode of literary criticism and as a means of revitalizing literary genres which are in danger of becoming exhausted. These critical and creative functions have been more fully explored in a recent study by Margaret Rose,[12] but only in relation to the modern self-conscious novel. The most recent and most important special study of parody is Linda Hutcheon's[13] – one which is full of profound insights not only into the phenomenon itself but into its broader implications for literary theory. However one unfortunate side-effect of reading it is that one rapidly forgets that parody is both funny and 'fun'. It would be wrong to blame Ms Hutcheon for this, since a major premise of her book is that parody is no longer merely a matter of satire or comedy: but I shall be arguing below that to stretch parody beyond the satirical is to complicate and blur a phenomenon which is already complex enough, yet whose unique effect a vigilant audience cannot fail to recognize and relish.

[1]Walter Jerrold and R.M. Leonard, eds., *A Century of Parody and Imitation* (London, Humphrey Milford/Oxford University Press, 1913).

[2]Dwight Macdonald, ed., *Parodies: An Anthology from Chaucer to Beerbohm – and After* (London, Faber & Faber, 1961).

[3]Simon Brett, ed., *The Faber Book of Parodies* (London, Faber & Faber, 1984).

[4]Gilbert Highet, *The Anatomy of Satire* (Princeton, Princeton University Press, 1962).

[5]Matthew Hodgart, *Satire* (London, Weidenfeld & Nicolson, 1969).

[6]Arthur Pollard, *Satire* (London, Methuen, 1970).

[7]John D. Jump, *Burlesque* (London, Methuen, 1972).

[8]D.C. Muecke, *The Compass of Irony* (London, Methuen, 1969).

[9]Wayne C. Booth, *A Rhetoric of Irony* (London, University of Chicago Press, 1974).

[10]J.G. Riewald, 'Parody as Criticism', *Neophilologus* L (1966), pp. 125–48.

[11]G.D. Kiremidjian, 'The Aesthetics of Parody', *Journal of Aesthetics and Art Criticism* XXVIII (1969), pp. 231–42.

[12]Margaret A. Rose, *Parody//Metafiction* (London, Croom Helm, 1979).

[13]Linda Hutcheon, *A Theory of Parody* (New York/London, Methuen, 1985).

7

Parody and the Satirical Mentality

Andrew Crisell

Why do satirists write satire? For more than two thousand years the reasons they have given have been invariably, compulsively, moral:[1] among many others Juvenal, Samuel 'Hudibras' Butler, Defoe, Pope and Swift have declared their motives to be the defence of virtue and truth and the chastisement of wickedness and folly. But the very frequency of these declarations may make us suspicious, particularly since satirists as a breed do not appear to have been especially virtuous or notably persecuted;[2] and their declarations often coexist with a certain relish for their work which does not seem to come wholly from the sober promptings of morality. As Geoffrey Grigson has pointed out, 'Whatever satirical poets may have said about their moral or reforming or punitive intentions – and they have made some rather grand claims – we may be sure that writing their satires never caused them pain. They have enjoyed it . . .'[3] This question of the satirist's motivation and mentality has been much discussed, but in this essay I would like to try a different approach – through parody. The approach looks promising since parody is satire which involves an element of imitation, and in taking pains to imitate what he[4] is satirizing the satirist will reveal a certain range of attitudes which will not be so evident in the more narrowly 'moral' denunciations of direct satire. Our immediate task, however, is to define parody in relation to satire because the degree of commonality between the two has recently been questioned. There would seem to be two main reasons for this. The first lies in the disjunctive nature of the parodic process itself, which has produced some slightly lopsided

[1]Robert C. Elliott, *The Power of Satire: Magic, Ritual, Art* (Princeton, Princeton University Press, 1966), p. 107.
[2]Leonard Feinberg, *The Satirist: His Temperament, Motivation, and Influence* (Ames, Ia., Iowa State University Press, 1963), pp. 23–41, 78–9.
[3]Geoffrey Grigson, ed., *The Oxford Book of Satirical Verse* (Oxford, Oxford University Press, 1980), p. v.
[4]Since the reader is unlikely to accept my defence that the pronoun 'he' is epicene, I will plead guilty to the charge of sexism and admit that I have a predominantly male notion of the satirist. The reason for this, which by no means reflects credit on the male sex, will become clear later in this essay.

claims about its effects: critics seem to be unable to decide whether parody is a form of homage or ridicule.[5] Secondly certain rather large critical and aesthetic functions have been ascribed to parody in recent years, one or two of which are considered to take it beyond the bounds of satire. Among these are the following four. (I) Parody acts as a subtle kind of literary criticism and one which is more imaginative than the conventional kind.[6] It makes comic entertainment out of the critical act.[7] (2) In demonstrating the effeteness of old literary forms parody opens new creative possibilities.[8] (3) It enables the relations between a literary norm and its original historical context to be more easily seen.[9] (4) It explores what significance these norms have for subsequent historical contexts.[10] In the view of critics like Linda Hutcheon these functions have been assigned to parody as part of the modernist attempt to come to terms with our somewhat overwhelming literary heritage, and so to see parody merely as a species of satire is unnecessarily limiting.[11] She points out that parody has not always been seen as exclusively satirical and in this follows Brower, who invokes Johnson to argue that the characteristic action of parody is not inherently comic: it is merely a form of imitation or adaptation.[12]

However true this may be, I would suggest that in the modern mind parody remains firmly associated with the idea of ridicule or mockery and that to extend the word to cover non-satirical processes would reduce rather than enhance its critical usefulness, leaving us without a term to describe its precise yet complex effects. Indeed, insofar as Hutcheon's own definition of parody – 'repetition with ironic or critical distance'[13] – does not presuppose that sardonic judgement which is the essence of satire, it is hard to see why such already-existing terms as 'imitation', 'adaptation' or 'pastiche' will not adequately cover the modernist treatments of previous texts she is concerned to describe. But even those recent theoretical discussions of parody which do not discount its unvarying satirical tendency and which on their own terms are pretty well indisputable seem to me to be misleading in giving the impression that parody is primarily, even exclusively, a sophisticated literary form – literature *about* literature. They tend to obscure the fact that it is a basic instinct which is immediately achievable by people of all ages and intellectual levels[14] and is discernible as

[5]Margaret A. Rose, *Parody//Metafiction* (London, Croom Helm, 1979), p. 28.
[6]J.G. Riewald, 'Parody as Criticism', *Neophilologus* L (1966), p. 129; G.D. Kiremidjian, 'The Aesthetics of Parody', *Journal of Aesthetics and Art Criticism* XXVIII (1969), p. 240.
[7]Riewald, 'Parody', p. 131; Patricia Waugh, *Metafiction: The Theory and Practice of Self-Conscious Fiction* (London, Methuen, 1984), p. 69.
[8]Waugh, *Metafiction*, pp. 64–5.
[9]*Op. cit.*, p. 66.
[10]*Op. cit.*, p. 67.
[11]Linda Hutcheon, *A Theory of Parody* (New York and London, Methuen, 1985), pp. 4, 10–11.
[12]Reuben Brower, *Mirror on Mirror: Translation, Imitation, Parody* (Cambridge, Mass., Harvard University Press, 1974), p. 4.
[13]Hutcheon, *Parody*, p. 6.
[14]Feinberg, *The Satirist*, pp. 348–50.

spontaneous behaviour which very much precedes its more formal cultural manifestations in writing, music, art, and so on. This is equally true of all the other forms of satire, yet we easily fall into the trap of discussing it only in its more refined and 'finished' guises: in the very first sentence of this essay I discuss satire as if it were purely a literary genre. It is therefore worth stressing that in common with all other kinds of satire, parody is a less cerebral and more commonplace activity than the critical theorists would seem to imply.

What, precisely, is parody? It is first and foremost an activity of imitation or simulation. It is a text or a series of actions which passes itself off as something else and is in this respect similar to two other forms of humour, the hoax and the pun. Its affinity with the hoax has been noted by Highet,[15] and since the latter is a practical joke this underlines the fact that parody has manifestations in the 'real' as well as the literary world. We see it not merely in Max Beerbohm's elaborate re-creations of Henry James but in the schoolboy's physical and verbal mimicry of his form master. In both parody and hoax something is created which pretends to be something else and whose aim is to discredit a victim, the difference being that whilst the parody may deceive the audience it cannot deceive the victim, whereas a hoax must always deceive its victim and may deceive its audience as an optional 'extra'. In both parodies and puns the utterance or 'text' pretends to be something other than it is: a pun on a word pretends to *be* that word, the parody of an original pretends to *be* that original. Parody, then, resembles a pun in that the pun establishes a verbal similarity as a means of disguising semantic difference:[16] 'Two girls went for a tramp. The tramp died.' Walter Redfern overstates the narrowness of parody's subject-matter in order to indulge his own little weakness for punning, but since he is an adept at it I cannot resist quoting his comparison of puns and parodies: 'Sex in both rears its tumescent head, for parody too is a codpiece.'[17]

But the comparison of parodies with hoaxes and puns is also illuminating in the sense that in all three the principle of imitation is only half the matter: an element of incongruity, of *difference*, is also essential. In a true hoax there must be some self-signalling element of absurdity, something to enable the reasonable person to deduce that it is a hoax, otherwise the victim cannot be discredited. Its purpose is to expose stupidity, the blindness or monomania of the person to be hoaxed, and if the hoax would deceive any reasonable person it will merely attract sympathy for the victim and contempt for the perpetrator. The element of incongruity is even more obvious in puns, although some people fail to notice when a pun is being made, and it reveals itself in parody in the form of exaggeration, reduction or distortion, the effect of which is always in some degree to mock or discredit the original. Yet despite the fact that its combination of imitation and distortion gives parody a very precise and particular effect, its potential

[15]Gilbert Highet, *The Anatomy of Satire* (Princeton, Princeton University Press, 1962), p. 92.
[16]Walter Redfern, *Puns* (Oxford, Basil Blackwell, 1984), p. 15.
[17]*Op. cit.*, p. 93.

scope is truly global. Hodgart argues persuasively that in its blend of realism and bias there is a sense in which all satire is parody.[18] Indeed, insofar as literature necessarily 'deforms' or distorts the reality it imitates one could argue that all literature, all *art*, is parody.[19]

Nevertheless, if we restrict our discussion to conscious and deliberate parody and if we can confine the term of imitations with a mocking or satirical purpose, an interesting psychological question arises. Given that imitation seems to be the sincerest form of flattery and that direct denunciation is always open to the satirist, why is he often moved to imitate something which he regards as absurd or even downright immoral? Two famous examples of parodies whose authors' intentions are unmistakably hostile can be taken from the eighteenth century: *Shamela* and 'Namby Pamby'. In 1740 appeared Samuel Richardson's novel, *Pamela*, the story of a modest maidservant who resists the strenuous attempts of her high-born master to seduce her. At last, impressed by her chastity, he condescends to marry her: for her, as the subtitle declares, it is a case of 'virtue rewarded'. Richardson's contemporary Fielding felt that a quite different set of inferences could be drawn from the story, that the heroine exemplifies Gay's maxim 'By keeping men off you keep them on', and that she is a calculating little hypocrite – a kind of whore who withholds herself until the price is right. This is the theme of his parody *Shamela*, but for all its air of hilarity and exuberance, his moral objections to the original are made quite explicit: 'Young Gentlemen are here taught, that to marry their Mother's Chambermaids, and to indulge the Passion of Lust, at the Expence of Reason and Common Sense, is an Act of Religion, Virtue and Honour; and, indeed, the surest Road to Happiness . . . All Chambermaids are strictly enjoyned to look out after their Masters; they are taught to use little Arts to that purpose . . .'[20] But some fifteen years before this the pastoral poet Ambrose Philips suffered an even more virulent parody. In the early 1720s he wrote a series of highly distinctive poems in trochaic four-stressed lines which were addressed to the infant daughters of the influential Lord Pulteney. Here is the beginning of 'To Miss Charlotte Pulteney in her Mother's Arms':

> Timely blossom, infant fair,
> Fondling of a happy pair,
> Every morn, and every night,
> Their solicitous delight,
> Sleeping, waking, still at ease,
> Pleasing, without skill to please . . .[21]

[18]Matthew Hodgart, *Satire* (London, Weidenfeld and Nicolson, 1969), p. 24.
[19]Rose, *Parody*, p. 102.
[20]Henry Fielding, *Joseph Andrews* and *Shamela*, ed., Douglas Brooks (London, Oxford University Press, 1970), pp. 355–6.
[21]David Nichol Smith, ed., *The Oxford Book of Eighteenth Century Verse* (Oxford, Clarendon Press, 1926), pp. 145–6.

Though the modern reader might see an unfortunate ambiguity in the first word of the second line, the sentiment is generally appropriate and the see-saw rhythm well-suited to the nursery; Dr Johnson was among those who admired its charm. It nonetheless aroused the ire of Henry Carey, who in the following year produced a parody entitled 'Namby Pamby'. The title was also his nickname for Philips himself and has remained in the language as an adjective meaning 'insipidly or affectedly sentimental; twee'. Here are two extracts:

> Namby-Pamby, pilly-piss,
> Rhimy-pimed on Missy Miss
> Tartaretta Tartaree,
> From the navel to the knee;
> That her father's gracy-grace
> Might give him a placey place . . .

> Namby Pamby's doubly mild,
> Once a man, and twice a child;
> To his hanging sleeves restored,
> Now he foots it like a lord;
> Now he pumps his little wits,
> Shitting writes, and writing shits,
> All by little tiny bits.[22]

In these 13 lines alone (and the entire poem is over 90 lines in this version) there are hints at paedophilia, place-hunting and senile dementia, and an association of Philips's writing with defecation. Carey's animosity towards his victim can hardly be doubted. Why, then, does he not employ straight-forward invective but go to the trouble of imitating the work of someone whom he so despises? In order to attempt an answer to this question we need first to consider what the effect of the imitation is. Adopting Highet's distinction,[23] we might describe 'Namby Pamby' as a *material* rather than a *formal* parody in the sense that it is in the poem's subject-matter or content that the element of ridicule lies, whereas the overall shape of the poem and its trochaic rhythms and couplets are a straight imitation of the originals. The distinction between form and content is, of course, difficult – perhaps ultimately impossible – to maintain: when inapposite words are fitted to Philips's trochees, the trochees too become ridiculous. Still, for analytic purposes it is a tenable one: and what seems to happen in the material parody of 'Namby Pamby' is that the imitative nature of the form actually serves to *mitigate* the ridicule of the content, acts as a kind of solvent upon the allegations that are made. This is true even of the allegation that Philips is a paedophile, for its expression in nursery rhythms and rhymes makes it seem a harmless bit of fun, mere poetic licence. It is hard

[22]Grigson, *Satirical Verse*, pp. 162, 163.
[23]Highet, *Anatomy*, pp. 69–72.

to take so serious a charge seriously when it is couched in the jaunty tetra-
meters of 'Tartaretta Tartaree,/From the naval to the knee'. Of course we
may feel that content – the choice of the words themselves – softens
the charge quite as much as the poetic form; but it is difficult to escape the
impression that this choice is closely determined by the form, by the
exigencies of the metre. Thus while much has been made of the critical
functions of parody,[24] I would suggest that in a parody such as this the
outer framework of imitation *lessens* the force of the criticisms within it;
that there is a sense in which the attacks on Philips are subordinate to the
impersonation of him, whereas these attacks would perforce be more
directly made, and less easy to discount, in other kinds of satire.

The imitative aspect of parody therefore seems to confess the satirist's
half-suppressed *admiration* for his victim, an attraction at the creative or
imaginative level to something which he feels impelled to denounce in
moral terms. Such absurd iteratives as 'rhimy-pimed' and 'placey place'
reveal Carey's contempt for the original, but his adoption of its trochaic
rhythms, even in the nickname 'Namby Pamby', also shows the extent to
which he is under its spell. In all of us the promptings of attraction and
repulsion are intimately connected, and there is a sense in which we are not
only drawn to what we regard as wicked or absurd but by the same token
oppressed by those principles of reason and morality which hold us in
check. Freud points out that an important purpose of all jokes is to release
instincts and desires which are normally restrained by inhibitions of a
moral or social nature – inhibitions which cannot be overcome in any other
way.[25] Parody is a mode of joking which allows a fuller release than other
modes, because instead of achieving it in a kind of hypothetical or fantasiz-
ing way it involves the actual impersonation of someone who is so absurd or
wicked as apparently to be free from such inhibitions. But the release can
never be total and the price that is exacted in parody is that the parodist
must retain a degree of dissociation from the original by ridiculing as well
as impersonating him. What the technique does, then, is to enable the
parodist to indulge a sub-rational or pre-moral desire to be just as serenely
stupid, ridiculous or vicious as his victim is – and to be so without offend-
ing his own conscience. A kind of demonic celebration of the victim's
characteristics is subsumed within what is, at the most 'public' level of the
satirist's consciousness, a powerful sense of revulsion and contempt.

Nevertheless it is widely agreed that not all parodies are written out of a
sense of revulsion and contempt: many, perhaps the majority, are what
might be termed genial, inspired by an affection for their originals. Whilst
I would not deny that this is true, I would suggest that it is not as self-
evidently true as may be supposed. Macdonald states flatly that most
parodies are written out of admiration rather than contempt, otherwise the

[24]Riewald, 'Parody', pp. 127–32; Kiremidjian, 'Aesthetics', p. 240; Waugh, *Metafiction*,
p. 69; Hutcheon, *Parody*, p. 1.
[25]Sigmund Freud, *Jokes and their Relation to the Unconscious*, trans. and ed., James
Strachey, revised Angela Richards (Harmondsworth, Penguin Books, 1976), pp. 144, 165–6.

parodist would not take the trouble to imitate:[26] but this is to under-estimate the diligence of animosity. Given that the aim of parody, as of all satire, is ridicule, it is strictly logical that the parodist will parody what he finds ridiculous, not what strikes him as admirable. Nevertheless strict logic does not apply in these matters. The relatively gentle tone of the parodies he writes will often suggest that the parodist is well-disposed towards his victim, and even as members of the audience we are well aware that we can enjoy ridicule of what we admire – all those travesties of Shakespeare, for instance. But perhaps the most cogent evidence is provided by that special class of 'secondary' parody known variously as the mock-heroic, mock-epic or high burlesque. Here the writer takes one or more of the most elevated literary forms, usually the epic or the Bible, but sometimes the lyric or pastoral,[27] and uses it to ridicule something ludicrously inappropriate to it – an insignificant person or incident. It is primarily, then, a mode of straight satire. Dryden used the epic form to ridicule a bad poet in *MacFlecknoe*, Pope to ridicule a petty quarrel in *The Rape of the Lock*. Linda Hutcheon distinguishes the mock-heroic from the conventional parody rather well when she says that whereas the latter treats its model as a target, the former uses it as a weapon.[28] But following Jack and Riewald she is insistent that the mock-heroic does not mock the heroic.[29] This is certainly not its primary purpose, but to argue that it does not do this at all would appear to set a false limit on the scope of the irony. In *The Rape of the Lock* Pope's primary purpose may be to write a satire on fashionable society, but his application of the epic form to the trivial events and preoccupations of that society results in an inevitable *debasement* of the epic, a distortion of it which falls within the definition of parody. The joke is not only that vacuous fops and belles should be depicted like epic heroes, but that in this process the epic ideal is itself debunked, travestied. As Matthew Hodgart puts it: 'the framework for satire is often a travesty or parody of the most serious forms of literature, and those most highly valued by the parodist himself . . . The effect of mock heroic is never simply the opposition of ancient and modern, the contrast of the good old with the bad new way that people live, although it usually includes such a contrast; it also gives the pleasure of seeing the traditional values, conventions and styles of epic turned on their heads. . .'[30] It would therefore be naive to suppose that Pope was unaware of this effect or did not intend it, although it is quite true, as Joseph Dane points out,[31] that the satiric and parodic elements of the mock-heroic cannot be construed at the same time but are an *ex post facto* synthesis: to see *The Rape of the Lock* as social satire

---

[26]Dwight Macdonald, ed., *Parodies: An Anthology from Chaucer to Beerbohm – and After* (London, Faber and Faber, 1961), pp. xiii–xiv. Cf. also Riewald, 'Parody', p. 128.
[27]John D. Jump, *Burlesque* (London, Methuen, 1972), p. 48.
[28]Hutcheon, *Parody*, p. 52.
[29]Ian Jack, *Augustan Satire* (Oxford, Clarendon Press, 1952), pp. 45, 51; Riewald, 'Parody', p. 125; Hutcheon, *Parody*, pp. 5, 10, 44.
[30]Hodgart, *Satire*, pp. 24–7.
[31]Joseph A. Dane, 'Parody and Satire: A Theoretical Model', *Genre* XIII (1980), p. 156.

we must take the epic form 'straight', and we must reduce the satire of fashionable society to an instrumental role in order to perceive the poem as a parody of the epic. But the main point I wish to make here is that in the case of Dryden and Pope at the very least, the parody is indubitably of what the writer admires. Being a convinced Christian did not deter Dryden from his parodic use of *Paradise Lost* in *MacFlecknoe*, nor of the Bible in *Absalom and Achitophel*. In the case of genial parody, then, the element of imitation is immediately understandable: far from being a half-conscious desire to be as ridiculous as the victim it is a fully-conscious and honest endeavour to imitate what is admired. But now we are assailed by a second question coming, as it were, from the opposite quarter to the first. Given that the writer is free to stop short at straight imitation and that the ultimate tendency of parody is always to make fun of, why is he moved to ridicule what he admires? I would suggest that it is the means by which the parodist reconciles himself to what he is incapable of producing in his own right. It is the means by which he can bring the original down to his own level, or, if we look at it another way, to go one better than the original – transcend it by both impersonating and 'improving' on it, giving it an extra, comic significance its creator had not intended. The poetic theories of Harold Bloom are of relevance here. He argues that the creative genius of the poet causes him to 'resent' the influence which previous poets have had upon him, since it denies him priority or original-ity. Consequently he makes imaginative space for himself by 'misreading' them: 'Poetic Influence . . . always proceeds by a misreading of the prior poet, an act of creative correction that is actually or necessarily a misinter-pretation. The history of fruitful poetic influence, which is to say the main tradition of Western Poetry since the Renaissance, is a history of anxiety and self-saving caricature, of distortion, of perverse, wilful revisionism without which modern poetry as such could not exist.'[32] Parody, then, could be seen as this act of 'creative correction' in its most deliberate and comic form, a way of coming to terms with an illustrious predecessor.[33] Margaret Rose makes a similar point when she argues that parody has an exorcizing function:[34] it is a means by which the limitations of the original and the genius of the parodist are simultaneously exposed, affording catharsis to the latter and to his audience. It may even be that having 'exorcized' the influence of his predecessor, the parodist can admire him the more wholeheartedly.

What are the implications of the parodist's use of a single technique both for what he admires and for what he dislikes? What insight does it afford us into the satirical mentality? The fact that he is prompted to imitate bad as well as good writing suggests that contempt and admiration are different sides of the same emotion, that the satiric and panegyric

---

[32]Harold Bloom, *The Anxiety of Influence: a Theory of Poetry* (New York, Oxford University Press, 1973), p. 30. Cf. also Harold Bloom, *A Map of Misreading* (Oxford, Oxford University Press, 1980).

[33]Hutcheon, *Parody*, pp. 4, 29.

[34]Rose, *Parody*, p. 63.

impulses are not far removed from each other. And on the other hand, since he does not confine his parodies to what he disapproves of but sometimes feels impelled to debunk what he admires, it suggests that the satirical impulse is not usefully discussible in terms of moral beliefs: it is a more basic, more purely psychological matter in which the primary, or at any rate the dominant, factor is an undiscriminating urge to attack. Even in a parody like Carey's, where the writer's first impulse seems to be imitative, the overall effect is of a coarse aggression which is not notably 'moral'. Why, then, do satirists more than anybody else insist on discussing their art in moral terms? Satire differs from many other art forms in one important respect. The latter often establish characters and situations towards which their creator is equivocal and which allow for some variance in the audience's attitudes. But whatever the ironies he may deploy the satirist's attitude will be unequivocal: he holds the victim in some contempt and if we do not share this attitude the satire will fail: it will be the satirist, and not his victim, who will be discredited. Hence in aiming for this precision of effect satire is highly rhetorical and propagandistic.[35] It is vital that the satirist win our assent to his attacks, but he must do so not by appealing to our aggressive instincts (which are by no means equally developed in all of us) but to our sense of good and evil (which is). Aggression is an urge which requires civilized restraint because it threatens the deserving and underserving alike. Its manifestation in satire is abuse, a kind of literary terrorism in the sense that it is gratuitous, violent and indiscriminate. Its effect is alienating and ultimately frightening – even, perhaps, to the satirist himself. As Edward Lucie-Smith puts it, 'The satirist is afraid of his own instincts; he is afraid that matters will get out of control.'[36] Consequently there can be few satirists who would allow that their motives are anything other than moral. Moreover their claims to be morally motivated are not merely a means of wooing the audience, they provide an important structural principle – give an air of coherence or consistency even to such wide-ranging attacks as those of Juvenal. And they can do more than this. They can cause the satirist to *reduce* the range of his attacks to the most 'deserving' cases and throw their faults into a sharper focus. We can see, then, why moral asseveration so often accompanies satire and why the genre seems an unusually self-conscious one – 'why', in the words of Lucie-Smith, 'the chastisement of manners and morals is intermingled with a discussion of the genre itself'.[37] Yet since we have learned from parody that we cannot make reliable inferences about the satirist's moral values purely from the objects of his attack – he may hate what he ridicules or he may love it – we retain the stubborn impression that in satire morals are, indeed, an *ex post facto* matter, a subsequent stage in the creative process which confers a retrospective decorum on the aggressive instincts of the writer.

[35]James Sutherland, *English Satire* (Cambridge, Cambridge University Press, 1962), p. 5.
[36]Edward Lucie-Smith, ed., *The Penguin Book of Satirical Verse* (Harmondsworth, Penguin Books, 1967), p. 13.
[37]*Op. cit.*, p. 13.

We must now look at these instincts a little more closely. Matthew Hodgart takes it as a matter of fact not surmise that aggression rather than an active sense of what is right and wrong prompts the satirist to write satire, that his activity is more a matter of biology, even of zoology, than ethics:

> the impulses behind satire are basic to human nature. Indeed they probably go back beyond human nature, to the psychology of our animal forebears. All social animals are aggressive to their own kind: each of their societies possess [*sic*] a hierarchy, sometimes known as a 'pecking order', by which its efficient functioning is maintained. To establish this order, two animals will use 'threat displays' against each other, until the inferior submits to the superior. The human expression of contempt, the curling lip and the mocking laugh, seem to be rooted in such threat displays; and the satiric impulse is probably more closely connected with this kind of aggressive behaviour than with overt attack, such as animals make against other species.[38]

Nevertheless the moral mantle worn by so much satire makes it difficult to demonstrate the truth of this assertion, and I would like to spend the last few paragraphs of this chapter looking at one or two satirical themes and strategies which seem to offer evidence, albeit of a somewhat disparate and circumstantial nature, that aggression rather than moral sense is the satirist's prime mover.

We might first of all expect that an activity which is morally motivated would deal mostly in universals and abstractions, provide such generalized portraits of vice and folly as those of the miser and the aspiring scholar in Johnson's 'Vanity of Human Wishes'. Yet a remarkable amount of satire concentrates instead on actual, historical cases – mentions real people by name or describes them unmistakably. This is always and obviously true of parody: its referent is something actual – an individual, a piece of writing, a work of art, or whatever, which exists in the real world: but the tendency exists in all kinds of satire. And given that nothing obliges the satirist to be specific it is surprising that he so often is, since specificity presents him with two problems. The first is that the number of those who appreciate his satire will be limited by their knowledge of the people and things he attacks (a problem frequently caused by the 'in' jokes favoured by the magazine, *Private Eye*). And secondly, specific satire is likely to be short-lived: with the passing of the people and things under attack, the satire itself fades into oblivion. These are, of course, particular problems in parody: despite assurances to the contrary[39] a parody cannot be properly appreciated without some knowledge, however vague, of what is being parodied. But they are present even in satires which are generally acknowledged to have transcended the specifics of their age. Pope's

[38]Hodgart, *Satire*, pp. 10–11.
[39]Walter Jerrold and R.M. Leonard, eds., *A Century of Parody and Imitation* (London, Humphrey Milford/Oxford University Press, 1913), p. v.; Simon Brett, ed., *The Faber Book of Parodies* (London, Faber & Faber, 1984), p. 23.

Dunciad, for instance, has survived, but only amid a scaffolding of explanatory notes and glosses. His friend Swift saw the dangers as soon as the poem appeared: 'The Notes I could wish to be very large, in what relates to the persons concerned; for I have long observed that twenty miles from London no body understands hints, initial letters, or town-facts and passages; and in a few years not even those who live in London.'[40]

As we might expect, the satirist is often concerned with specific actualities not simply to illuminate a general moral truth but to influence his audience's attitudes and conduct *towards* those actualities. There is thus a sense in which satire, unlike many other art forms, transcends the purely artistic sphere. Swift's *Drapier's Letters* and *A Modest Proposal* were not intended merely to illustrate corruption and callousness *per se*, but to force action on the Irish Question; for satire is an unusually *conative* form of writing. It is not surprising, then, that a great deal of it has been concerned with politics since, as Hodgart shrewdly remarks, 'There is an essential connection between satire and politics in the widest sense: satire is not only the commonest form of political literature, but, insofar as it tries to influence public behaviour, it is the most political part of all literature'.[41]

Satire's tendency to portray actualities and to try to influence practical affairs presents literary theory with some unusual problems. First, the element of actuality challenges traditional notions of what constitutes 'literature', since whilst satire often contains fantastical distortions of the world which typify literature's general concern with things imaginary, and whilst it expresses them through such familiar literary forms as poetry and fiction; it also deals with real people, events and institutions in a campaigning way that is reminiscent of journalism and which lacks that measure of autonomy we regard as characteristic of most works of literature. As Pat Rogers puts it, 'The form is unable to live off its private resources. It is radically impure, non-reflexive, dependent on agencies outside itself. . . . A mode of writing where the text so abjectly prerequires a context is hard to reconcile with our fashionable concerns whether as practitioners or critics of literature.'[42] Secondly, its conative tendency seems to challenge received notions of literary value. We consider many satires to be great works of literature or art, yet how far can they be subject to a purely artistic assessment when they insist that their purpose is to influence attitudes and behaviour in the world 'outside' art?

But mercifully the significance of all this for our enquiry is limited. It is simply that we feel that a disinterested promotion of virtue would not entail so many and such vitriolic attacks upon real individuals and institutions – especially since the attacks actually threaten the intelligibility and durability of the satirist's work in a way that a more generalized approach would not. One is drawn to the likelihood that the

[40] Harold Williams, ed., *The Correspondence of Jonathan Swift - Volume III: 1724-1731* (Oxford, Clarendon Press, 1963), p. 293.
[41] Hodgart, *Satire*, p. 33.
[42] Pat Rogers, 'Reviling in Rhyme', *Times Literary Supplement*, 12 September 1980, pp. 981–2.

satirist is fired by something more instinctual and combative than a wish to advance morality.

Further evidence of the satirist's aggressive instincts might be adduced from his choice of subject: it has often been remarked that a great deal of satire consists of attacks on women, but if this is not in itself especially significant the particular nature or tone of many of those attacks assuredly is, and it is here that satire's moral pretensions are at their most threadbare. They usually take one of two forms: the satirist feels a duty to correct men's absurd idealization of women, and/or he feels a need to expose woman's true nature – her insatiable lust and depravity. But even if we allow the dubious proposition that women are morally responsible for the fact that men idealize them, we must also allow that the nature of these attacks, their peculiar virulence and preoccupation with unsavoury physical details, quite exceeds the call of duty. In the misogynistic satires of Swift, for instance, we gain the distinct impression that what women are really being reproached with is not any moral failing but the physical fact of being female. The effect is, in a strange way, not so much one of moral condemnation as sexual assault. The phenomenon of misogynistic satire has been helpfully discussed by Edward Lucie-Smith:

> The reasons why writers should often dislike other writers are plain enough; but the reasons why satirists should persecute women perhaps need disentangling. It is not generally realized, even today, how large a part aggressive instincts, using this phrase in a Freudian sense, have to play in the creation of works of art. Since satire is itself an aggressive form of writing, the Freudian impulse appears more nakedly here than elsewhere. The symbolic rape is common in satire – we find it in the coarse poems against women written by Rochester and Swift. Misogynistic satire is often distinguished by a peculiarly nagging tone. Images recur in a way which suggests, not writers borrowing consciously from one another, but a common stock in the collective male sub-conscious. A writer like Robert Gould presents us with a picture of the fantasies which the male has about the female, and also the fears – of deception, castration, loss of identity. Sexual guilt leads him to paint women as repulsive physically; satire against women often seems to dwell with special emphasis on diseases, and on bodily functions and malfunctions.[43]

There seems little doubt, then, that misogynistic satire is primarily motivated by an amoral aggression, but irrespective of subject-matter we might feel that such aggression is generally more characteristic of males than females. The whole question of gender differences and similarities is, of course, dauntingly complex and generalizations are dangerous; but this would seem to be the case at least at the biological level. Male sexuality involves an invasion of the female which is in some sense aggressive; and there seem good behavioural grounds for assuming that this aggression is

[43]Lucie-Smith, *Satirical Verse*, pp. 21–2.

reflected at the psychological level. In most societies males have traditionally assumed the more belligerent roles of warrior and hunter, and even in the modern world, where the distinctions between genders are held to be altogether more complex and sexual stereotyping is deplored, it is not uncommon to hear feminist complaints about aggressive behaviour in males. Linda Hutcheon offers an Oedipal explanation for the writing of parody[44] which seems to enshrine the belief that artistic creation is 'aggressive' and which has traditionally been regarded as more applicable to accounts of the male than the female psyche. In any event, if overt aggression is indeed more characteristic of males than females, it seems of relevance to our suggestion that satire is an especially aggressive form of writing to point out that there appear to have been many more male than female satirists, even when we allow for the fact that cultural and political inequalities have produced fewer female artists.

Finally I would suggest that the *strategy* of the satirist often betrays a kind of aggression, a deployment of arguments which seems fundamentally destructive. I pointed out earlier that as part of his need to win the audience over to his side he almost always claims a moral motivation. Closely bound up with this is another, though usually tacit, claim to be a man of common sense and plain reason. His pose is of the ordinary decent person (like you and me) who sees the world in a rational way and expects it to conduct itself sensibly. Nevertheless it is not uncommon for a satirist to invoke reason and common sense to gain his audience's confidence and then to 'ambush' it by using these faculties to attack the values it normally holds dear. What occurs, then, is a kind of subversive extension of conventional wisdom, as when with simple logic Swift portrays romantic love in *Gulliver's Travels*, and Voltaire religious practices in *Letters Philosophiques*, as a form of madness. And it is this strategy which creates the paradoxical impression of the satirist as conservative and orthodox (his premises are often familiar and he argues in a straightforward and conventional way), yet at the same time radical and iconoclastic (his audience feels that *all* established values, customs and institutions are potentially under threat).[45] We may suspect that there is something mischievous in this 'ambushing' technique – that the satirist is prompted not so much by genuine moral conviction as by a belligerent desire to shock or unsettle his audience: but such a technique is by no means inconsistent with moral conviction. The real trouble begins when the satirist (and again Swift is a prime example) advances two separate arguments of equal plausibility which flatly contradict each other and give us little idea of his own moral position or that which he assumes in us. The difficulty which he likes to exploit is that while they are virtually indistinguishable in many contexts logic and reason, or the way of the intellect on the one hand, and common sense, the way of the world on the other, have an unexpected knack of diverging and becoming incompatible. The former takes too little account

[44]Hutcheon, *Parody*, p. 77.
[45]Elliott, *The Power of Satire*, pp. 273–5.

of expediency and the 'human factor', the latter often lacks consistency and moral integrity. We can see the satirist exploiting this divergence in *A Tale of a Tub*, yet more clearly in *An Argument Against Abolishing Christianity*, and we are ultimately overwhelmed by it in the fourth book of *Gulliver's Travels*, where Swift extrapolates man's most noble and virtuous attributes – and comes up with a species of saintly horses and a man who holds his nose in disgust whenever a fellow human approaches. He thus has it both ways: the world is made ridiculous by the standards of reason, rationality is made ridiculous by the standards of the world. Hence the satirist may not only invoke reason to ridicule popular prejudices or vicious pragmatism: on the grounds that, as Joe Orton put it in *What the Butler Saw*, 'You can't be a rationalist in an irrational world. It isn't rational', he will invoke common sense to laugh at the irrationality of reason. In life as we experience it, logic itself seems absurdly incongruous. This strategy of equivocation involves an element of imitation which is reminiscent of the imitation involved in parody, since one (or both) of its arguments is feigned; but the general effect differs from that of parody since we do not know for certain *which* of them is being feigned and which (if any) is being seriously put forward. It is even more like the mock-heroic in that its elements ridicule each other in the way that the heroic ideal ridicules the pettiness of the contemporary world and the contemporary world ridicules the quixotic absurdity of the heroic ideal. But whereas in the mock-heroic one element, the heroic, is something 'given' or pre-existing, an established idiom or genre, in the strategy of equivocation both elements are arguments which have to be established, or at least implied, within the terms of the work itself.

What all these strategies point to, however, is not so much a consistent moral attitude on the part of the satirist as a kind of non-moral aggression – a mischievous, destructive determination to leave no one secure or unscathed, least of all his ally the audience. And this aggression is confirmed by his common preoccupation with particular, actual people and institutions and his frequent hostility towards women. However moral his conscious intentions may be, it seems ultimately more helpful to perceive the satirist's work in terms of a temperamental or psychological predisposition than as something initiated by a sense of right and wrong.

Note

This chapter draws on three main theoretical strands, work in Linguistics, in Semiotics, and certain ideas from psychoanalytic theory. The latter comes from the work of Jacques Lacan; a readily available selection of his work, including 'The Mirror Stage', can be found in *Ecrits*, translated by Alan Sheridan, (London, Tavistock Publications, 1977). Judith Williamson's *Decoding Advertisements* draws in part on that tradition; but it is included here to represent semiotically influenced analyses of advertising texts. Although the book by Bill Bonney and Helen Wilson deals with Australian materials in its applications and descriptions, it provides an excellent and generally usable synthesis of theoretical work drawn from the strands mentioned and from the political economy of the Mass Media (including advertising). The linguistic work drawn on here is that first developed in *Language as Ideology, Language and Control*, both published in 1979 by Routledge, and further developed in publications by a number of writers, including my own recent *Linguistic Processes in Sociocultural Practice* published in 1985 by Deakin University Press, in Geelong, Victoria.

The following sources may all be of interest to the reader seeking further referent material.

Bonney, W. and H. Wilson, *Australia's Commercial Media* (Melbourne, Macmillan, 1983).

Davis, H. and P. Walton (eds.), *Language Image Media* (Oxford, Basil Blackwell, 1983).

Hartley, J., *Understanding News* (London, Methuen, 1982).

Kress, G.R., *Linguistic Processes in Socio-cultural Practice* (Geelong, Vic., Deakin University Press, 1985).

Kress, G.R. and R.I.V. Hodge, *Language as Ideology* (London, Routledge and Kegan Paul, 1979).

Lacan, J., 'The Mirror Phase' *New Left Review* No. 51 (1968).

Williamson, J., *Decoding Advertisements* (London, Marion Boyars, 1978).

8

Educating Readers: Language in Advertising

Gunther Kress

Language, culture and advertising

Language is the most fully articulated system of cultural values, norms and meanings; it is everywhere entirely intermeshed with social and cultural processes and it gives expression to the meanings of those processes. Consequently the intuition that there is a close correspondence between linguistic form and social context is well-founded. However, the nature of the connection between a particular institution and its characteristic language uses bears some reflection. The manner in which that connection is usually (and usually implicitly) articulated, as a search for the language 'of' education, 'of' the mass-media, 'of' persuasion, or 'of' advertising, enshrines a fundamentally misconceived view of society and of language. It assumes that there are discrete and autonomous areas of social life, with their own sets of practices, meanings, values and forms of language corresponding to these. There is some truth in this: particular configurations of social practices, around specific professions for instance or in (sub) cultural groups, lead to the emergence of meanings which are specific to these groups. Such meanings are coded in specialized vocabulary (popularly referred to as 'jargon') or in characteristic grammatical uses. On the whole however, the larger structures and meanings of, say, the education system, or of the legal profession, or of advertising, are those of society at large. The kind of education system that we find in a particular society bears a very close relation to the structures and meanings of that society, with all its contradictions reflected quite precisely in the contradictions inherent in a particular education system.

Advertising is no exception. Its very ubiquity ensures that in its structures, processes and meanings it is a serviceable mirror to the society in which it operates. Every culture has the kind of advertising that it deserves. There is little point in railing at the excesses, distortions and practices – or conversely marvelling at the inventiveness, creativity and beneficial effects – of the advertising industry without railing – or marvelling – at the excesses, distortions – inventiveness, creativity – of the larger culture and society in which it operates. That suggests that we can expect to find in advertising and in its practices what we expect to find in society at large. In other words, there is no point looking for the language 'of' advertising; rather we need to explore the operation of language 'in' advertising, as one aspect of the operation of language across and 'in' all of society.

Advertising cannot be seen as a kind of grotesque deformity grafted onto the otherwise sound fabric of the social and cultural body. In this chapter I will explore some of the strategies of deployment of linguistic forms and processes which, while they may be characteristic of advertising, are nevertheless the forms and processes of language use in society generally.

I start the argument therefore with an attempt to characterize linguistic processes as one kind of social and cultural process, and describe the close intermeshing of all of these processes at all times. In particular I wish to draw attention to the formation and positioning of social subjects in and by these processes, in order to be able to demonstrate the very close affinity of the uses of language in advertising and indeed their dependence on the processes and strategies of language use in society at large.

The training of readers: preparing audiences for advertisers

Our encounters with language, our participation in linguistic activity, is always an encounter with and a participation in the formation of texts. In texts we encounter language organized in particular ways: in specific social situations, deployed around the structures of those situations, organized by the functions of those situations and the purposes of the participants. Because our encounter with language is always in the form of texts, and because text is always language organized from a particular point in social and cultural structure, language learning and the learning of culture are aspects of one larger process; they are two sides of one coin. To understand the strategies of language use in advertising we need to understand the processes involved in the formation of texts, and the positioning of writers and readers in relation to them.

Here is an advertisement, the text printed on a bottle of household cleaner:

AJAX SPRAY N' WIPE
All purpose solvent cleaner
Cleans without rinsing

I want to ask a question which may seem both too banal and too obvious to warrant its being put, particularly in relation to such a simple little text: how does it work? My analysis moves right away from the usual search for an explanation located in individual linguistic features and their meaning. The account which I will give places linguistic activity in the broadest social and cultural context, it asks about the action and interaction of writers and readers, and about their formation. To do so I will take a slightly circuitous but, I believe, necessary route, and attempt to show how readers as social agents are formed in the processes of learning a culture and learning a language. The pervasive metaphors for my account are those of education, of training and of instruction: whether in the formal institution of the education system, or in other educational institutions such as the family, the media and, indeed, advertising. And so my first two example texts are chosen from educational institutions: the first one from a child-care centre, and the second one from the early years of secondary school. This will enable me to develop a somewhat complex answer to my simple question.

Here is the example (an extract from a much longer text) from the child-care centre.[1] The participants are the (female) supervisor, and two children, Sarah (who is four years and six months old) and Aaron (who is four years and five months old).

	Teacher:	Look at this (pointing to picture of mother and young rhino)
	Sarah:	His mother a lot of toothes.
	Teacher:	How many teeth? How many have they got?
5	*Sarah*:	one two three, four
	Teacher:	What are they up the top?
	Sarah:	One two three four five
	Teacher:	Five at the top and four at the bottom
	Aaron:	No they're pimples
10	*Teacher*:	Do you think they're pimples?
	Aaron:	Yeah
	Teacher:	But they're where his teeth should be . . . do you think they're just a different colour?
	Aaron:	Well . . . that . . . those are pimples cos those are
15		pink
	Teacher:	Um . . . could be too . . . and what do you call those things there?
	Sarah:	Whiskers
	Teacher:	You do too and what's that Sarah?
20	*Sarah*:	A ear
	Teacher:	It's a funny looking ear isn't it?
	Aaron:	Yes . . . a little ear
	Sarah:	Thats got two . . . one, two . . . two ears
	Teacher:	Do you think they'd be friendly? . . . these
25		rhinoceroses?
	Aaron & Sarah:	No
	Teacher:	Why not?
	Aaron:	Cos they'll eat people
	Teacher:	How do you know? What makes them look
30		unfriendly?
	Aaron:	Their teeth . . . they can eat people
	Teacher:	They *are* big. What about this animal?

[1]This extract is a transcript from the author's tape. The names of the children have been changed.

Sarah:	That hasn't got any teeth
Teacher:	Hasn't he?
35 *Sarah*:	No
Teacher:	Do you think he'd be friendly?
Sarah & Aaron:	Yes
Teacher:	Look what he *has* got
Sarah:	He's got little claws
40 *Teacher*:	Claws
Sarah:	See . . . but that . . . but he's still our friendly . . .
Teacher:	He's still friendly even if he's got claws?
Sarah:	Look . . . they're not flendry
Aaron:	Yes they are
45 *Teacher*:	Do you think lions are friendly Aaron?
Aaron:	Yeah . . . because . . . if they . . . if people hurt them they hurt them back
Teacher:	And it's quite safe you think if you don't hurt them?
50 *Aaron*:	Yes
Teacher:	I don't know

Although the situation is not that of formal schooling, the text never-theless has all the features of a lesson: it is, first and foremost, about instruction, both in the sense of 'being informed' about cultural classifica-tions, and 'being commanded' to attend to a particular topic, to knowledge and to authority. The cultural classifications at issue here are complex. Superficially, they concern physiological, behavioural charac-teristics of animals. More significantly, they concern modes of reasoning: for instance the teacher's 'But they're where his teeth should be . . .', 'do you think they're just a different colour' (12–13); 'how do you know? What makes them look unfriendly?' (29) or Aaron's 'those are pimples cos those are pink' (14–15) and '. . . because . . . if they . . . if people hurt them they hurt back' (45). What is at issue here are both valuations of modes of reasoning, and what are culturally acceptable premises. Because this is outside the context of formal schooling, the 'teacher's' power is not asserted as strongly as it might be in a classroom lesson; her challenges to the children's classifications are indirect, modulated: '. . . do you think they're just a different colour' (12–13); 'Um . . . could be too . . .' (16); 'They *are* big' (31) (offering one classificatory principle which might plausibly support the children's judgement), and 'Look what he *has* got' (37) (suggesting that the children should shift the focus of their attention, or search for relevant principles). Nevertheless the children are instructed: it is the 'teacher' who selects and changes the topic, directs the interaction, accepts an answer or leaves its evaluation up in the air. Above all the children learn, through processes of this kind, particular attitudes to authority and to knowledge, about who has knowledge and how it is asserted, and about their own place in relation to authority and knowledge. They learn that there are those who have the right to decide what are important, relevant, even permissible topics ('Look at this', 'How many teeth', 'What are they . . .'); and they learn that their role is to respond, either in acquiescence: Sarah's 'one two three, four' (5), or, changing her mind under the teacher's pressure, 'Look . . . they're not flendry' (42); or by attempted subversion: Aaron's 'No they're pimples' (9); 'Yes they are' (43) contradicting both the teacher and Sarah.

There are two points here that I wish to draw out particularly. One is the fact that all aspects of the text's construction, and of its final form are intimately related to the wider socio-cultural structures and processes – structures of authority and forms of power, assumptions about the place of individuals in relation to culture, and of course, culturally given classifications of knowledge. Even here, where the power of the adult is not strongly and overtly asserted – though nonetheless present – the close interrelation of power and knowledge is obvious. Having power conveys the ability to determine what will count as knowledge; the possession of culturally validated knowledge conveys power. The other point is that language is not merely a reflection of social and cultural structures and meanings. It is the very means by which these structures and meanings are produced and reproduced. Aaron's challenges may come to nothing here; in a different situation, among his peers, or as a more powerful adult later on, they will have their effect on those structures and meanings – however minutely that effect may register on the larger system.

But, most significantly, in these processes, the two children come to be who they are and will be, as socially and culturally formed subjects. For instance, in this text there is a distinct difference between Sarah's and Aaron's responses, Sarah willing to cooperate and acquiesce, while Aaron attempts to interrupt and subvert the smooth flow of the text's construction. Whether this is a sign of an already established gender-difference is impossible to establish from this text alone. The constantly insistent repetition of a vast range of experiences of this kind leaves individuals formed in particular ways, as social agents and as writers/speakers and readers/hearers of a certain kind. It leaves them with quite precise knowledge of textual forms, and trained in their roles as writers/speakers or readers/hearers in relation to texts. They have learned, or will soon have learned, that knowledge and power are distributed in particular ways, so that those who have power have knowledge; and that those who have control of texts have both power and knowledge. From there it is a short step towards seeing the text itself as the location of power and of knowledge. That of course is one essential pre-requisite for the effectiveness of advertising texts. To pause momentarily and reflect on my question about the little advertisement: in part it works because readers have been trained to read texts as locations/expressions of power and knowledge.

The text I have just discussed is a spoken text, constructed by more than one participant. Power is distributed unequally, so that a greater degree of control of the text lies with one participant; the other participants have the task of 'reading' the developing text and constructing their position and their contribution in response. This allows for the possibility of 'reading against the grain', as Aaron seems to have done. At any rate it involves a knowledge of what the possibilities of positioning are, a knowledge which Aaron may or may not have had. What applies to spoken, interactively constructed texts, applies no less to written, seemingly monologic texts. Writers construct positions for the readers of their texts to occupy, positions which the readers may or may not assume depending on a complex of social factors. Among these are, as I have mentioned, questions of power, and matters such as gender, age, or other factors determining the reader's social positioning. For instance, if I am a certain kind of male, I won't consider myself as an appropriate reader of the household cleaner ad, it does not position me in any way. Clearly I need to have had the appropriate linguistic and cultural instruction for a particular reading position. Without such instruction (and my acquiescence in it) no text and no writer can position me as a reader. Here I want to focus on the mechanisms which are at work in constructing appropriate subjects for particular reading positions.

Because 'instruction' is the pervasive metaphor of my argument I will take an explicitly instructional text as my next example. It consists of two brief extracts from a geography textbook intended for students in the early years of secondary school in the New South Wales education system.[2]

The influence of Brisbane in northern New South Wales

There was at one time a strong agitation in the northern part of New South Wales to form a new state to be called New England. At the time when Queensland was separated from New South Wales,
5 the boundary originally suggested was latitude 30°S.

Find this line on a map. What towns now in New South Wales would have become part of Queensland? What is the present border (a) in the west, (b) in the east? Why is the eastern part of the present boundary more satisfactory than latitude 30°S, with
10 the possible exception of the coastal strip? . . .

The researchers next undertook extensive investigation of actual trade by distributing a questionnaire in the main towns of the region. They received the remarkably good result of a 90 per cent return, and so were able to estimate totals of wholesale purchases
15 from Sydney and Brisbane for each town. These results were recorded as in Fig. 5.12 and then mapped in Fig. 5.13.

Name two towns where the actual trade influence of Brisbane was greater, and two where it was smaller, than the theoretical model indicated.

The ambiguity of 'instruction' as both 'informing' and 'commanding' which I mentioned above is overtly marked here; lines 1–8, and 16–24 are ostensibly about informing the reader, and lines 9–15, and 25–27 are

---

[2]Harris, D.D. and Stehbens, I.R., *Settlement Patterns and Processes* (Melbourne, Longman-Cheshire), 1981.

equally about commanding the reader to carry out specific tasks. This text is remarkable only because of this startlingly overt marking of these two aspects which are characteristic of all texts. It may be that in the context of the education system the distinction of informing and commanding does not appear as an ambiguity; that is, in education or in educational texts there is no difference between commanding and informing: 'informing' might be seen as a command to act in a particular way, that is, to take up a particular position vis-a-vis knowledge (to accept/internalize it), and 'commanding' may be seen as information about how to adopt certain social positions, and how to internalize kinds of knowledge. In an institution which is founded on the identity of power and knowledge, one all-important instruction to readers (and to social subjects) may be *not* to attend to that distinction, or not to accept a distinction as existing in that domain.

What applies to education, what is learned there, can be transferred to advertising. In that way the cleaner ad, in presenting information to no one in particular (no one is addressed by the ad), nevertheless succeeds in commanding those who see themselves as appropriate readers to act in a particular way.

It is clear on the one hand that the co-writers of the text-book (attempt to) position their readers quite precisely. Readers, on the other hand have to be trained to recognize not only the positioning, but also the sanctions which support this attempted positioning. Not to accept the reading-position in this situation has the severe consequences of failure in tests or in end-of-year examinations. In this context it is interesting to note that many advertising texts spend much energy on establishing that there are sanctions surrounding a refusal to be positioned as a reader: a disapproving mother-in-law or a disappointed mother looking at grubby bathroom tiles, or the foregone satisfaction of receiving the envious glances at the sparkling sink by the lady from next door.

This example serves well to illustrate the intimate linkage of power and of the reader's possibilities in relation to reading positions: the greater the power of the writer (whether mediated via institutions or expressed more directly) the less the reader's opportunity to read against the grain without attracting such sanctions as exist in the particular area. The less the writer's power in relation to the reader, the greater the latter's opportunities to resist the writer's positioning.

In most texts, as for instance in the cleaner ad, the positioning is not quite so apparent, nor the ambiguity around 'instruction' quite so overt as in this text-book extract. Here is another extract from the same textbook.

Regions

The area round a town in which its urban functions exert a strong influence can be described as a *functional region*. In highly urbanized countries this is probably the most useful way of division
5 of large areas into smaller units for study. We need to remember, however, that the boundary of a region can be defined precisely only in terms of one factor, and then only if that factor can be

expressed as a quantity. We can talk of part of northern New South
Wales as within the region of 50 per cent or more commercial
10 orientation to Brisbane: we can also talk of that part where 50 per
cent or more of the people take in Brisbane daily newspapers; the
boundaries are different, but they both mean something precise.
To speak of the 'Brisbane region' without any indication of the way
it is defined is vague indeed. In Chapter 2 the boundary of a
15 population density region was defined from statistics in a precise
way.

Here the reading-position is constructed by a series of syntactic devices.
Take, for instance, the agentless passives 'can be described' (3–4), 'can be
defined' (9). 'can be expressed' (11), 'was defined' (22). As with all
agentless passives there is a question for the reader about the identity of the
absent agent. In this text that question has a double answer: the agent is
the scientist / geographer *and* the student / reader, who is (positioned by the
curriculum as) an aspirant to the status of fully fledged member of the
community of scientific geographers. So the text has a place for the reader
to adopt, and that place is one which identifies her or him at once with a
particular community, that of geographers. Adopting the reading-
position therefore at once confers membership of a community, a
membership which is constructed, via the pressures of the educational
system, as a desirable goal. Other syntactic grammatical devices have the
same effect: for instance, the nominalization 'division' (6) (which relates
to a full clause 'someone divides something') invites the reader to be the
'divider'. The 'we' in 'We need to remember . . .' (7–8), 'We can talk
. . .' (11–12), and the verb 'mean' (18) invite the reader to be a member of
some unspecified group, and to be the subject to whom this meaning is
'something precise'. Interestingly, this text also has a 'prohibited' or
'negative' reading-position, for those who are not members of that
community. For instance, the non-finite verb '*to speak of* the Brisbane
region . . .' (18–19), and the nominal 'indication' (19) both have a
missing agent-place, for those who are not scientific geographers. Hence
the other, the outside community is also already constructed into this text.

The cleaner ad makes use of very similar syntactic devices. Here, as in the
textbook extract, there are a number of subject / agentless verbs, 'spray',
'wipe', 'rinsing'; in each case the reader is invited to take this position: 'I
spray, . . . wipe, . . . rinse'. The noun 'purpose' similarly invites the
reader to identify him / herself as having these purposes. Although not as
clearly articulated as in the textbook, even this small text implicitly holds
out to the reader the promise of membership of a community, the
community of 'Ajax mums' perhaps.

Turning readers into consumers

The choice of 'instruction' as the focal metaphor for my argument has led
me to use 'educational' texts as central examples. The linguistic processes
which are perhaps particularly sharply in focus in educational institutions

are no less present in other institutions. While education is the institution which is concerned, par excellence, with the reproduction of central aspects of culture, advertising is also an institution which is central in the processes of cultural (re)production in capitalist societies. The force of my argument is to demonstrate the close homology of linguistic and other processes across the whole complex of cultural and social structures.

Any one society has a finite number of kinds of occasions of social inter-action, and therefore a finite number of textual types which arise in these occasions. Following traditional usage I call these text-types genres. Challenging traditional usage somewhat I assume that the form and meaning of genres have a social explanation and origin. Genres are among other things the encodings of modes of social interactions, and repo-sitory of certain cultural meanings. Competence in language use and competence in culture both depend equally on a full knowledge of the stock of the generic types of the social and cultural groups to which a speaker belongs. That competence is the result of the kinds of training and instruction which I have sketched so far.

Advertisers, like other producers of texts, are bound by the possibilities of the range of generic forms in any one cultural group, and by the kinds of social positionings which these generic forms project and make available. Advertisers need to draw on the training, the instruction which readers have, in the attempt to (re)position readers as consumers. The economic metaphor of production and consumption, and of commodities has of course frequently been used of 'cultural commodities' – texts, meanings, literary works, and so on. And the fact that as readers social subjects are already consumers is not a trivial matter. It means that the task of advertisers is already more than half completed. Take as one further example around the commodity of household cleaners the following two texts: one again from a high-school textbook, the other an advertisement for a cleaner in a women's magazine.

Home management and house care

> . . . powder, or by a combination of these methods. In some instances electrolytic action will remove tarnish, e.g. silver dip cleaners.
>
> 5   Light soil is easy to remove while it is fresh. When allowed to accumulate, it hardens and harsher treatments are needed to remove it, which may harm the surface underneath. Regular clean-ing is quick and easy and involves only simple inexpensive cleaning supplies. The task can be lightened further if simple sturdy
> 10   materials are chosen for the various household surfaces.

Household cleaners

> Abrasives
> These are mechanical cleaners which abrade or grind the surface, assisting in removal of soil, tarnish, stains, etc. Unless chosen and
> 15   used carefully, they may damage the surface.

Examples
Fine abrasives – volcanic ash, feldspar.
Medium abrasives – whiting, powdered pumice or rottenstone.
Coarse abrasives – sand, quartz.

20 Absorbents
Some fine powders can absorb liquids or grease and when they are removed, by brushing or vacuuming, the soil goes too.

Examples
Cornflour, talcum powder, french chalk, bran, fuller's earth.

25 Acids
These have the power to dissolve tarnish and other deposits and may also act as bleaches. They are often used in conjunction with an abrasive substance such as salt or scouring powder.

Examples
30 Lemon juice, vinegar, cream of tartar, oxalic acid.
Hydrochloric acid (spirits of salts) is a very strong acid used for drastic cleaning, e.g. lavatory bowls, brick fireplaces.

Alkalis
These react with grease and make it into an emulsion which dis-
35 solves in water, carrying soil with it. They also soften hard water by changing its mineral salts to soluble forms, thus preventing scums forming.

Examples
Ammonia, a solution of ammonia gas in water (household
40 ammonia).
With a little soap added, this is sold as cloudy ammonia. If the latter is used, rinse well to avoid leaving a film. Used for cleaning carpets, upholstery, brushes. Avoid on aluminium, sisal, and test on coloured fabrics first.
45 Baking soda (sodium bicarbonate), a mild alkaline powder used as a fine abrasive for enamel, porcelain, plastic.
Borax (sodium tetraborate), mild alkali, water softener and fine abrasive. Uses as for baking soda.
Caustic soda (sodium hydroxide), a very strong alkali. Will
50 corrode aluminium, enamel and porcelain glazes.
Trisodium phosphate, a moderately strong alkali, effective as a water softener and for removing grease. It is the active ingredient in some paint removers. Avoid excess as this may harm some surfaces.
Washing soda (sodium carbonate), cheap and effective as a
55 grease solvent and water softener, but can harm wood, metal, paint etc. if not used in correct proportions, or rinsed away completely.

Bleaches
These are often used to lighten discoloured surfaces or to remove stains. Apply only as directed, as misuse can be harmful.

Examples

60 Chlorine bleaches, formerly only available as liquids, but now also in powder form. Also called household bleaches, they contain sodium hypochlorite and are strong bleaches used to whiten wood, baths and basins, white cottons and linens. Not suitable for silk, wool, synthetics, drip-dry or crease-resist finishes. Chlorine
65 bleaches also act as disinfectants.

Hydrogen peroxide is a mild bleach useful for whitening baths and removing stains from all fabrics. It must be fresh, as it loses its effectiveness with time.

Sodium perborate, a mild powder bleach, suitable for all fab-
70 rics. It works slowly at cool temperatures and requires longer application.

Grease solvents
This class of cleanser acts by dissolving grease and evaporating, carrying the soil with it. Use with caution, as they are often
75 flammable, or poisonous, or both.

(Emily E. Carpenter, *Home Management and House Care*, Whitcoulls Publishers, New Zealand, 1977, pp. 108–9)

Helps remove stains in the wash
With BIO JOY most stains come out in the wash
Just put it in with your normal detergent
And for more difficult stains there's a simple chart on the back of the pack
Used either as a detergent booster in the wash or as a laundry soaker.
BIO JOY docs the work for you

(*New Idea*, 6.9.1984, p. 124)

The 'Home management' text shows the kinds of syntactic features that I have discussed in the Geography text-book extracts and the 'cleaner' ad. The very many agentless verbs invite the reader to assume the position of subject-agent: '. . . is easy for *you   You* remove it . . .' (4), 'When allowed by *you* . . . and harsher treatments by *you* are needed for *you* to remove it . . .' (4–5), etc. etc. The informational aspect of this text is about the classificatory system of household cleaners, though in establishing the system of cleaners it also establishes indirectly the more important classi- fications of *types of activities* which define 'housecare'.

To take one example, 'Abrasives'. In the course of this description (lines 12–14) a number of activities are mentioned, 'cleaner', 'abrade', 'grind', 'assisting', 'removal', 'chosen', 'used', 'damage'. So in the course of describing the members of one classificatory system (the 'informational' aspect of the text) the set of activities which are of relevance in this domain is established. The latter, through the implicit assignation of agency of those actions, constitutes the 'commanding' aspect of the text: 'If you are to act appropriately in this domain, you will need to act in the following way.'

However not all actions have the reader as their implied subject-agent. In the three lines 12–14 the reader is the implied subject/agent of 'removal' ('you remove the soil . . .'), 'chosen' and 'used' ('by you'). The implied subject-agents of 'abrade' and 'grind' is 'mechanical cleaners' or 'abrasives' which is also the subject-agent of 'damage'. Throughout this text there is a systematic distinction between agency assigned to the reader as the human agent, and agency and agentive power assigned to 'cleansers'. Some other examples of the latter are 'electrolytic action will remove tarnish . . .' (2), '. . . fine powders can absorb liquids . . .' (20), '(Acids) . . . have the power to dissolve tarnish . . . and may also act as bleaches' (25–6). This is very much like the Ajax ad, where the Ajax is the 'cleaner', and is the subject-agent of 'cleans' ('cleans without rinsing'). Indeed, the human subject-agent is only involved, literally, at the margin, in applying the cleaner and wiping it off, after 'it' has done 'its job'.

In other words, the way in which agency is assigned in the 'Home management' text establishes some actions as being outside the scope and ability of the human agent; consequently the human agent who cannot supply all the necessary power and activity 'has a need' for the additional and, as it turns out, central power of the household cleaners. The school text-book identifies a lack on the part of the consumer, which the household cleaners can and will fill. The BIO JOY advertisement draws on these processes, and on the preparation which the readers of this text have undergone. The assignment of agency is kept more vague in the BIO JOY ad than in the Home management or AJAX texts. For instance, agency is left vague syntactically in line 2, that is, 'stains' is the subject of 'come out' without any explicit agency being indicated. Readers are left to carry out the task of making the causal connection of 'with BIO JOY' to 'come out', and the indication of *where* this happens (rather than *how*) 'in the wash'. So it isn't quite clear who is being helped (line 1): are the stains helped in coming out, is the detergent helped in being boosted, or is the human agent helped in 'removing stains'? Without the careful preparation from countlessly many texts such as the 'Home management' example, readers/consumers might not be so readily positioned by a text such as the BIO JOY advertisement.

Ideology and the construction of the consumer

The pervasive vagueness on the question of agency of the BIO JOY text allows us to see the ideological constructedness not only of this text, but in particular of the 'Home management' text. At first reading the 'Home management' text may seem to present 'things as they are' in a transparent manner. However, the equivocation of the BIO JOY text on the matter of agency shows that the clarity of the 'Home management' text is not unproblematic and natural, but is one particular and ideologically motivated structuring of this particular domain. For instance, it is entirely possible to give household cleaners a different syntactic role: not that of 'agent' (as it is here) but of 'instrument'. Lines 12–14 might then read 'These are substances with a mechanical action which you can use to abrade or grind the surface, assisting you in the removal of soil . . . Unless you chose the appropriate one for the job you have in hand you could damage the surface.'

That rewriting represents a different ideological structuring, with different assignment of causal powers, and with a different relation to the ideological structurings of wider social systems. The ideology of the 'Home management' text has a particular fit with a larger ideological system with certain discourses of economic organization, of class-structures, and with specific kinds of discourses around gender. It makes assumptions about the socially formed subjectivities of its readers – how possibilities of action are distributed between men and women, what values attach to notions of 'the home', 'the family', or 'work' and 'career' for men and for women. In marginalizing human agents it fits into discourses which valorize consumption and technological aids and it therefore provides a closer fit with texts constructed by the advertising industry. In those texts the reader is turned into a (potential) consumer by the syntactic construction of a need, a lack, as I have pointed out, which only the acquisition of a particular commodity can overcome. Both the BIO JOY and the Ajax texts insist on the necessity of the presence of the human agent '(You) just put it in . . .' or '(You) spray n' (you) wipe' and on the centrality of the agentive powers of the commodity 'BIO JOY does the work for you', '(Ajax) cleans without (your) rinsing'. Given the ambivalence around women's roles – whether as merely reproductive domestic labour, or as fully autonomous participants in social life – these texts have to negotiate the difficult line between asserting the need for (marginal) female labour, and the assertion that technologically sophisticated commodities have freed women and made it possible for them to join the productive workforce. Hence the reality of women's labour has to be acknowledged on the one hand – lest men lose some of their power – while on the other hand it has to be insisted – whether by the pedagogical ideologue or by the advertiser – that women's domestic labour is no longer in any serious sense real labour, because technology (in the form of commodities) has intervened in the structure of domestic life and has taken away the need for women's domestic labour.

Producing consumers: advertising and the mass media[3]

The social, economic and ideological tendencies that I have described in the textbook example and in the advertising texts coincide neatly with the needs of the capitalist system for ever-increasing production and, consequently, consumption. It is the economic and ideological function of

[3]This section had to be revised following the refusal of permission to reproduce extracts from a magazine.

the advertising industry to meet this need, by producing consumers. Perhaps it is surprising that the school text-book's language does fit quite so well with these economic and ideological requirements; or perhaps that simply illustrates the close ideological fit of the major components of social and cultural structures.

While the education system produces culturally competent subjects and potential consumers, it is the function of the advertising industry to provide the fine tuning that ensures the matching of subjects/consumers with commodities. It is here that the mass-media play a crucial role. Not only do they act as carriers of advertisements, they work to position their readers appropriately as audiences for advertisers, and as consumers for specific commodities. It is well known that many or most newspapers are designed around the advertisements which they carry, literally in terms of actual layout and in terms of often far-reaching editorial policy. The same applies to commercial television and radio.

The point could be made and sustained that all texts in a magazine, whether that publication is for a trade, hobby, or other specialist audience, serve to 'prepare' readers, to position them as potential consumers of advertisements and of their commodities. Here I'll attempt the merest sketch of how this might happen in a women's magazine. Imagine the kind of magazine aimed at an audience of young women, perhaps in the 19–29 age group. Apart from the advertisements that it carries, it has texts in a very wide range of genres, from the instructional ('How to get on at work') to the advisorial/informational (say, a 'life-style' feature) to entertainment (say, the usual short-story/novella). My classification is of course a massive over-simplification, for, as I've pointed out, the writer–reader relation pointed to in 'instructional' is as likely to occur in the entertainment text as in the more explicitly instructional one.

So in a feature on how to succeed in the office, a writer might put forward a number of stereotypes: the sex-object dolly-bird, a Miss Plain Jane, the career woman, and so on. Each will provide a characterization which, while it is likely to be a caricature, is likely to put forward a description of a human being in highly objectified terms; characteristics and actions of a person turned into and presented as object-like entities: dazzling smiles, fluttering eyelashes, alluring lips, seductive curves, sparkling teeth, etc., etc. Being object-like they can be used mechanically, as instruments: Miss Dazzler can flash a dazzling smile, or pout with her alluring lips, and so on. This caricature is likely to be held up for disapproval. And yet, another stereotype, let's say, Ms Successful, is likely to be described in terms which are fundamentally the same; that is, again as an assemblage of object-like attributes, which can be used instrumentally when needed. The attributes are different: unassuming manner, poise and self-assurance, well modulated speech, coordinated yet subdued outfit, her confident personal style, and so on.

Two points can be made in relation to such texts. First, they are always descriptions of humans as bundles of attributes and possessions, and hence subject to acquisition. It is the discourse of possessive individualism with a vengeance, where human beings are themselves described as a collection of attributes seen as possessions. The point of texts of this kind, and of the ideology that gives rise to them is to suggest that any deficiency in such personal possessions can be made good. And just as one can dispose of undesirable attributes so one can acquire desirable ones. From here there is a very short (metonymic) step indeed to the suggestion that commodity X or Y will bring about such desired changes. Second, the descriptions of such caricatures are always constructed from the male point of view. Despite frequent apparent attempts in such texts at accommodating feminist analyses, they are always constructed in sexist discourse; that is, women and their desires are defined in terms of the power and the desires of men. Indeed, at the core of all such texts is a sexist construction of the male. The fulfilment of his supposed needs/desires becomes the source of the apparent desires of the female. The gap between the male's desire and the female's possibility of meeting them is assiduously cultivated and constructed in all the texts of the magazine; it is filled by the commodities advertised in the magazine. Clearly, the more the needs can be proliferated, and the more specific they can be made, the greater the need for the proliferation of specific solutions the greater the need for commodities. The extraordinary objectification, commodification of the human body and psyche is driven by the insatiable desire of advertisers for 'needs', which in its turn is driven by the constant demand by producers for the production of new kinds of demands for commodities.

The relations between language-as-text and the wider socio-economic structures are very direct, very specific in magazines of this kind. Straightforwardly, an article on one page might suggest to (female) readers what men like by way of gifts; the opposite page will feature advertisements for precisely such gifts. A reader might be told that a present has to be very precisely calibrated to the state of a relationship – not too little, not too much –, lest she frighten off her 'guy'. In this way female readers are told both that the success of a relationship is secured via commodities, and that the changing state of relationships needs to be registered by them through the purchase of commodities. Most significantly such and (all) other texts establish that women and their conduct are constructed around the desires of men, and that their success is always subject to the judgement of men.

A new kind of genre to emerge in women's magazines is one that fuses the formerly distinct genres of advertisement and of feature. This might be a text that describes how fashion models fix flaws in their bodies or faces. The text might consist of snapshot photos of a fashion model, with comments scribbled on them seemingly by the make-up artist. The objectification and fragmentation of the human body – narrow face, eye area, the outer brows, a sultry, wide-eyed look, the eyelids, the middle of the eyelid, the under-eye, the lashes, etc., etc. – is accompanied by advertisements for commodities precisely matched to the remedy of these deficiencies printed in and around the texts.

Educating resistant readers

Although I have drawn my examples largely from one area of advertising and from one type of magazine, my analysis applies across all the uses of advertising. The specialist magazine that addresses plumbers, or bikies, or bodybuilders, draws on the same linguistic and cultural processes, uses the prior construction and disposition of subjects as readers, engages in the same construction and proliferation of needs. There are differences in degree: the trade-magazine for the plumber deals with someone who is both more prepared as a reader through his professional training, and better able to resist certain positionings through his detailed knowledge of practices in the area. He (or less frequently, she) is less open to mystification. Nevertheless, the advent of new technology – as a new material, a new tool, a new set of practices – always leaves him anxious too: and hence exploitable.

Both the plumber/reader and the reader of the women's magazine come already prepared, not only as readers in the general sense, but prepared in the quite specialized way of the plumber. Even though the latter has not had the plumber's formal training, she (or less frequently, he) has been trained by countlessly many experiences, in childhood, as a young adult, at work, through the family, school, peer-group, employment. And she feels the 'needs' that are presented in the magazine as tangibly as the plumber feels the need for appropriate materials and tools. Readers come to the mass media, or to specific sections of the mass media, already well prepared, anxious to be members of the group or community projected and constructed by the magazine, the television station or programme, the newspaper.

I said at the beginning of this paper that advertising acts as a serviceable mirror to society; and suggested therefore that we should not look for the special characteristics of the language *of* advertising. Nevertheless, advertising as a practice of construction of texts, while everywhere employing processes common to all textual production, does have special features. But these do not emerge as characteristics of individual texts; rather they emerge when we look at advertising texts in relation to other texts produced in a society. What we then discover is that there are systematic absences in advertising texts. These absences register precisely the function of advertising, that of producing consumers to meet the insatiable need of continuously expanding production of commodities in a capitalist economy. That function explains both the nature of advertising texts, and the complete absence in advertising of texts that question, challenge, subvert the dominant ideology, texts which point to alternatives to the fragmentation, alienation and commodification of human beings projected by advertising texts in capitalist societies.

All texts carry in them the signs of conflict, contestation and contradiction. Indeed, as I pointed out, advertising texts depend on the existence (or the manufacture) of a gap between reality and some textually constructed ideal which can be turned into a perceived lack and hence a 'need'. The 'making faces' text for instance shows that even those who come closest to the ideal suffer from serious defects which need some remedy. However, in advertising texts these contradictions are consistently handled at the level of the individual. There is no hint of the effects of class in causing needs; there is no mention of gender differences in causing inequities of a kind that are further entrenched by the operation of such texts. In this advertising is a powerful device in sustaining and reproducing the hegemonic structures of a society riven by differences of gender, class, ethnicity, race, age.

Advertising texts are not merely reflective and reproductive of a status quo. They have a central role in producing specific ideological effects in a society, a partial and therefore a distorting view. That distortion, being amplified and incessantly transmitted by the mass media, has a hugely powerful effect as a cultural force. If we are happy with society as it is then my account here serves simply as an analysis of this area of social life. If we wish to effect changes to advertising practices, then my account suggests that that entails at the same time an effort to bring about wider social changes. The total inter-connectedness of the textual practices of advertising with all aspects of wider cultural practices and with the social and economic system means that they cannot be uncoupled: it is not possible to operate on advertising texts in isolation. Strategies designed to bring about changes will have to calculate the strength and kinds of resistance that will be encountered in such attempts. One strategy within the realm of the possible for all those concerned with the issues raised in this book is to educate readers able to resist the positionings of advertising texts: readers more, much more, like the plumber and her mate.

Note

The issues touched upon in this article are very wide-ranging, and for that reason it is hard to provide a neatly delimited introductory bibliography. The following are the sources to which I refer in the article; they include some of the most important work done on the topic of political television.

R. Barthes, *Mythologies*, selected and trans. from the French by Annette Lavers (Frogmore, Paladin, 1973).

J. Blumler and D. McQuail, 'The Audience for Election Television', in J. Tunstall, ed., *Media Sociology* (London, Constable, 1970).

A. Clarke, I. Taylor, and J. Wren-Lewis, 'Inequality of Access to Election Television', in D. Robbins *et al.*, eds., *Problems in the Sociology of Inequality* (London, Gower, 1978).

G. Dyer, *Advertising as Communication* (London, Methuen, 1982).

Glasgow Media Group, *More Bad News* (London, Routledge, 1980).

S. Hall, I. Connell, and L. Curtis, 'The Unity of Current Affairs Television', in *Working Papers in Cultural Studies* 9 (1976).

S. Hall *et al.*, *Policing the Crisis* (London, Macmillan, 1978).

J. Hartmann and C. Husband, 'The Mass Media and Racial Conflict', in S. Cohen and J. Young, eds., *The Manufacture of News* (London, Constable, 1973).

D. Hobson, 'Housewives and the Mass Media', in S. Hall *et al.*, eds., *Culture, Media, Language* (London, Hutchinson, 1980).

C. Hovland, 'Reconciling Conflicting Results Derived from Experimental and Survey Studies of Attitude Change', *The American Psychologist* 14 (1959).

P. Lazarsfeld *et al.*, *The People's Choice* (New York, Columbia University Press, 1944).

J. Lewis, 'Decoding Television News', in P. Drummond and R. Paterson, eds., *Television in Transition* (London, BFI, 1985).

J. Wren-Lewis, 'The Story of a Riot', *Screen Education* 40 (1981-2).

In addition to the works cited in the footnotes, the following are recent collections of mass media studies that relate to the issues we address in our article:

S. Cohen, J. Young, eds., *The Manufacture of News* (London, Constable, 1973).

J. Curran *et al.*, eds., *Mass Communication and Society* (London, Edward Arnold, 1973).

J. Curran *et al.*, eds., *Bending Reality* (London, Pluto Press, 1986).

M. Gurevitch *et al.*, eds., *Culture, Society and the Media* (London, Methuen, 1982).

W. Schramm, ed., *Mass Communications* (University of Illinois Press, USA, 2nd edn., 1972).

J. Tunstall, ed., *Media Sociology: A Reader* (London, Constable, 1971).

Below is a small sample of texts that raise the issue of media bias in relation to specific aspects of current affairs:

C. Aubrey *et al.*, *Nukespeak: The Media and the Bomb* (London, Comedia, 1982).

P. Beharrell, G. Philo, *Trade Unions and the Media* (London, Macmillan, 1977).

P. Cohen, C. Gardner, *It Ain't Half Racist, Mum* (London, Comedia, 1982).

D. Douglass, *Tell us Lies about the Miners* (Doncaster, DAM-IWA 1985).

L. Curtis, *Ireland and the Propaganda War* (London, Pluto 1984).

R. Harris, *Gotcha! The Media, the Government and the Falklands Crisis* (London, Faber & Faber, 1983).

C. Husband, ed., *White Media and Black Britain* (London, Arrow 1975).

I would like to thank Janet Gillian for her critical comments, which were of great help to me in revising an early draft of this article.

9

The Politics of 'Bias': How Television Audiences View Current Affairs

Rosalind Brunt and Martin Jordin

One of the most common arguments about mass communications in Britain is that they are in some way 'biased'. 'Bias in the media' is usually taken to refer to television because of its current dominance and obvious 'visibility' in terms of the amount of viewing-time and size of audience it receives. Higher responsibilities are placed on television, whereas the press is understood and expected to take a partisan editorial stance and there has always been a sense in which 'you can't believe everything you read in the papers'. But more credibility is expected of television, both because of its unique capacity to convey sound and pictures direct from the scene of an event in an apparently transparent 'window on the world' way and because of the requirement that all British broadcasting be 'impartial' and 'balanced' in its current affairs coverage.

Arguments about bias tend to take the form of accusations that this requirement has not been maintained in a particular programme or range of output. The most common accusation made by an aggrieved party is that couched in political terms: a programme has been 'too' left- or right-wing, for instance. The other party to the bias dispute, the broadcasting organization, then typically defends its production values and professional practices by responding that, since current affairs coverage is regularly accused of being biased in both directions, broadcasting must have got it straight-down-the-middle in the first place and all such accusations only reconfirm its independence from all political pressures.

But when disputes about bias become particularly acute and prolonged then a third party enters the arena, the mass media researchers, who offer themselves as the only really independent adjudicators of bias. The typical form in which they test for bias is some version of content analysis, most usually of a quantitative type, according to measures of frequency of items. So for instance in the most recent debate about bias concerning the broadcast coverage of the 1984–85 Miners' Strike, items like camera shots of police and pickets' injuries, camera positions behind or in front of police lines, terms used in commentaries like 'moderate' or 'militant' or references to 'today's return to work figures' have been added up in order to compute whether current affairs coverage has indicated support

141

or opposition to the strike.[1]

But precisely because such debates have tended to involve academics engaging the arguments on the same terms as their immediate protagonists, the aggrieved parties and the defending professional communicators, the notion of 'bias' itself has been increasingly challenged as an inadequate formulation. The challenge has come since the early 1970s from a strand of media studies that has been concerned with the development of theories of ideology. The argument here has been that the notion of 'bias' assumes some non-existent middle ground of political reporting, an illusory neutrality and a naive realism that looks for an impossibly transparent reflection of real life. By contrast, the critics emphasize the importance of starting with a recognition that recording reality is always a matter of mediation, selection, agenda-setting, inter-preting-for-values. From this standpoint, the aim of any media research that claims to be politically effective is to understand how the 'encoding' process works, rather than to establish the existence or otherwise of some mythical 'bias'.[2] Furthermore, it is maintained that the notion of 'bias' smacks too much of deliberate conspiracy, despite attempts to refer to 'unintended' or 'structural' bias; or, finally, that it is a way of displacing the blame for the real problems of society onto television because of the way current affairs coverage highlights 'the bad news'.[3]

As media researchers ourselves, we would support such criticisms of the disputes about bias and agree with the reformulation of questions about media content in terms of 'ideology'. At the same time, we consider that the detailed systematic monitoring of current affairs output, particularly the work carried out by the Glasgow University Media Group since 1974,[4] which has aimed to explore and expose bias, has made an important polemical contribution to the debate. Precisely because such research has taken the broadcasting institutions seriously on their own terms and asked whether their coverage lives up to the claims made about balance and impartiality, it has provided enough sustained evidence to the contrary to encourage some journalists within the broadcasting organizations them-selves to re-examine their own professional protocols.

Our own research in this area starts at the opposite, receiving, end of the

[1]See for instance, G. Cumberbatch *et al.*, *Television and the Miners' Strike* (London, Broadcasting Research Unit, 1986) and for an alternative view, Len Masterman, 'The Battle of Orgreave' in L. Masterman, ed., *Television Mythologies* (London, Comedia, 1985).

[2]'Key' texts here include: J. Halloran *et al.*, *Demonstrations and Communication: A Case Study* (London, Penguin, 1970); S. Hall *et al.*, 'The "Unity" of Current Affairs Television', *Working Papers in Cultural Studies*, no. 9, Spring 1976, p. 51.; C. Brunsdon, D. Morley, *Everyday Television: Nationwide* (London, British Film Institute, 1978); D. Morley, *The Nationwide Audience* (London, BFI, 1980).

[3]This argument is advanced in I. Connell, 'Blaming the Media' in L. Masterman, ed., *Television Mythologies*. Other versions of it are discussed in A. Goodwin, 'Striking Contrasts: Media Studies at Northern College', *Screen*, vol. 26, no. 5, October 1985, p. 92.

[4]Studies by the Glasgow University Media Group include: *Bad News* (London, Routledge Kegan Paul, 1976) *More Bad News* (London, RKP, 1980) *Really Bad News* (London, Writers and Readers, 1982) *War and Peace News* (London, Open University, 1985).

media professionals and broadcasting organizations: with the audiences of current affairs programmes and the terms in which they define the dominant political discourse of such programmes. Do they too employ the vocabulary of 'bias'? And if so, what part does it play in their under-standing of how these programmes, and the media generally, actually operate?

Our interest in these questions derives from a particular research project we were involved in concerning the media coverage of a parliamentary election in the industrial North Midlands town of Chesterfield in February 1984.[5] The newsworthy importance of this local election was that it was the first since the General Election of June 1983, which had returned a Conservative Government, and that the candidate selected to replace the sitting Labour MP after his sudden resignation was Tony Benn, at that time the most famous left-wing member of the Labour Party, who had lost his own seat in the previous General Election.

One of the main aims of the research project was to examine, via the use of both large-scale survey and small discussion-group methods, how the Chesterfield electorate thought about both the progress of the political campaign and the way it was presented in the media. In the process we expected normally taken-for-granted and infrequently vocalized attitudes about both 'politics' and 'the media' to become more widely articulated and elaborated to the extent that the amount of national attention being focused on their town was giving its inhabitants a sense of occasion: 'the media' were putting 'politics' on the agenda in a way which encouraged the expression of personal opinion, position-taking and fierce debate. In particular, a stance had to be taken towards the Labour candidate, who, ever since his selection in December had been defined by the media as a 'controversial' choice.

The 'controversy' referred to a long history of Tony Benn's being labelled 'extremist', with additional connotations of 'madness' arising from his identification with labour-movement causes since the late 1960s and with moves to democratize the Party constitution since the late 1970s.[6] Furthermore, the candidate himself had widespread experience of the media first as a former television producer then as Post-Master General, the minister responsible for broadcasting in the mid-1960s Labour Government, and subsequently the Left's most well-known critic of media bias, most famous for the statement he made in 1968 that 'Broad-casting is too important to be left to the broadcasters'.[7]

[5]R. Brunt, C. Critcher, M. Jordin, J. Lewis, 'Media, Polls and the Public: A Case Study of the Chesterfield By-Election, 1984.' Funded by the Economic and Social Research Council, Great Britain 1984.

[6]See Glasgow University Media Group, *Really Bad News*, p. 67, chapter IV, ' "Pushed about by the Left": Labour Politics on Television' which discusses the way in which the left of the Labour Party was personalized as 'Mr Benn's supporters' and equated with 'troublemakers' and 'extremists'.

[7]*Guardian*, 19 October, 1968; and discussed in J. Halloran *et al.*, *Demonstrations and Communication* p. 19.

This view was reconfirmed for Benn by the first BBC programme on the Chesterfield campaign. Immediately after the broadcast he issued a statement that 'The BBC think they can take over the election. They want to beat Labour in Chesterfield'.[8]

The programme was *Newsnight*, BBC's regular 'flagship' current affairs programme, regarded as influential and opinion-leading in political circles. It had opened by referring to Chesterfield as 'one of the historic by-elections of the century. And the result, in this normally safe Labour seat is not at all a foregone conclusion. . . .' Because it had gone on to make repeated allusions to the possibilities of 'tactical voting' for a third-party force, the recently formed Liberal–Social Democratic Alliance, Benn had accused the *Newsnight* reporter, Vincent Hanna, of being effectively the Alliance candidate in the election. He had countered by saying that his programme was merely reflecting how the candidates themselves saw the election: 'The politicians, not the BBC, set the agenda'.[9]

Because the 'media bias' issue was so central in the campaign we decided to include a showing of the *Newsnight* programme in our discussions with groups of the Chesterfield electorate following more general discussion with them about politics-and-the-media.

In the event, Tony Benn became MP with a slightly reduced majority on the previous year.[10] And overnight he was transformed from 'the controversial candidate' into the new owner of a parliamentary seat which, of course, had been a 'safe' and 'natural' Labour constituency all along. The media caravan left Chesterfield. But for the duration it had provided the context for a case-study of political television coverage with the added element of a protagonist who was himself both a key target and critic of media bias. What sense would the local groups we worked with make of all this? And could we start to draw any general conclusions about media audiences from what they said?

Our interest in working with discussion groups in the first place was that it allowed us to acknowledge the extent to which public opinion is an active formation, shaped in and through social interaction. In contrast to the survey methods also employed on the project which highlighted the individual, 'spontaneous' and immediate response, the discursive approach encouraged the more sustained and elaborated response and enabled the research to take account of the ways in which attitudes are 'negotiated' in a socially dynamic, often contradictory, process. We also believed that group discussion created a solidarity among group members that could better resist the imposition of our own academic priorities and encourage the groups' own frames of reference and system of relevances to

[8]V. Hanna, 'At the Chesterfield By-Election', *Listener*, 23 February 1984.
[9]V. Hanna, *Listener*. Also cf. the Labour Party's own discussion of the issue of media bias: S. Weir, 'Hanna in Wonderland', *New Socialist*, May/June 1984.
[10] Chesterfield election figures: General Election, 1983: Labour: 23,881; Conservative: 16,118; Liberal: 9,705. By-election, 1984; Labour: 24,633; Liberal, 18,369; Conservative: 8,028 votes.

determine the discussion agenda.[11] This was why we decided to work with groups which were not constituted by us but already had some social existence as community groups.

During the three weeks of the election campaign we taped a total of 13 one to two-hour discussions, out of which we have selected five to highlight a range of attitudes to the politics of bias. These are:

(1) A group of miners, all members of the Labour Party and, after initial doubts relating to support for another candidate from their own union, enthusiastic supporters of Benn. They were currently involved in the overtime ban that preceded the national strike.

(2) A group of women shop stewards from the National Union of Public employees working in low-paid domestic and care-assistant jobs. One was a member of the Labour Party; the others, after some qualms and consideration of the Alliance, had come to support Tony Benn. They were concurrently involved in a campaign against National Health Service cuts.

(3) A group of houseworkers, unemployed and retired people who met every week in a community centre to discuss topical issues in a session called 'Behind the News'. All but one Alliance supporter were supporters of Labour.

(4) A group of women keep-fit enthusiasts, mothers of small children, retired women and part-time workers who defined themselves as all 'don't knows', were extremely hostile to the Labour Party and favoured a coalition government.

(5) A mixed-sex group of catering students in their first year of technical college. Only two members expressed an interest in voting, probably for Labour, but the main characteristic of the group was their disenchantment with all forms of politics.

Regardless of their own political positions, the starting-point for all the groups we taped in any discussion of the relationship between 'politics' and 'the media' was that the media were biased. Indeed, this was such a routine, taken-for-granted assumption that no one in the groups expected it to be a matter of argument or debate. That was simply how it was. While there might be disagreement about the ways and directions in which the media were biased, there was no question that bias actually existed.

What 'bias' meant to all the groups in the first place was that 'the media' could not be trusted. Basically, they were 'out to get' their audiences by manipulation and distortion. Specifically in the case of television this meant, inevitably and always, that it would not be impartial. So the main point of judging any political programme would be to look out for, and expect to find, examples of bias.

This view was most forcibly expressed by the miners, who were able to refer to the greatest number of other newsworthy events they had themselves participated in. From that vantage point, they talked of media

[11]For further discussion of our choice of working with groups, see M. Jordin, R. Brunt, 'Constituting the Television Audience: A Problem of Method', paper presented to the International Television Studies Conference, London Institute of Education, 1986 (Conference papers published by the British Film Institute).

'exploitation' and how 'you've only got to look at who owns and controls the media: they're no friends of ours.' The miners saw bias as obviously against the Left and the working class. A miner who had been a local Labour councillor referred to an argument he had had with the reporter of the *Newsnight* programme and put it this way:

> Hanna – I had a brush with a couple of years ago, like and I was saying you know, It's biased and he said, 'Well, funny enough, all the letters we get say it's biased towards the left, like.' I said, 'Well, you're bound to aren't you? they're probably more articulate than the working class are – understandably. They've got more routes as well to get to these places.'

For the keep-fit class of women at the other end of the political spectrum, 'the media' combined with 'politics' to produce an alien world imposing itself on their own locality: 'a complete *insult* to Chesterfield and its people!' They had been invaded by a 'circus' of professional smooth-talkers, politicians and journalists alike, who aimed to distort and cheat on the assumption that the Chesterfield electorate would know no better. The group imagined them thinking, 'Oh they're Northerners, thick as planks, they won't know anything!' But on the contrary: 'We think a lot for ourselves. We're not soft!'

Distrust for the media, then, derived from a clear sense of 'Them' and 'Us', whether this was expressed in class terms, as with the miners, or, as more usually, in terms of locality: 'we the ordinary people of Chesterfield' as against those who were presumed to inhabit a more cosmopolitan, London-oriented world. In constantly referring to the media as an anonymous 'they' who try and 'put one over' on 'us' the audience groups reiterated a strong sense of the distance of the media from their own experience.

This view was demonstrated more specifically in relation to the television coverage of Chesterfield itself as instanced by the first *Newsnight* programme on the election which set out to introduce the-town-and-its-people to a national audience alongside portraits of the three main party candidates. All the audience groups were participants in the situation being described to them on the *Newsnight* programme: not only did they live where this 'historic' election was happening but it was they who had the decisive electoral power to affect its outcome. Yet the unanimous response to the programme was that theirs were the voices excluded from the *Newsnight* discourse. Obviously, the programme had to address a nationwide audience. But it was not simply that the groups felt themselves outside of this address; rather that the programme bore no relation to their own experience of living in Chesterfield, nor did it 'recognize' them as the people most immediately involved in the election. The way in which the programme concentrated on the candidates and their party machines and speculated on likely electoral outcomes and the results of opinion-polling meant that 'the Chesterfield voters' were only invoked as the passive, non-political subjects of others' – 'the three main parties' '– political action.

Accordingly, everyone rejected the programme's portrayal of politics along with its presentation of Chesterfield.

Each group made the point that there was 'another side' to the *Newsnight* description of their town. Where the reporter had noted 'prosperity' for instance, they drew attention to 'rising unemployment'; where he had stayed in the town centre, they referred to the outlying areas where people actually lived; while he concentrated on the famous 'landmark' church with the twisted spire and the only electors he interviewed were the vicar and bellringers, they speculated who indeed belonged to the church's congregation. Throughout they noted the absence of 'ordinary people like us' on the programme – except when used as 'background' to the candidates canvassing in the streets.

For instance, the catering students thought the programme made Chesterfield 'look like a medieval, cobbled little town . . . They chose market day. That scene was saying "we attract visitors to Chesterfield" – that sort of thing.' The NUPE shop stewards also picked up on the touristy image and linked it to their perception of the programme's failure to recognize the predominantly working-class composition of the town. But it was the 'Behind the News' group who had had most experience in 'decoding' types of media output who developed the politics of bias most extensively in terms of the absence in the programme of any points of identification. To start with the group considered the one-sidedness of the programme in relation to what 'they' had left out:

- I think the spire were nice. It was nice to see that on television.
- But why has it got to show you the bellringers and the people in church because . . . they were in a minority, aren't they, the people that go to parish church?
- I think they didn't do justice to Chesterfield or, they'd left it, very, a very thin covering of Chesterfield. You know, I mean they never mentioned unemployment, they never showed you the queues waiting to sign on. They never showed you the pits as are being closed down. . . .
- They made it sound very posh . . .
- I think they should have shown you the empty shops and the run-down factories and things like that as well.
- And people walking round the streets.
- Which is really painting a rosy picture of Chesterfield under a Tory government isn't it?
- It did say, didn't it, that owing to its diverse – er – manufacturing complexes . . . what was it? You know, one thing or another, that we hadn't suffered as much as other areas, didn't it? He said that. Of course that was the reason he was putting that Chesterfield was, like middle of the road, sort of in the past, and this was why we'd had a moderate MP in the past.

It was this group which was most aware of the way the programme's presentation of Chesterfield imputed a political stance of 'moderation' to the electorate. They then went on to consider what other versions of the town the programme could have presented and whether a bleaker picture would merely offer another form of one-sided bias:

-   If they had spoken bad about Chesterfield everybody would be up in arms, wouldn't they, saying 'Oh why did they show us this nasty thing and that nasty thing?' They had to show it nice. I mean it'll bring more trade to Chesterfield anyway, making a nice picture of it, won't it?
-   But it's not a nice place to live if you're unemployed.
-   It could have been a more balanced picture . . .
-   But it doesn't want to be shown in a nasty light does it?
-   It could have been a lot worse. I mean, they could have taken a line, 'This is just a crumbling old Northern industrial town; therefore, whoever they vote in, it's out of date, they're living in the past.'
-   But they didn't show you the ravages caused by a Tory government.
-   And we need someone like Tony Benn to put it back on its feet!
-   I mean we're not saying that they should *only* show you that. (general assent) Because then it would be biased the other way wouldn't it? (general assent).
-   It's a Labour town, though, and look what they've done for the town even so – made it look nice, haven't they? They've done all sorts for it.

When the discussion reverted to Chesterfield coverage for the final time it was this last point that was elaborated. The group then reached the position that, when the reporter failed to show the 'negative' things about the town, he also failed to place Chesterfield within an overall political context of government policies and their effects. But again, in presenting his 'positive' version of Chesterfield, which the group conceded in the end was not such a bad idea, he had still not established an adequate political context. He had attributed the attractiveness of the town and the recent restoration work done on its centre to its political moderation – whereas, in the group's view, this was the result of Labour militancy:

-   I think it always comes across very well when they photograph it.
-   It's photogenic Chesterfield really.
-   Thanks to the Labour Councils! (laughter)
-   Yeah, I thought, you know if he had had the chance to go much more in depth into Chesterfield he could have mentioned the fact that they'd had that campaign which stopped the whole of the centre of Chesterfield you know. . . . There was this marvellous campaign which showed that it wasn't *at all* moderate in a sense which made them change their minds about the centre completely. You know, it's a town where you could say that, you know, *action* and *extremism* have led to produce the town.

All groups, then, had a sense of 'the people' as being somehow absent from *Newsnight's* construction of their town in a way which rendered it primarily a consumerist spectacle for tourists. The 'Behind the News' group presented the most 'politicized' version of this view by suggesting how the programme could have offered an emphasis on 'the people' as active agents in the political processes which had made their town and included the parties, local councils and community campaigns. Their version would have supplied the missing social and historical explanations for 'photogenic' Chesterfield as much as for 'the empty shops and the rundown factories.'

In this instance, the groups' experience of their home town preceded the media images of it. But in the case of the Labour candidate's arrival on the scene, the situation was reversed. The media stereotype of Tony Benn as the key representative of 'the loony Left' of the period preceded any personal knowledge of him. So how did the groups cope with this widely circulated stereotype in relation to the novel presence in their community of 'the real man'?

The most frequently repeated phrase we heard in the town during the campaign was: 'but when you actually meet him . . .'. The speaker would then give an illustrative anecdote of some encounter with 'the controversial candidate', the point of which was to highlight the very dramatic contrast between the media version and the real-life persona. Nearly everyone in our groups had either met Benn face-to-face or attended a campaign meeting he had addressed. In this they were not untypical of the electorate as a whole, since Benn had made direct 'voter contact' with the majority by the end of the campaign precisely because his party had decided their main strategy must involve counteracting the media image. Moreover, given the massive media-generated interest in him anyway, there had been a revival of the old 'pre-television' public rallies in the town attracting audiences of thousands eager to 'judge for themselves'.

The discovery that, far from being 'mad', Benn was polite, affable and above all 'sincere' and 'genuine' furnished for most of the groups we spoke to the most damning and dramatic evidence they had encountered to reinforce their existing belief in media bias.

For instance, the miners felt their experience with Benn proved conclusively all they'd been saying about distrusting the media:

– All they want, it's like the old cliché, if a dog bites me it's not news but if I bite that damn dog, it's grand, we'll print that. And that's what it's all about: they're waiting for Tony Benn to drop a clanger. And Tony Benn's acted like a perfect gentleman – as he is!
– He must be!
– But talk to him – there's nobody can see, they can sense but that man is genuine. They can look into a man's eyes and tell whether he's genuine – and I think that . . . They've done such a job on him. . . . if I didn't know him I'd have thought he'd got horns on his head.'

The NUPE shop stewards saw the problem of bias against Benn in terms of the selection of material about him. As one woman put it:

> I think, er, Tony Benn first-hand is a lot different to Tony Benn second-hand after he's been through the media process. I think when you watch him on the television. . . . it's selected, you know, you only get to hear or to see all those particular bits that whoever edits the political programme feels that, er, they think you *ought* to see. But if you go and see for yourself then you get to see the whole thing, the whole man. . . . You don't get a true impression of anybody just by seeing them for a few seconds or a few minutes on certain programmes. . . . I feel you'll always get a distortion of that kind. But sometimes it's even made worse by the fact that it's willingly done.'

The group then went on to discuss whether bias was an unwitting or deliberate distortion – they reached no conclusions but gave instances of both – before returning to their 'first hand' impression of Benn. All agreed with the view of one speaker that, 'He speaks in a language you can understand – you know, working people. No airs and graces you know. Very clear-cut.'

But although these groups prized the values of direct face-to-face encounter to dispel distorted media images, it had not been primary contact alone that had affected them so dramatically. The 'real' Benn had proved convincing only to those who had some other knowledge or practical experience of politics 'on the ground'. For those who felt entirely alienated, both from this election and from anything they construed as 'politics', direct contact with a candidate was not sufficient in itself to make them change their minds and reconsider media images anew. Yet at the same time, those groups who saw least disparity between the Benn they encountered in Chesterfield and his media image were also the ones most critical of the media as a whole.

It was the catering students who offered the most wholesale rejection of all current-affairs journalism. 'Bias' for them resided in the way the media presented all politics. As they saw it, every politician simply used the media to make propaganda and the 'manipulative' media simply obliged: 'media' and 'politics' were in cahoots to produce distortion. They found the *Newsnight* programme boring and thought that it, like the rest of the media, had simply gone 'giddy' about politics and were having 'a field day' at Chesterfield's expense:

> – They've blown it out of all proportion and everything.
> – Television probably looks at it in more reality than a paper does. But still it's also fantasy and everything.
> MJ: How do the rest of you feel about the media?
> – Waste of time!
> – Waste of money!
> – Overdoing it!

In addition, the group felt you couldn't trust either the press or television because their news stories of the same event always differed in significant details anyway. Yet for all their explicit rejection of media manipulation, this group was the one most tightly implicated in media images of politics. They were cynical about 'the politicians' on precisely the media's own terms. Some of them had been to the all-party political forum in the college but the experience had only confirmed their view that all politics belonged to a media world of silly games and electoral manoeuvres and that politicians were the ultimate con-artists.

They felt that Tony Benn had come to the college 'on a big publicity stunt'. He was a very intelligent person who could 'twist his words and make them sound like they're genuine' – enough to deceive most of their fellow students who were ignorantly clapping and cheering him and attacking the other two candidates. Politics as a whole amounted to 'that many people saying things' that you couldn't afford to waste time listening to them all. Indeed, there was no real difference between local politics and politics as presented in the media:

- If you go to a meeting where there are several candidates, after about 10 minutes of discussion – a slanging match.
- It's like *Question Time* – has anyone seen that?
- It's like that wrestling on Saturday afternoon!
- As I say, it's pointless going unless you're after entertainment really.
- They talk about the young ones of today: they're punks and that. You should see some of those politicians!
- Take Michael Foot . . .
- Yeah, *you* take Michael Foot!

'Taking Michael Foot' (who had been the leader of the Labour Party at the last General Election and received much media criticism for his apparently careless mode of dressing) became something of a running gag for the group and indicated the extent to which their main reference points for politics were those adopted almost 'straight' and uncritically from a media discourse based on stereotyping and personalizing:

- Personality definitely does come into it. I mean I made a joke last year that I wouldn't vote Labour for the simple reason that I couldn't stand to see Michael Foot on television. . . . You've got to have somebody that, you know, you like.
- Appealing . . .
- Take foreign policies. I mean Michael Foot would be off to other countries and people would take one look at him and think flipping heck, if that's what English people look like, you can keep England! (general laughter).

The group had all encountered Benn face-to-face, but, like all politicians in their eyes, he had proved he was no different from his media image as con-artist. They had indeed spent the whole morning preparing their department for his visit and then he had swept through it without speaking to them. People were reacting to the likes of Benn as if they were 'pop stars' when in fact they were nothing but 'bloody Labour politicians':

  - It's like Ronald Reagan isn't it?
  - It's like people idolizing Hitler – yeah!

For this group there were no differentiations to be made in the world of politics: it was all an alien spectacle disconnected from their lives and linked to a media world 'out there' that every so often reached out to manipulate ordinary people. The students had some idea of a politics that could be related to their experience and on those grounds they all concurred with the view that all Benn 'ever said was *de*structive; nothing was *con*structive. Nothing was sort of connected with us.' But this remained an incipient, undeveloped view because none of the group had any knowledge of political activity to draw on outside of the framework provided by the media coverage of politics.

For similar reasons, the women in the keep-fit class were also both extremely cynical of media coverage of current affairs whilst at the same time remaining within the bounds of the media's own definitions of politics. They did not, however, adopt the same tone of jokey and flippant detachment as the students. Their cynicism was suffused with moral indignation on the lines that, although you could never trust either 'the politicians' or the media, nevertheless you *ought* to be able to. Again, they had all met Benn; he had stopped to chat to them outside the class, but their impression was that he was simply being condescending, and like all politicians, simply 'using' the occasion for electoral advantage. They had 'seen through' him – but in a way that served only to reconfirm the dominant media image of him as irrational demagogue. Indeed, it was with this group that we encountered the only 'pure' expression of the media-promulgated view that Benn was literally mad. But it was presented to the group as a spontaneous discovery, based, in one woman's case, on her experience of mental nursing, and in another's by the sudden revelation, on glancing through her daughter's history homework, that Benn had a similar personality to Hitler's. For both women, what had struck them was an odd look in Benn's eyes. In the course of retailing these anecdotes, no one in the group made any reference to pre-existing media stereotypes of Benn and all other such 'extremists'. For these had simply come to be inhabited as the women's own views in the absence of any apparent alternatives. And they were now too deeply embedded to be dislodged by any immediate encounter with 'the real man' behind the image.

It was groups like these women and the students who, while rejecting the influence of the media most emphatically, displayed least resistance to television's addressing them as political spectators. They showed least interest in how *Newsnight* covered politics because they did not define themselves as actively 'political' in the first place. By contrast, those groups who saw themselves as participants in the election and who had highlighted the differences between their immediate and mediated impressions of Benn, did engage with the programme's presentation of politics and had a wide variety of opinions about the way they saw it working.

Since they assumed that bias was routinely embedded in the programme, the problem for discussion was fixing it in relation to which 'side' *Newsnight* and its presenter could be discovered to be taking. Determining the 'side' became a matter of how the groups interpreted the programme's mode of presentation which was based on an accumulation of witty juxtapositions of scenes from the election interspersed with shots of Chesterfield 'sights' and a 'knowing' style of commentary that concluded, 'It shows you there's nothing *new* in politics.' In our view, the approach derived from a particular strategy of current affairs broadcasting that actually upholds the canons of impartiality and balance by assuming a distancing spectatorist 'take' on all positions it covers, thereby demonstrating itself as party to none of them. In *Newsnight's* case the strategy produced an ironic mode of presentation and a perspective based on cynicism towards all politics and politicians.

All the audience groups recognized that the stance of the programme had the effect of 'showing up' different political positions. What could not be agreed upon was whether that 'showing up' amounted to deliberate distortion or necessary revelation. This was because members of the groups tended to assume that the presenter's cynicism was a transparent reflection of reality when it was used to describe politics they opposed and a manipulative fabrication when it referred to what they supported. Thus for Labour supporters, the programme's presentation of the Liberal and Conservative candidates was more or less accurate since they deserved to be shown up. But with Benn it was different: a cynical stance implied a deliberate attempt by the programme to do him down.

We do not however conclude from such remarks that the discussion groups fit a 'uses-and-gratifications' model of a media audience.[12] This model assumes that media messages are uncoded and 'open' to any interpretation that audiences make on the basis of pre-existing psychic disposition. From this standpoint, it asks only that audience members 'rank' and 'rate' their preferences; it does not ask what they mean by them.

Because the starting point of our own research assumed that being a member of a media audience involved an active social process of decoding meanings, our use of the discussion-group method enabled us to go beyond the point where 'uses-and-grats' would have rested its relativistic case to probe further at what the attributions of 'bias' might entail.

Thus, in charting the ensuing discussion about the location of bias in the programme we noted that the groups began to run into difficulties of 'squaring' their accounts with any satisfactory evidence of active political partisanship. The outcome was that each group began to question the adequacy of a notion of 'bias' based on 'taking sides' and started to

[12]See for instance, D. McQuail *et al.*, 'The Television Audience – A revised Perspective' in D. McQuail, ed., *Sociology of Mass Communication* (London, Penguin, 1972).

consider other explanations from their own reading of the programme in terms of the use of professional codes and modes of presentation.

It was all the easier for groups to move to this position because they had viewed the programme as a fragmented entity in the first place. Picking up bits of the message that they agreed with, discarding aspects they disagreed with, they had never identified with *Newsnight* as a whole. Its particular mode of presentation, its ironic distancing held no coherent appeal for them; and once they had placed themselves outside the programme's overall frame of reference the groups could start to shift the argument to what an alternative election programme might look like.

In the first place, the groups argued, they would present all the candidates in a manner least 'mediated' by existing professional protocols as possible and, in particular, dispensing with the distanced-spectator role to allow the maximum direct access to all political messages. But secondly, in so far as professional intervention could not be avoided, they asked that it be explicit in both declaring its standpoint and connecting it in some way with 'the real world'. Thirdly, they would ensure that viewers could 'make up their own minds' by estimating for themselves concrete and visible demonstrations of support for each candidate 'on the ground' and in public meetings instead of via the 'stage-management' of press conferences, journalistic speculation or the 'discredited' methods of opinion-polling.

This last point was made most forcefully by the 'Behind the News' group arising out of the group's probing of the apparent ambiguities of 'bias':

MJ I mean, on the one hand you were saying that the programme didn't do justice to Tony Benn. On the other hand, you said it showed up the Liberal and Conservative candidates in a bad light. Would you still say then that it's biased?

– Yeah. Yeah, it showed up the lack of support on the streets for the – er Liberals and Tories but it didn't show the *amount* of support on the street for the Labour candidate – which is a totally different thing.

– It shown you the Liberal candidate on a walkabout. And it shown you the Tory candidate on a walkabout. Now it *did* expose their amount of support on these walkabouts – there was nobody at all around them – *at all*! But it didn't show you Tony Benn. If Tony Benn had been on a walkabout in Chesterfield he'd have had 500 people around him!

We can obviously make no large generalizing claims on the basis of this one particular case study. But we do suggest that the discursive method we have attempted may have highlighted certain aspects of how a socially varied range of audience groups may regard questions of bias.

Summarizing these, we would point in the first place to the way in which all the audience groups used attributions of bias to register a strong *resistance* to the mass media's, and particularly television's, coverage of current affairs. This took the form of a deep distrust of the media's power to 'mediate' and a suspicion that the media belonged to 'them' and not 'us' in a way which inhibited identification with both the content and codes of media messages.

Where resistance to the media took the form of outright *rejection* of current-affairs coverage, we noted that this might leave viewers still inhabiting the political frames of reference adopted by the media to the extent that they assumed them as their own commonsense wisdom. But where audience members had other knowledge of politics derived from their own participation in the community, they were able both to engage and 'negotiate' with television's version of politics and present alternatives to it.

It was not surprising that, on the way to developing alternatives, the groups should get caught up, indeed, bogged down, in the dominant discourse of bias and use the term as if it was some kind of entity to indicate deviation from a standard baseline of truth. But in working through the problems associated with this essentialist notion of bias we considered that there was an attempt to move towards a more productive formulation of the groups' own 'readings' of television coverage, albeit still based on the existing vocabulary.

That is, the questions audiences were starting to address were not crudely whether or not 'bias' existed in a programme and if so, where? But rather, thinking of "bias' in terms of the *politics of representation*: asking, 'who speaks for us and on what terms?' The groups saw the media using definitions of politics that ignored their own experience. 'Ordinary people' were not only excluded from access to television; they were in all senses, 'not in the picture'. Nor did they appear to have any 'rights' to representation, in that they witnessed no recognition of support for their interests.

In attempting to work out a different construction of politics from that adopted by *Newsnight*, the audience groups were hammering out a notion of 'representation' that would be contextualized, empirical, based on a belief in 'seeing and hearing it for yourself' and responding to a view of politics as immediate, practical and popular. From this perspective, 'bias' stood as a coverall term for all the instances where 'the media' had somehow failed to 'represent the people' while arrogantly insisting on their supreme right and professional duty to do so.

Note

The issues touched upon in this article are very wide-ranging, and for that reason it is hard to provide a neatly delimited introductory bibliography. The following are the sources to which I refer in the article; they include some of the most important work done on the topic of political television.

R. Barthes, *Mythologies*, selected and trans. from the French by Annette Lavers (Frogmore, Paladin, 1973).

J. Blumler and D. McQuail, 'The Audience for Election Television', in J. Tunstall, ed., *Media Sociology* (London, Constable, 1970).

A. Clarke, I. Taylor, and J. Wren-Lewis, 'Inequality of Access to Election Television', in D. Robbins *et al.*, eds., *Problems in the Sociology of Inequality* (London, Gower, 1978).

G. Dyer, *Advertising as Communication* (London, Methuen, 1982).

Glasgow Media Group, *More Bad News* (London, Routledge, 1980).

S. Hall, I. Connell, and L. Curtis, 'The Unity of Current Affairs Television', in *Working Papers in Cultural Studies* 9 (1976).

S. Hall *et al.*, *Policing the Crisis* (London, Macmillan, 1978).

J. Hartmann and C. Husband, 'The Mass Media and Racial Conflict', in S. Cohen and J. Young, eds., *The Manufacture of News* (London, Constable, 1973).

D. Hobson, 'Housewives and the Mass Media', in S. Hall *et al.*, eds., *Culture, Media, Language* (London, Hutchinson, 1980).

C. Hovland, 'Reconciling Conflicting Results Derived from Experimental and Survey Studies of Attitude Change', *The American Psychologist* 14 (1959).

P. Lazarsfeld *et al.*, *The People's Choice* (New York, Columbia University Press, 1944).

J. Lewis, 'Decoding Television News', in P. Drummond and R. Paterson, eds., *Television in Transition* (London, BFI, 1985).

J. Wren-Lewis, 'The Story of a Riot', *Screen Education* 40 (1981–2).

I would like to thank Janet Gillian for her critical comments, which were of great help to me in revising an early draft of this article.

10

The Framework of Political Television

Justin Lewis

The power and status of political television

The role of the media – and television in particular – in shaping peoples' political attitudes has been a subject for research and debate since audience research began. Lazarsfeld studied the effects of political television on the American voter over 40 years ago[1] and, in so doing opened up one of most popular fields of inquiry in the field of media research.

There are two major questions for this research to answer: does political television have an effect on the viewer/voter and, if it does, how? Most audience research in the last three or four decades has been too busy grappling with the first of these questions to offer any detailed account of the second. The main problem was that the research done has repeatedly come up with contradictory results. This made exploration of the *way* that viewers/voters were influenced by political television seem premature.

What I propose to do here is to assume that political television has a level of influence in order to examine ways in which it can work. This influence is not simple but it is profound.

In a perceptive review of media research written over 25 years ago, Carl Hovland demonstrated that the conflicting results research produced could be traced back to the way it was done. Briefly, those surveys which were able to measure a controlled exposure to media (i.e. before and after exposure) yielded more positive results than those sample surveys that simply attempted to draw correlations between exposure to media and attitude[2] where 'before and after' controls are difficult or impossible. Typical of the latter was Trenaman and McQuail's work on the 1959 British general election, which concluded that:

> within the frame of reference set up by our experiment, political change

[1]P. Lazarsfeld, *et al. The People's Choice* (New York, Columbia University Press, 1944).
[2]C. Hovland, 'Reconciling Conflicting Results Derived from Experimental and Survey Studies of Attitude Change', *The American Psychologist* 14 (1959).

was neither related to the degree of exposure nor to any particular programme or argument put forward by the parties.[3]

Any attempt to relate fairly short periods of media exposure with simple changes in attitude or behaviour is unlikely to be successful, partly because ways of thinking may be influenced in ways that do not easily correspond to, say, particular political orientations, and partly because it will completely neglect the long-term influence various media have in shaping our perceptions of the world. As Gillian Dyer points out, when writing about the influence of advertising:

> It is more than likely that an advertisement's effects are diffuse and long-term, and there is some evidence that advertising plays a part in defining 'reality' in a general or anthropological sense. For instance, the sex-role stereotyping common to many advertisements – the 'little woman' as household functionary thrilling to her newly polished table or whiter-than-white sheets, or the masterful, adventurous male – act, many social scientists argue, as agents of socialization and lead many people, young and old, to believe in traditional and discriminating sex roles.[4]

Similarly, Hartmann and Husband's work on the media and attitudes to various racial groups strongly suggests that, in areas where people do not have experience of those racial groups, the media play a crucial role in gradually building up a collection of images, attitudes and stereotypes about them.[5]

Hartmann and Husband's work gives us an insight into the status of political television in our lives. The world of politics – and frequently, the world of TV News generally – is about a world of which we have (or think we have) no experience. My own research in this area[6] would suggest that viewers are not only outside but alienated from this world. The viewers may accept the agenda constructed by politicians, broadcasters and 'experts' *within the world depicted behind the screen*, but they will not necessarily be able to make coherent connections between *that* world and their own. Dorothy Hobson's work on Housewives and the Mass Media, for example,[7] demonstrates how women working at home are fundamentally *distanced* from the world of TV news. This alienation effect has made political education a massive problem in Britain today. Most viewing/voting citizens are unable to make anything more than superficial connections between politics *as it exists in the world* of TV news, and the effect of political

[3]J. Blumler and D. McQuail, 'The Audience for Election Television', in J. Tunstall, ed., *Media Sociology* (London, Constable, 1970), p. 457.
[4]G. Dyer, *Advertising as Communication* (London, Methuen, 1982), pp. 77–8.
[5]J. Hartmann and C. Husband, 'The Mass Media and Racial Conflict', in S. Cohen and J. Young, eds., *The Manufacture of News* (London, Constable, 1973).
[6]J. Lewis, 'Decoding Television News', in P. Drummond and R. Paterson, eds., *Television in Transition* (London, BFI, 1985).
[7]D. Hobson, 'Housewives and the Mass media', in S. Hall *et al.*, eds., *Culture, Media, Language* (London, Hutchinson, 1980).

decisions on their employment, wages, their system of education, the conditions of their environment, the choice of public or private amenities available to them and, ultimately, the peaceful continuation of their whole way of life. This distance from the political world revealed to us on our television screens simultaneously strengthens and weakens its power over us. On the one hand, it is likely to provide us with a particular framework for understanding what politics is. On the other, this framework will only intrude into our own world when we are required to comment on it, as we are during occasional but important moments like general elections.

An example of the power and the distance of political television is the 'problem' of inflation, which preoccupied broadcasters and politicians throughout the 1970s. British public opinion correspondingly put infla- tion at the top of the agenda of 'important issues facing Britain' in the run- up to the 1979 General Election. Yet, incredibly, had opinion pollsters asked the British public (or, for that matter, many broadcasters or politicians) *why* they thought inflation was a problem – given that wage rises had more than kept pace with prices, producing a corresponding rise in most people's standard of living – the vast majority would not have had a sufficient knowledge of economics to be able to answer. Many economists, indeed, would have argued that a level of inflation below 10 per cent (as it was in 1979) was a comparatively minor problem for an economy to live with – particularly if that economy was faced with the possibility of extremely high levels of unemployment.

The implication I am making is that the framework of political television and the concepts used to inform it will largely define our response to it. The subsequent question is: how do those frameworks and concepts work? How are they articulated? I shall, in what follows, attempt to explore aspects of this question.

The government of political television

Political television and parliamentary politics have a close and, usually, reflexive relationship with one another. The political 'agenda' drawn up by the leading politicans in the main political parties (i.e. what they are concerned with and the way they talk about those concerns) is reflected by television and translated through codes of 'news value'. These 'news values', moreover, will sometimes reflect the values or priorities of politicians. At the same time, the concerns of politicians will be shaped by the framework used by television. For example, the winter before Thatcher's first victory in 1979 saw a series of industrial disputes in the public sector. This series of disputes became highly newsworthy, being inscribed in history as the 'Winter of Discontent'. The news value attributed to these disputes derived partly from the Labour Government's emphasis upon the need for a 5 per cent limit in wage increases (in order to bring down inflation), and partly from the newsworthiness of certain types of disruptive industrial disputes. The Conservative Party, in turn, made the 'issue' of trade unions and the law (i.e. as the party who could 'control' the trade unions) their most prominent election issue,[8] a prominence duly reflected by television.

I use this example because it demonstrates how the reflexivity between politicians and political television produces a political world that we respond to – one response being to vote Conservative, because that would appear to be the party best able to solve the trade union problem – but which does not necessarily make any sense outside the conceptual limits of that world. In this instance, trade-union disputes were seen as politically important during the 'Winter of Discontent' because they were conceived by the Labour Government as inflationary, i.e. wage rises = price rises. In other words, the trade union 'problem' was part of the more general problem of inflation. This made the disputes of 1978–9 of considerable political news value. Now, according to this logic, because inflation was a major issue in the 1979 election (as it had been throughout the 70s), the control of wage rises, and therefore of the trade unions, was also a key issue. It was, apparently, entirely coherent for the Conservative Party to concentrate upon this issue. Since they, unlike the Labour Party, were prepared to use the law to control trade union activity, their strategy appeared both serious and forceful to the viewer/voter (especially when compared to the Labour Government's failure to impose 'voluntary' agreements).

What appears here to be a stable set of political developments hides a vital inconsistency. The 'problem' of trade union activity during the Callaghan/Healey Government was couched entirely within the more fundamental problem of inflation, i.e. wages rises = prices rises. This is a framework documented in great detail by the Glasgow Media Group. The debate about whether to restrict trade union power to strike for 'excessive' wage demands by agreement or by law, was therefore given its significance during the election campaign, by the problem of inflation. In 1979 Thatcherite economics, however, *attached little importance to the link between wages and prices*.

The Conservative Party position was spelled out fairly clearly in their 1979 manifesto. This sees wage rises in the private sector as unproblematic, and wage rises in the public sector as a problem only in the context of public spending. The opposition here is between public sector unions and the 'Great British taxpayer':

> Pay bargaining in the private sector should be left to companies and workers concerned. At the end of the day, no one should or can protect them from the results of agreements they make.
>
> Different considerations apply to some extent to the public sector, of whose seven million workers the Government directly employs only a minority. In the great public corporations, pay bargaining should be governed, as in private ones, by what each can afford. There can be no question of subsidizing excessive pay deals.

[8]See A. Clarke, I. Taylor, and J. Wren-Lewis, 'Inequality of Access to Election Television, in D. Robbins *et al.*, eds., *Problems in the Sociology of Inequality* (London, Gower, 1982).

Wage rises were clearly *not* seen as a problem in the context of inflation. However, it was inflation and not public sector spending that was a dominant election issue in 1979.

Consequently, their attack upon the legal 'immunities' of trade unions was given considerable weight by a discourse – wage inflation = price inflation, therefore the high wage demands of one union are to the detriment of all – that was irrelevant to Thatcherite economics at the time. The conceptual framework on political television worked to mask rather than reveal this inconsistency. Given Thatcher's decisive victory in 1979, it is plausible to speculate how the character of political television might have facilitated this. In the analysis that follows, I shall be examining a political discourse whose limitations were not questioned at one point in history, yet seriously interrogated at another. In so doing, I shall try to demonstrate how and why a conceptual framework can become appropriate or inappropriate to political television. My focal point will be the issue of 'law and order'. This is an issue that has continually punctuated the British political world in recent history. It has taken various forms, from violence on political demonstrations in the 60s to the 'mugging' crisis of the 70s to the urban riots of the 80s. How 'law and order' issues are articulated, interpreted and understood in the world of political television clearly affects our own perceptions of those issues.

1979: 'The whole basis of civilized society'

In *Policing the Crisis*[9] Stuart Hall *et al.* described the construction of a societal model grounded upon notions of 'law and order', an authoritarian populism based upon 'image clusters which stand as collective representations of order against which images of crime and the criminal are counterposed'.[10] This discourse was developed from the specific to the general, until it encompassed a whole range of human activity within its vast moral strictures. This development was achieved not by the complex mapping out of determination and causality, but 'by sliding quite different things together beneath a single rubric',[11] to create a discourse based upon a whole range of associations, a paradigm rather than a grammar. The basic antagonism – law and order versus the criminal and the chaotic – was gradually expanded to form a whole chain of 'equivalent' antagonisms; law, order, democracy, policy, Judges, moderates, freedom versus muggers, anarchy, chaos, strikers, demonstrators, extremists, left-wingers. This discourse, the authors argue, provided a means of mobilizing popular support for policing the crisis of the capitalist state. When the Thatcher government came to power, riding high upon a wave of law and order rhetoric, this model (stretched to its paradigmatic limits) was a crucial component of the triumphant Thatcherite strategy.

9S. Hall *et al.*, eds., *Policing the Crisis* (London, Macmillan, 1978).
10Hall, *Policing the Crisis*, p. 149.
11Hall, *Policing the Crisis*, p. 249.

The framework used by parties of the right to understand law and order issues have tended to dominate the framework used by political television. However in the space between 1979 and 1981, this framework shifted decisively. The two periods I shall focus on occurred the day after violent police/civilian clashes had hit the news headlines – the Southall demonstration of 23 April 1979 against the National Front (at which Blair Peach was killed), and the Brixton riots of 11–12 April 1981. Both, therefore, offered Thatcher the opportunity to spell out the 'law and order' view of events.

In 1979, on the day after the Southall troubles, Mrs Thatcher appeared on television in Huddersfield and declared that:

> I think we ought to say a word about the dreadful and tragic events in Southall last night, which really were, which really were a disgrace to democracy, and they must be dealt with by the full might and power of the law. We welcome the enquiry that's been set up, but as Conservatives, we all recognize that the whole basis of civilized society is: respect for the law, and support by each and every citizen for the police, and the difficult and dangerous work that they do, and we're very mindful of the risks they clearly undertake, on our behalf. We totally condemn the racial policies of the National Front, and we've no sympathy whatsoever with any extremist group. But the way to deal with them is by the ballot box, and not by bricks or by bombs.

A powerfully articulated series of equivalences enables Thatcher to interpret the 'dreadful and tragic events in Southall last night' within a central antagonism: law and order, the police, civilization and democracy versus 'extremists' (or any other group outside the legitimate realm of civilization and democracy). The effectivity of this antagonism relies upon the widening of the scope of the original term – law and order, symbolized by the police – so that it can be seen to represent not just a specific set of interests, but 'each and every citizen', or civilization itself. Consequently, whoever is unlucky enough to be represented on the other side of the antagonism is defined by an opposing set of terms – barbarism, totalitarianism, anarchy and criminality. In an interview with Denis Tuohy the same day, Thatcher gave this amorphous group a sinister title – 'the Great Destroyers . . . who wish to destroy the kind of free society we have'. The threat is named but not identified.

This law and order discourse relies upon a mythical conception of causality: 'a criminal is criminal is criminal' or 'an extremist is extremist is extremist', a tautology that replaces causality with repetition.

As Roland Barthes put it:

> one takes refuge in tautology as one does in fear, or anger, or sadness, when one is at a loss for an explanation . . . a magical act which . . . believes itself to be even with causality because it has uttered the word which introduces it.[12]

[12]R. Barthes, *Mythologies*, selected and trans. from the French by Annette Lavers (Frogmore, Paladin, 1973), pp. 152–3.

'Outbreaks' of violent civil unrest, like outbreaks of smallpox, just happen – they have no history, just as 'the Great Destroyers' have no biographies. If the law and order discourse offers no explanations, its solutions have a rock-solid presence – the strengthening of the agencies of law and order in proportion with the level of lawlessness or disorder. As Mr Justice Melford Stephenson, drawing upon the law and order lexicon put it on *News at One* two days after Southall, civil unrest was part of:

> a malignant and growing cancer, and you don't cure malignant cancer by putting on an area of flannel lined with vaseline, which is the sort of remedy which is usually suggested.

The troubles at Southall must therefore 'be dealt with by the full might and power of the law'. This, of course, allows no space for explanations involving police harassment or provocation, explanations which are certainly necessary to account for events at Southall. The fact that the worst problems occurred *after* the arrival of massive police reinforcements makes the solution offered by Thatcher – 'the full might and power of the law' – at best inappropriate, and, at worst, an inversion of the truth.

Nevertheless, it is a testimony to the character of the 1979 General Election campaigns that Thatcher was able to appropriate the undeniably tragic events at Southall to inform her own party's articulation of the law and order 'issue'. Denis Tuohy, despite attempts to challenge her on most issues, allowed Thatcher to define Southall as an instance of 'the Great Destroyers' in action, and to assert that (in spite of Blair Peach's death):

> The police do a fantastic job, and we must support them in every way possible.

The untainted terrain of the police, and the Great Destroyers conspiracy theory, were assumptions that were appropriate at the time, assumptions couched within the law and order framework. Those on television who were asked did not dislodge this framework, and those who would were not asked.

1981: Filling out the space

When, two years later, Thatcher was interviewed to express her views on the Brixton riots (amongs other things), the climate had changed. For other explanations and solutions to come into play, to challenge the law and order framework, the site of the problem needed to shift – and shift it did. Against the backdrop of an immobilized trade union movement, mass unemployment and a shrinking Welfare State, the focal point of events like Southall and Brixton could be re-articulated as *significations* of problems rather than problems *in themselves*. The advocates, in the Labour Party and elsewhere, of a more liberal politics were able to fill out the space ignored by the law and order discourse, and shift the debate onto the terrain of causality. Television, having diligently documented the rise in unemployment and the drift into recession, was now in a position to represent Brixton not so much as a problem of law and order, but a problem of Thatcher's Britain.

Once this space had been opened up (on prime-time television news), explanations directly subverting the law and order framework – of racist and oppressive policing – were given access to challenge its symbolic range of legitimation. For the first time on television news, the character of policing was significantly questioned.[13] It is in this context that we must view the Alistair Burnet interview with Mrs Thatcher on ITN on 13 April 1981.

The 'inappropriate' nature of the law and order framework to represent Brixton is clearly revealed by Burnet's questions – all of which operate outside the scope of the law and order problematic. Thatcher's position is consequently decidedly shaky. On the one hand, she cannot endorse either the discourses alluding to social causality – whose consequences imply more public spending and the expansion of the 'unproductive' sector of the economy – or the discourses critical of policing – which deny her whole moral conception of society. On the other hand, a full-scale reiteration of the antagonisms constructed in 1979 would reinforce her critics' case against her 'uncaring' attitude. She begins the interview, therefore, by attempting to shift the debate onto her own terrain (and consequently by *relocating* the problem as a problem of law and order) while avoiding a straightforward denial of notions of social causality. Her tone, during this part of the interview is sympathetic and cautious.

Burnet: Prime Minister, do you accept that there is deep disaffection among many young black people, especially towards the police?

Thatcher: I think there's probably . . . deep disaffection . . . a number of problems . . . whatever the problems, nothing but nothing justifies what happened on Saturday and Sunday night. It is totally and utterly wrong, with all the ways of protest and demonstration and democratic methods we have, that anyone should attempt to take it out on the police, on the citizens of the area by turning over cars, looting property, setting it alight and throwing bombs and missiles at the police – nothing justifies that, and I cannot condemn it too strongly. (All said in soft tone.)

What Thatcher succeeds in doing here is to rearticulate the sociological discourse informing the question in terms of a moral discourse. The issue of explanations is not so much refuted as belittled by the introduction of the notion of justification. Her second sentence attempts to inform this rearticulation by listing various forms of criminal behaviour ('turning over cars, looting property') rather than the explanations behind them. Her distinction between those taking part in the riot and 'the citizens of the

13See J. Wren-Lewis, 'The Story of a Riot', *Screen Education*, 40 (1981–2).

area' is an attempt to resurrect an antagonism that enables her to position herself *and* the 'citizens of the area' on common ground. Once the riot is no longer seen as a product of *certain conditions within a community*, she is able to represent the rioters as antagonistic to (and therefore beyond the boundaries of) that community, i.e. once involved in criminal activity, such people are no longer 'citizens of the area'.

At this point in the interview, Thatcher has not only succeeded in answering a question about the problems behind the riots in terms of the moral/legal problem *of the riots themselves*, but has also negotiated a position identifying her interests with those of the people of Brixton. At the same time, she has avoided a straightforward reiteration of the law and order discourse by acknowledging the existence of space beyond it – 'a number of problems'. Nevertheless, despite her nimble word play, her position is extremely unstable, an instability revealed as the interview develops.

Their next exchange demonstrates the extent to which discourses of social causality had infiltrated the media professional's discursive repertoire. Thatcher's skilful relocation of the problem is ignored by Burnet, who asks her about unemployment:

B: Do you think that high unemployment is a primary cause?
T: No, I don't somehow think that that's a primary cause. After all, we had much higher unemployment in the 30s, but we didn't get this behaviour in any way. I know that . . . among young West Indians, there is a higher rate of unemployment, there tends to be . . . many of them are unskilled, and its not always easy to get a job for the unskilled at the moment, but I don't accept that that justifies what happened on Saturday and Sunday night.
B: What do you intend to *do* about high unemployment among young blacks, bad housing, bad environment?

This exchange effectively undermines Thatcher's moral discourse. Burnet's question – 'What do you intend to *do* about high unemployment . . .?' – subverts Thatcher's *negative* answer to her previous question, by assuming a *positive* response had been given.

This places Thatcher in an extremely awkward position. She is being asked to fill out a space she had previously avoided – a space beyond the law and order frame of reference. Her answer is entirely contradictory:

T: As far as high unemployment among any young people is concerned the answer is the same. We have stepped up the amount of money and the number of job chances we are trying to give – over 4,400 thousand this year – because there are an unusually large number of school leavers, and that applies to anyone. It doesn't matter, whatever your background, if you're a young person and haven't got a job, then we try to find some work experience for you, under that scheme. But you know, money has been poured into Lambeth: it's one of those areas where we have what's called a partnership scheme between government and local authorities, this year some £9m goes to that; there's quite a high rate support grant into Lambeth; there's a lot of money – I think something like £40m going on housing this year. So, I think it would be a mistake to think that *money* . . . can solve the problems. Money can't buy either trust . . . or racial harmony, we have to try to go about it in a different way. You must get trust – we've set up almost every known voluntary organization and institution – they're helped by funds. But trust takes a very much longer time to develop, and is very much two-way, and you allow the leaders of *that* community to try to get it, as much as leaders of the voluntary organizations.

She begins by accepting the frame of reference implied by the question. In short, she affirms that she *is* doing something about the social problems precipitating the riots, she is increasing *public spending* on Youth Opportunities Schemes. This position is untenable within a framework of Thatcherite economics. An endorsement of an (albeit paltry) expansion of the Welfare State upsets the chain of antagonisms between public money and private money, government intervention and free enterprise, individual economic freedom and state bureaucracy, the people and the power bloc.[14] She subsequently changes position in mid-stream by (effectively) denying *the importance* of what she is doing 'about unemployment', and asserting that 'it would be a mistake to think that money can solve the problems'. She is then forced to set about the different task of *redefining* notions of causality while maintaining the basic oppositions involved in the economic and moral/legal discourses she is committed to:

> Money can't buy either trust or racial harmony, we have to try to go about it in a different way.

Apparently abstract terms like 'trust' and 'racial harmony' enable Thatcher to locate Brixton's problems on an emotional level. This allows her to fill out the space beyond the law and order framework *without* trespassing upon the level of the economic.

For a brief moment, Thatcher attempts to rearticulate a solution *within* the antagonisms of Thatcherite economic policy; stressing the importance of 'voluntary organizations' that are 'helped by funds' as opposed to the government's own agencies/social/services. The implication here is that *public* money won't solve the problems, but private money will. This analysis is clearly extremely difficult to sustain, and Thatcher doesn't attempt to develop it further.

At this point then, having been forced into the level of causality (outside the law and order problematic), she has more or less succeeded in defining this space without jeopardizing the discourses fundamental to Thatcherism. In terms of the interview, however, she has relinquished her

---

[14]The 'people versus the power bloc' antagonism is an important part of Thatcherite populism, and in opposition she attempted to speak for 'the people' against the 'power bloc' of the corporate state (incorporating the TUC and a large public sector).

authority to speak. The subject constructed in Burnet's question ('what do you intend to do') is endowed with power to act, to solve problems, to right wrongs. If the receiver of the question does not wield this degree of power, the question becomes meaningless. By answering the question in the way she does, Thatcher's reply constitutes herself as a very different subject – one without such power – precisely *in order* to make Burnet's question meaningless. This is a significant moment. The Prime Ministerial interview is an important event in televisual history, because it is based upon a subject whose authority to speak derives from his/her power to act (as opposed to the Leader of the Opposition, whose power is hypothetical – 'what *would* you do if?'). If the Prime Minister refuses to identify with such a subject, the whole *raison d'être* of the interview collapses. In this instance the subject of the Prime Ministerial interview is clearly in direct conflict with the Prime Ministerial subject of a government based upon a *laissez faire* politics.

Thatcher's shift towards powerlessness is indicated by the substitution of the pronoun 'we' with the pronoun 'you'. 'We' is the subject of the social causality discourse she begins with ('we have . . .', 'we try . . .'), the powerful subject; 'you' is the subject of the discourse on 'trust' she ends with ('you must . . .', 'you allow . . .') a subject who has implied power *outside* his/her self.

Burnet's next question acknowledges this shift in identity, while revealing the consequences of Thatcher's position:

B: But it hasn't worked – so do you agree with Mr Enoch Powell in the Commons today that 'we've seen nothing yet'?

In other words: given your refusal to intervene; the situation must inevitably deteriorate. The question effectively lays bare Thatcher's refusal to accept a position of power – it projects a negative set of conditions to a subject who is 'required' to give a positive response, but is unable to do so. Thatcher's position, at this point, is decidely precarious. She has to renegotiate a position of authority, to reassert her power to speak, without facilitating the discourses that would enable her to do so. The difficulty of this task is reflected in what is undoubtedly the weakest answer so far.

T: I heard him say that, and I thought it was a very, very alarming remark, and I hope with all my heart that it isn't true, and I hope that we can get far more trust, and try to work out these problems better than we have. Its quite true that we had Bristol a year ago, but I do stress, trust is a two-way business, it only comes with people who want it, who positively want to solve the problems. It only comes with people who want to live as true and honourable and upright members of society. I don't know quite how to get it, except we just have to go on working at it, and I do know this; sometimes too much money doesn't help to solve problems, it causes more troubles. It has to be contact between people – people who . . . really have some kind of aptitude for this work, to get the confidence of the young people. You know, when I was Secretary of

> State for Education I hated enormous schools. I thought . . . you
> learn far more, you get far more trust, you're taught far more, if you
> had a much, much smaller school, a much, much smaller group of
> people – if they were in difficulty in particular – with one teacher.

For a Prime Minister to leave the problems of Brixton to 'people who really
have some kind of aptitude for this work', is, at the very least, rather lame.
We can, nonetheless, understand Thatcher's answer as an attempt to
rebuild a platform from which to speak.

It is symptomatic of Thatcher's confusion that she shifts between 'we'
and 'I' and back to 'you' again – almost as if she is no longer sure *who* she
is speaking for. Certainly, the discourses represented here do not seem to
construct subject positions as clearly as those based on well defined
antagonisms ('us' versus 'them'). Her powerlessness is signified by the
dominance of the first person (singular), used *ten* times in this section. In
other words, she is unable to speak for, to represent, she can only assert her
own subjectivity in 'commenting' on events.

Amidst this confusion, she makes two bids for power. Firstly, she tries to
return towards the terrain of the law and order problematic:

> trust is a two-way business, it only comes with people who want it, who
> positively want to solve the problems. It only comes with people who
> want to live as true and honourable and upright members of society.

The concept of social causality is denied in terms of the classic
Tory/Christian subject – the free agent possessing free will. The implication is, of course, that if the rioters in Brixton don't appear to 'want to live
as true and honourable and upright members of society', then they can be
dismissed, banished to the realm of the criminal, beyond law and order.
Secondly, she lays claim to speak from a place 'in the know' by referring to
her Ministerial experience at the Department of Education. There is
nowhere she can go from here. From the moment her interviewer forced
her on to the space behind the law and order discourse, Thatcher's
authority steadily diminishes. The antagonisms that inform the various
discourses of Thatcherism sanction what she can and can't say, and, in this
instance, deny her the power to speak. Her attempt to avoid a full-blooded
burst of law and order rhetoric, undoubtedly fails – the limitations
imposed by those antagonisms (inscribed within a law and order framework and an economic framework) leave her floundering. That failure is
finally consolidated in their final exchange (on this subject). Thatcher's
only mean of regaining control, of reasserting her authority, lie within the
confines of the law and order discourse. Thus, when her interviewer
provides her with an opportunity to return to these confines, she willingly
accepts. Burnet points out to her that:

> B: But there's no trust with the police – at the moment, it appears, in
>   Lambeth, I mean somebody said today that the police in Lambeth
>   were behaving like an army of occupation.

In so doing, he has turned the law and order discourse on its head, forcing

Thatcher towards a straightforward refutation. This refutation is made easier by the way in which the question is phrased. Burnet makes two charges; firstly 'there's no trust with the police'; secondly, the police in Lambeth behaved like 'an army of occupation'. To connect these two statements, the second statement needs to be contextualized. The 'army of occupation' quotation refers to police presence *before* the rioting, to police operations like *Swamp 81*. There is not enough information, in Burnet's formulation, however, to make this connection. The second statement is thus allowed a certain degree of ambiguity (which Thatcher is able to exploit).

> *T:* (Contemptuously) What absolute nonsense, and what an appalling remark, and I condemn the person who made it. Had there been any question of the police withdrawing from Lambeth, as they had temporarily to withdraw from Bristol, they'd have been subject to the gravest criticism, they would have been totally wrong. The job of the police is to protect the citizen, and they *did* protect the citizens in Lambeth to the very best of their ability, and they were absolutely right to do so. No one must condone the violence, no one must condone the disgraceful events that took place in Lambeth, it should not have happened. They were *criminal* . . . criminal, and they should never have occurred, and the police's job is to protect citizens against criminal activity.

The 'army of occupation' statement is seen to refer not to the level of causality, but to the *moment of conflict itself*. This shift of referent allows the law and order problematic to come back into play.

The vehemence of Thatcher's condemnation is further facilitated by Burnet's failure to name the voice behind the allegation. The probable source was the Report commissioned by Lambeth Council (under David Turner Samuals, QC) into police/community relations – whose findings were reported on *News at One* earlier that day. By replacing this semi-official souce with an unnamed voice in the wilderness ('somebody said that . . .'), Thatcher is able to safely re-establish a law and order antagonism by setting herself up against this unknown 'other'. This formulation allows her to identify herself with 'the police' and 'the citizen' in a blanket condemnation of the 'other', who is subsequently *reinterpreted* as 'condoning the violence'.

Thatcher, finally, having struggled to fill out a space beyond the tautology of the law and order 'explanation' of Brixton, gives up the attempt, in a straightforward rearticulation of that 'explanation'. The events were '*criminal* . . . *criminal*, and they should never have occurred'.

The limits of political television

What the interview with Alistair Burnet reveals is the power of political frameworks in shaping political discussion on television. In 1979, the framework for understanding breakdowns in law and order was firmly inscribed within a discourse that did not seriously address any notions of causality. The only terrain for debate was how to catch/constrain/clampdown/punish the offender. This framework was informed by police chiefs and the judiciary, who were, by their very function, appropriate to its confines. Two years later, the focal point had shifted quite dramatically. Questions were addressed to the cause of lawlessness – 'high unemployment . . . bad housing, bad environment – . . .' – rather than the lawlessness itself. There was, in short, a movement from a moral discourse to a sociological discourse. The first involves notions of *justification* and *punishment*, the second involves notions of *explanation*. By 1981, Thatcher's attempt to invoke the moral discourse ('it is totally and utterly wrong . . . nothing justifies that') – developed so successfully in the 1979 election campaign – had become almost anachronistic. Her foray into the field of explanation, during the Burnet interview, finds her powerless and lost. The political world on television had clearly changed. This change was informed by the relation between the television and parliamentary worlds. The period between April 1980 and April 1981 saw a dramatic and serious rise in unemployment, from 1.3 million to 2.4 million, a rise unprecedented since the 1930s. The size and rapidity of the increase became highly newsworthy. Each new set of monthly unemployment statistics became a news story in its own right. Unemployment became *the* political 'issue' of the period. The government, accordingly, were held accountable and responsible for the increase – in parliament and on television. During the second half of 1980 and 1981, the opinion polls registered government popularity at an all-time low. It is in this context that Thatcher's TV encounter with Burnet took place. Burnet, as a broadcaster and journalist, had no choice but to operate within the existing political news framework. Unemployment had dislodged 'law and order' from the agenda. What I have tried to demonstrated is that, once dislodged, it could not easily be shifted back. The old concepts were no longer applicable. In this sense, the fact that a law and order perspective was no more appropriate to *explain* what happened on Southall in 1979 than it was to Brixton in 1981 is not important. The world of political television structures what can and cannot be said. This, in turn, will play a part in structuring how we, the viewers/voters, think about an issue or event.

This process is, in a democracy like Britain, potentially dangerous. The power of television to shape the political world *as the viewer/voter understands it* is, in this context, a problem. The viewer/voter is only given access to ways of understanding the world *when* those frameworks become appropriate. In 1979, as we have seen, the viewer/voter was not informed on the level of *explanation* about events like those at Southall, which were presented and interpreted within a 'law and order' framework. The existence of such a framework in 1981 was contingent upon the presence of a news story (in this case, unemployment) that shifted the focal point onto the level of social causality. In short, if unemployment had not been newsworthy, Mrs Thatcher may have been able to impose a law and order framework on events at Brixton with complete success. The range of political discourses used to interpret the political world on television is clearly limited. What is worrying is that this limitation is governed by the rules of political television, rather than the nature of events being reported or interpreted.

Notes on Contributors

Rosalind Brunt teaches mass communications and women's writing at Sheffield City Polytechnic. She is course leader of the MA in Women's Studies and director of the newly opened Centre for Popular Culture. She co-edited with C. Rowan, *Feminism, Culture and Politics* (Lawrence & Wishart, 1982) and contributed to *Popular Fiction and Social Change*, ed. C. Pawling (Macmillan, 1985) and *Television Mythologies*, ed. L. Masterman (Comedia, 1985).

Andrew Crisell is senior Lecturer in English and Communication Studies at Sunderland Polytechnic. His research interests are in satire, especially of the eighteenth century, and the mass media. His book *Understanding Radio* was published by Methuen in 1986.

Chris Emlyn Jones is Lecturer in Classical Studies at the Open University. His main academic interests are in early Greek philosophy and literature. His book *The Ionians and Hellenism: a Study of the Cultural Achievement of the Early Greek Inhabitants of Asia Minor* was published by Routledge in 1980. He has published articles on Herakleitos, and on Homer as literary and oral poet, and is at present working on *Speech and Persuasion in Fifth Century Athens*, to be published by Routledge in 1988.

Jeremy Hawthorn is Professor of Modern British Literature at the University of Trondheim, Norway. He has published books on literary theory, Virginia Woolf's *Mrs Dalloway*, Joseph Conrad, and on multiple personality. His most recent book is a study of Charles Dickens's *Bleak House*, published by Macmillan in 1986. With John Corner he is joint editor of *Communication Studies: an Introductory Reader*, the second edition of which was published by Edward Arnold in 1985.

Martin Jordin teaches sociology of literature and film studies at Sheffield City Polytechnic. He is course leader for the Polytechnic Certificate in Cultural Studies and on the management committee of the Centre for Popular Culture. He contributed to the *Popular Fiction and Social Change* volume and is currently co-editing with A. Cashdan, *Communication Studies: A Reader* for Blackwell, to be published in 1987.

Gunther Kress teaches courses about language in the context of awards in Communication Studies at the New South Wales Institute of Technology, in Sydney. As editor, co-author and author he has published a number of books and articles, including *Language as Ideology* and *Language and Control*, both of which were published by Routledge in 1979; *Literature, Language and Society in England 1580–1680*, published by Gill and Macmillan in 1982; *Learning to Write*, published by Routledge in 1982, and *Linguistic Processes in Sociocultural Practice*, which was published by Deakin University Press (Victoria, Australia), in 1985.

Justin Lewis is a researcher and writer in Media and Cultural Studies. His work has covered many aspects of this varied field, although he is particularly interested in reception and the audience. He is currently working for the London Strategic Policy Unit.

John M. MacKenzie is Senior Lecturer in History at the University of Lancaster. He was educated in Zambia, Scotland, and Canada, and has taught in the universities of British Columbia, Liverpool, Zimbabwe, and Lancaster. He is the author of *The Partition of Africa*, which was published by Methuen in 1983; *Propaganda and Empire*, which was published by Manchester University Press in 1984; editor of *Imperialism and Popular Culture*, which was published by Manchester University Press in 1986, and co-author of *The Railway Station, a Social History*, which was published in 1986. He is General Editor of the 'Studies in Imperialism' series published by Manchester University Press. He is currently working on studies of hunting and imperialism, and Orientalism in the late nineteenth and early twentieth centuries.

Jan-Ola Östman has an FL in English Language and Literature from Åbo Akademi (Finland), an MA in Linguistics from Reading University, and a PhD in Linguistics from the University of California, Berkeley. He is now an Assistant in the English Department, Åbo Akademi, and at present acting Associate Professor in the same department. In addition to having written a number of articles on various pragmatic issues, he is also author of the monograph *You know: A Discourse-Functional Approach*, published by John Benjamins (Amsterdam) in 1981. He is editor of *Reports on Text Linguistics: Semantics and Cohesion*, published by the Research Institute of Åbo Akademi in 1978, and is also the co-editor of *Journal of Pragmatics*.

Michael Pickering is Senior Lecturer in Mass Communication at Sunderland Polytechnic. He is the author of *Village Song and Culture*, which was published by Croom Helm in 1982 and which won the 1983 Katharine Briggs Memorial Award. He is also co-editor of *Popular Song and Vernacular Culture*, to be published by the Open University Press in the course of 1987. His research interests are in the areas of cultural history and the sociology of culture.

Kevin Robins is Senior Lecturer in Communication Studies at Sunderland Polytechnic. With Frank Webster he is co-author of *Information Technology: A Luddite Analysis*, which was published by Ablex in 1986. His research interests are in the political economy of information and information technology.

John L. Smith worked for some years in industry and commerce after leaving school and before studying psychology at Leicester University. He subsequently carried out research for his doctoral thesis at the Medical Research Council's Social and Applied Psychology Unit at Sheffield University. He is currently Senior Lecturer in Psychology at Sunderland Polytechnic.

Frank Webster was educated at Durham University and the London School of Economics. He has taught at the University of California, San Diego, and at presently holds the chair in Sociology at Oxford Polytechnic. He is author of *The New Photography: Responsibility in Visual Communication*, which was published by John Calder in 1980 and, with Kevin Robins, of *Information Technology: A Luddite Analysis*, published by Ablex in 1986.

Gordon Williams is Senior Lecturer in the Department of English, Saint David's University College, Lampeter. Besides numerous articles on Elizabethan and World War topics, he has written a book on *Macbeth* which was published by Macmillan in 1985, and is preparing another on *Coriolanus*.

Index